PERSPECTIVES ON SCHOENBERG AND STRAVINSKY

REVISED

Edited by

Benjamin Boretz and Edward T. Cone

The Norton Library

W · W · NORTON & COMPANY · INC ·

NEW YORK

W. W. Norton & Company, Inc. is the publisher of current
or forthcoming books on music by Putnam Aldrich, William Austin,
Anthony Baines, Philip Bate, Sol Berkowitz, Friedrich Blume, How-
ard Boatwright, Nadia Boulanger, Paul Brainerd, Nathan Broder,
Manfred Bukofzer, John Castellini, John Clough, Doda Conrad,
Aaron Copland, Hans David, Paul Des Marais, Otto Erich Deutsch,
Frederick Dorian, Alfred Einstein, Gabriel Fontrier, Harold Gleason,
Richard Franko Goldman, Noah Greenberg, Donald Jay Grout,
James Haar, F. L. Harrison, Daniel Heartz, Richard Hoppin, John
Horton, Edgar Hunt, A. J. B. Hutchings, Charles Ives, Roger
Kamien, Hermann Keller, Leo Kraft, Stanley Krebs, Paul Henry
Lang, Lyndesay G. Langwill, Jens Peter Larsen, Jan LaRue, Maurice
Lieberman, Irving Lowens, Joseph Machlis, Carol McClintock,
Alfred Mann, W. T. Marrocco, Arthur Mendel, William J. Mitchell,
Douglas Moore, Joel Newman, John F. Ohl, Carl Parrish, Vincent
Persichetti, Marc Pincherle, Walter Piston, Gustave Reese, Alexander
Ringer, Curt Sachs, Denis Stevens, Robert Stevenson, Oliver Strunk,
Francis Toye, Bruno Walter, J. T. Westrup, Emanuel Winternitz,
Walter Wiora, and Percy Young.

Library of Congress Cataloging in Publication Data
Boretz, Benjamin, comp.
  Perspectives on Schoenberg and Stravinsky.

  (The Norton library)
  Essays, principally reprinted from Perspectives of new music.
  Discographies: p.
  1. Schönberg, Arnold, 1874–1951. 2. Stravinskii,
Igor' Fedorovich, 1882–1971. 3. Music—Addresses,
essays, lectures. I. Cone, Edward T., joint comp.
II. Title.
ML55.B663P5 1972   780'.92'2   72-7395
ISBN 0-393-00618-2

ACKNOWLEDGMENTS

The music examples in these essays are reprinted by kind permission of the copyright owners as follow:

Associated Music Publishers, Inc., New York. Stravinsky:

Concerto in E♭ (*Dumbarton Oaks*)
Copyright 1938 by B. Schott's Söhne, Mainz.

Symphony in Three Movements
Copyright 1946 by B. Schott's Söhne, Mainz.

Boosey and Hawkes, Inc., New York. Stravinsky:

Agon
Copyright 1957 by Boosey & Hawkes, Inc.

Petrouchka
Copyright by Edition Russe de Musique.
Copyright assigned to Boosey & Hawkes, Inc.
Revised edition copyright 1947 by Boosey & Hawkes, Inc.

Octet
Copyright 1924 by Edition Russe de Musique; Renewed 1952.
Copyright & Renewal assigned to Boosey & Hawkes, Inc.
Revised version copyright 1952 by Boosey & Hawkes, Inc.

The Rakes Progress
Copyright 1949, 1950, 1951 by Boosey & Hawkes, Inc.

Le Sacre Du Printemps
Copyright 1921 by Edition Russe de Musique
Copyright assigned to Boosey & Hawkes, Inc.

Symphony of Psalms
Copyright 1931 by Russicher Musikverlag; Renewed 1958.
Copyright & Renewal assigned to Boosey & Hawkes, Inc.
Revised version copyright 1948 by Boosey & Hawkes, Inc.

Symphonies of Wind Instruments
Copyright 1948, 1952 by Boosey & Hawkes, Inc.

Abraham and Isaac
© 1965 by Boosey & Hawkes Music Publishers, Ltd.

Variations
© 1965 by Boosey & Hawkes Music Publishers, Ltd.

Requiem Canticles
© 1965 by Boosey & Hawkes Music Publishers, Ltd.

ACKNOWLEDGEMENTS

Introitus
© 1965 by Boosey & Hawkes Music Publishers, Ltd.

H.W. Gray Co., New York. Schoenberg:

Variations on a Recitative, Op. 40
Copyright 1947 by H.W. Gray Co., New York.

C.F. Peters Corp., New York. Schoenberg:

Fantasy for Violin with Piano Accompaniment, Op. 47
Copyright 1952 by C.F. Peters Corp.

Five Pieces for Orchestra, Op. 16
Copyright 1922 by C.F. Peters Corp.
Copyright renewed 1960 by C.F. Peters Corp.

G. Schirmer, Inc., New York. Stravinsky:

L'histoire d'un Soldat
Copyright 1924 by G. Schirmer, Inc.

Les Noces
Copyright 1922 by J. & W. Chester, Ltd. London.

PREFACE

THIS BOOK constitutes the first conjunction of Schoenberg and Stravinsky as subjects of a volume on this scale, the first collected representation of the recent thoughts on their music from within the community of American composers, and the first of a projected series of anthologies derived principally from PERSPECTIVES OF NEW MUSIC. The pictures of Schoenberg and Stravinsky that emerge from this collection—even from the mere fact of their unique juxtaposition here—are vastly different from their public images, or from those to be inferred from the current pedagogical or historical literature.

The coupling of these names is acceptable today not only because of Stravinsky's evolution toward serialism, but also because his recent works have forced us to listen to his older works anew, and we now realize that the distance between Vienna and St. Petersburg (or Paris) was not so great as we had surmised. Besides, as the late R. P. Blackmur was fond of pointing out, distance blurs distinctions in art as well as in nature. Styles that when new seem unrelated or even opposed often lose their sharp contours as they recede into the past, so that after the passage of years we can perceive the similarity of their general outlines.

The views of the two masters here presented perhaps reveal important aspects of contemporary American composition as much as they generate insight into the works actually under discussion. Here one will find composers (and other musicians closely associated with them) discussing the twin mainstreams of contemporary musical tradition, of which their own work represents a unique confluence. This confluence is, in fact, a wholly American characteristic, to be found nowhere in recent European music; and thus the presence of Schoenberg and Stravinsky as live musical issues is equally particular to the current American scene. Here, too, one will find the constant awareness of Schoenberg the great teacher and Stravinsky the still profoundly exploratory colleague, whose most recent works are invoked and discussed with a remarkable degree of concern and assimilation.

A final note. This collection is in no way intended as a definitive examination of the significance of Schoenberg's and Stravinsky's music. In the first place, work on Schoenberg and Stravinsky is necessarily work in progress; and in the second, the essays themselves were not originally written at the prompting of an "Aspects" survey, but only out of their authors' immediate and particular interests. Their selection by the editors was an attempt to exhibit the range of such interests arising naturally within the community of contemporary (American) musicians.

Princeton, N. J.   B. A. B.
October 1967   E. T. C.

PUBLISHER'S NOTE TO THE
NORTON LIBRARY EDITION

In addition to minor corrections, this edition incorporates a new study of Stravinsky editions prepared by Claudio Spies, and replaces the now outdated discographies of the first edition with a revised and corrected Stravinsky discography, first published in the Stravinsky memorial issue of *Perspectives of New Music*, IX/2–X/1 (1971).

CONTENTS

CONTENTS

PERSPECTIVES ON
SCHOENBERG AND STRAVINSKY

SCHOENBERG'S FIVE PIECES
FOR ORCHESTRA

ROBERT CRAFT

I

The Editions

THE conductor must compare no fewer than five texts: the original
1912 score; the two-piano arrangement, by Webern, dated 1913;
the reduction for chamber ensemble, by Schoenberg and Felix
Greissle, of the first, second, fourth, and fifth pieces; the "new,
revised" full orchestral score dated 1922; and the "new edition for
normal orchestra" dated 1949 but published in 1952. Of these, the
1922 score is the most accurate and reliable. It overhauls the original
edition in matters of articulation and dynamics (including muting).
And it implements two important revisions: the expansion of the
ending of the second piece; and the addition of speed changes, numerous and significant enough in the case of the fourth piece—played in
one unmodified tempo originally—to affect the whole character of the
music.

Titles appear for the first time in the 1922 score, too, though the
composer had chosen them a decade earlier, before publication of the
original score, as an entry in his diary, January 1, 1912, reveals:

Letter from Peters, making an appointment with me for Wednes-
day in Berlin, in order to get to know me personally. Wants titles
for the orchestral pieces—for publisher's reasons. Maybe I'll give
in, for I've found titles that are at least possible. On the whole,
unsympathetic to the idea. For the wonderful thing about music is
that one can say everything in it, so that he who knows under-
stands everything; and yet one hasn't given away one's secrets—
the things one doesn't admit even to oneself. But titles give you
away! Besides—whatever was to be said has been said, by the
music. Why, then, words as well? If words were necessary they
would be there in the first place. But art says more than words.
Now, the titles which I may provide give nothing away, because
some of them are very obscure and others highly technical. To wit:

I.   Premonitions (everybody has those)
II.   The Past (everybody has that, too)
III. Chord-Colors (technical)
IV. Peripetia (general enough, I think)
V.   The Obbligato (perhaps better the "fully-developed" or the "endless") Recitative.

However, there should be a note that these titles were added for technical reasons of publication and not to give a "poetic" content.

Schoenberg's stated purpose in preparing a new edition, in September 1949, was to reduce the size of the orchestra. But only six instruments—an oboe, a bassoon, a clarinet, two horns, and a trombone—are economized, and of these the trombone is forgetfully re-included at the end of *Peripetia*. The horn reduction affects only *Peripetia*, but there drastically, full harmonies in the unmixed sonority, a fundamental idea of the piece, no longer being possible. The curtailing of the clarinets likewise affects only one piece (apart from doublings in *Das Obligate Rezitativ*), but there, in *Vorgefühle*, just as crucially, for the color of the eliminated contrabass clarinet is irreplaceable. The actual notes played by the six excised instruments are of course supplied by other winds and strings; but the reduced wind families are not always able to absorb all of the linear content of the absentees, and in *Farben* the original scheme of timbres has been compromised (cf. mm. 248-49; I should mention that several errors have crept into the 1949 edition in this passage). The substitutions, apart from a few cases in which the balances have been realigned as well, are achieved without introducing new effects.

The 1949 edition does not presuppose a substantially smaller body of strings, I think, but the string parts, at least in the first piece, are more radically revised than the winds. All the second violins, violas, and cellos now play *spiccato* the figures (Exx. 8 and 9) formerly played *spiccato* by the halves of these sections, and *pizzicato* by the other halves. This change, which of course affects the sound of the piece as a whole, was instituted to facilitate the new very fast tempo, I believe, rather than to simplify the *quality* of the articulation; but having said that, I should add that the new score relinquishes several other *divisi* primarily in the interests of clarity and definition.

The amendments in the string parts in the other pieces are all concerned with orchestral balances. One of them, the erased cello doubling of the violins in *Peripetia* at mm. 296-97, is puzzling, the part having been strong enough only in the 1912 score, where it was assigned to violins, violas, and cellos together, and marked *fortissimo* and *crescendo* to boot.

On most counts the 1922 score is to be preferred to the 1949, and it is the version conductors should elect to perform. The 1949 score can then be used as a reference, and certain of its corrections,[1] of dynamics especially, incorporated in the 1922 edition. The "H" and "N," primary- and secondary-voice, priority ratings which the composer added to all of the pieces in 1949, can be incorporated as well, but they are helpful, in my opinion, only in *Das Obligate Rezitativ*, which is where he first introduced the idea, in bracket form, in the 1912 edition. The most valuable information in the 1949 score is in the metronome marks, and this in spite of errors. (There are no metronomes at all, oddly enough, in the 1922 edition, but Webern's *Klavierauszug* contains a sprinkling of them, presumably with Schoenberg's authority.) The $\bad J = 130$ at m. 193 is an error. So, too, I think, is the $J = 56$ at m. 173 (*pace* Webern, who gives the same marking; to me, at any rate, the faster tempo at this point is jarring, but the point is arguable). The added *allargando* at m. 300 and the new *accelerando* at m. 323 are indisputable improvements, however, and the newly posted metronomic roadsigns throughout *Peripetia* help to define the form. At the same time, other changes of speed, at mm. 312, 313, and 317, to which we are accustomed, and convinced as necessary, by the 1922 score, are now unaccountably missing, though I think only by carelessness.

Concerning *Vorgefühle*, which poses the most difficult problems of tempo in the entire opus, the 1949 edition only contributes to the confusion. This new score specifies the initial *molto allegro* as $J = 88$, which is fast. At m. 24, however, the same (*sic*) *molto allegro* becomes $J. = 112$. (Incidentally, the 1949 score omits the *langsam* of the 1922 score in two places near the beginning where it is indispensable; and at m. 14 it prints a wrong note in the third trombone.) But greater difficulties are propounded at m. 26, the starting line of the principal development section. Here both the 1912 and 1922 scores give the direction "very fast," following two pivotal measures, 24 and 25, marked merely "fast." But in the 1949 score no speed change occurs at m. 26 and "fast" and "very fast" are not differentiated. Now to my ear, the eighth of the "very fast" tempo should approximate the sixteenths of the merely "fast" tempo. Nor am I

[1] It fails to correct more than it corrects, however; the erroneous time-values in m. 296 (horns), for instance; and the unmeasured *crescendo* in m. 276 (should it equal the *crescendo* in m. 273?). And it neglects to give assurance in such cases as the E♮ in the first violins at m. 77, a perennial question-raiser, for which reason the natural sign was parenthesized in the chamber orchestra score.

deterred by the failure of the autograph sketches and manuscripts to endorse my contention, for apparently Schoenberg was undecided about the notation himself. His calculations in search of a metronomic prolation between the two tempi are found on a copy of the printed score in the legacy, but nothing conclusive is discovered from them except that he himself conducted, or thought of conducting, the "very fast" in two; which means that his own tempo was probably very slow. Support for my argument is advanced, however, or so I think, by performances that neglect to shift into higher gear at the "very fast." They sound convincingly wrong.

I should add, since all of the scores are innocent of the composer's exact intentions, that the same relationship obtains in reverse, going from sixteenths to eighths, near the end of the piece (mm. 122-25). But this does not apply at m. 120; there the overlapping eighths should continue in the old *langsamer* tempo; the new *rascher* tempo is meant only for the sixteenths. The manuscripts do not confirm this either, but then, like the 1912 score, they allow only one unvarying speed for the whole latter part of the piece. Webern's reduction lends some weight to the idea, however, and so does an oral tradition among Schoenberg's European pupils (one of whom, Max Deutsch, possesses a recording of Schoenberg conducting the *Five Pieces* in the French capital in 1922, a document of great interest concerning many of these points, and a monument, of a sort, to Parisian musical manners). I regret the failure of my own recording (Cleveland Orchestra) to follow it, as I feel certain now that it is correct.

II

An Unscientific Digression

The circumstance that Schoenberg was a painter as well as a composer invites consideration, if only because his principal achievement in the former capacity dates from the period immediately following the *Five Pieces for Orchestra*. One turns to the visual side of his artistic expression not in search of analogy, however—which in any case would be concerned with function[2]—but of homology, in the sense of the conceptual development of forms. And as Schoenberg himself has touched on the relationships between the two media (in a recorded interview), a definition of his affiliations as a painter might help to illuminate a part (at least) of the mind which composed the *Five Pieces*.

[2] Cf. Von Neumann's analysis of "analogy mechanisms" in *The General and Logical Theory of Automata*.

First, a culture cliché. Music rather than painting is the "German" art, or so Hegelian tradition has it, though I repeat the blurb only because Schoenberg himself insisted on the essential "German-ness" of his musical make-up. Schoenberg surely would have agreed that the "German" artist, pictorial or otherwise, tends to create his forms from "inner visions" or the "soul," rather than, like the "Latin" artist, to find them in objects of nature. (This is an untenable generality, of course, otherwise Dürer, for one, would have to be counted a "Latin," and Rimbaud, for another, a "German"; but it suits my restricted purpose in Schoenberg's case.) Moreover, the phrase "inner visions" could serve as a collective subtitle to nearly the whole of Expressionist[3] painting, of those paintings in which the artist attempts to sever or suspend identifying relationships to exterior objects and "the world of appearances." Form, color, the material qualities of paint itself, are world enough for him, he avers; and so, for his ends, they may be; no matter that we complain of arbitrary deprivations.

But what of the other term of the comparison? Can the composer "subjectify" himself as the painter has done? Can he in ascertainable fact, which is more than an attitude, divorce himself more deeply from "the object," which has never existed in music in the first place, or existed merely as a matter of ephemeral and loosely defined conventions? Schoenberg the composer transformed the whole musical identity system, though hardly, I think, only in the pursuit of a more profound "subjectivity"; and in so doing greatly expanded the musical language (whereas the Expressionist painter narrowed his). In fact, the vocabulary of Expressionism in music extends without limits through the whole range of the art, and the vocabulary is also the emotion; which in the case of Expressionist painting appears, in comparison, to be very one-sided. Furthermore, the kind of emotional intoxication that Expressionism seems to require is less naturally sustained in painting than in the time-art and the actively performed-art of music. But Schoenberg the composer overqualifies. To be sure, the normal body temperature of all of his music is an almost suffocating febrility; but the Expressionist label is too small for him, nevertheless. It is unable to encompass an art which embodies, as his does, the whole of tradition.

This is Schoenberg the composer. Schoenberg the painter is not limited by the label but very aptly pinned to it. With the exception of a few landscapes, the hundred or so paintings and drawings by him are either inner visions, whether so titled or not, or inward-turn-

---

[3] The contemporary, *Blaue Reiter* sense of the word, not Grünewald.

ing self-portraits; all issue alike from uncharted interiors rather than from the conventional bailiwicks of observed nature and fact. The *Five Pieces for Orchestra* are also "inner visions," and their headings —*Vorgefühle, Farben, Peripetia*—might have been borrowed from almost any of the paintings. The music, too, especially of *Vorgefühle* and *Peripetia*, will suggest to some people, as the paintings avowedly do, a world of dream experience, though, being music, it need not suggest or relate to anything, but only be.

Program annotators *are* expected to relate, however, and to place a work "in the composer's whole development." This being too tall an order in Schoenberg's case, in which each opus is a turning point in music itself, I will merely warn anyone who actually does wish to come to the *Five Pieces* in chronological sequence, not to dig as far back as the *Gurre-Lieder* or even the First Quartet. He will uncover origins in these early masterworks, and learn much or little, according to his own lights, about the uses of the past. But that past will hardly be recognizable to him in the first and last (at least) of the *Five Pieces*, which, together with the contemporary *Three Pieces for Piano*, represent Schoenberg's largest leap into Schoenberg to that date, and the first works in which Wagner or some other composer is no longer visible pacing in the wings. The listener must leap, too; he will never catch up by walking.

III

THE *FIVE PIECES*

Vorgefühle

> *Life surges from a center,*
> *expands from within outwards.*
> *—Rodin*

It was Schoenberg's lifelong practice, and not only in the twelve-tone compositions, to expose at the outset the basic and, to an unprecedented extent, all-inclusive materials of a work. The "all-inclusiveness" is retrospective, of course; composers do not generally begin with full knowledge of every consequence of their initial ideas. Yet at the same time Schoenberg had at least a far-reaching intuition of possibilities before his considered awareness of them. The speed with which the *Five Pieces* were written would alone bear that out; it certainly indicates that the original act of conception was of great depth.

For Schoenberg, then, to compose was to develop, or derive from, materials exposed at the beginning; and to develop them in close structural relationship, at least as close as a fugue in relation to its subject. A whole work thus grown from, and in considerable detail identified with, its originating cells would attain—so Schoenberg held—a new degree of consistency and unity. Thus, too, the shape of the whole would represent a larger, more comprehensive expression of the logic of the fundamental ideas; which is also a way of saying that the composer would be governed by inherited form-patterns only insofar as his background chemistry had been determined by them, and they were genetically unavoidable.

The elements of *Vorgefühle* are set forth in an introductory dialogue-recitative. The principal ones—which are links to the other pieces as well, for the pieces are closely interrelated—occur in the first three measures:

Ex. 1

The three-note motive[4] repeated in melodic sequence on the upper line describes an augmented triad on the longer and therefore emphasized notes F, A, C#. This augmented triad is a dominant characteristic of the *Five Pieces* (as well as of the *Three Pieces for Piano*), in something of the same sense that whole-tone structures were a characteristic of the Chamber Symphony Opus 9. Note that the excerpt is in the "key" (begging allowance for the levity of the terminology) of D-minor.[5] It is not an unequivocal statement of that tonality likely to have set *maître* Franck aglow with recognition, to be sure, but is less cloudy, nevertheless, than a first-time listener might expect, after all the threats of atonality that have been put about. The D-minor is a reference rather than a tonal-harmonic root, of course, but the ear remembers it as a tonic key in the usual sense; of the other pieces,

[4] Cf. Sir Kenneth Clark, *Studies in Western Art*, Vol. IV (Princeton University Press, 1963), for an admirable disentangling of "motive," "theme," "subject," though my own discovery of this essay was too late to help me here.
[5] Cf. Opus 11, No. 1, the final chord.

all except the third, which is a contrast in other ways as well, take their bearings from it.

From the "key" frame of Ex. 1 and, specifically, the last chord of m. 3, the composer extracts the pedal harmony,

Ex. 2

which underlies the whole of *Vorgefühle* from m. 23 to the end. The same chord is held over as the "key" of the second piece where, however, it is used in a more traditional and functional way; and it serves as an interrelating device at the beginnings of both *Peripetia* and *Das Obligate Rezitativ*. The fifths in Exx. 1 and 2 are another such device. Featured throughout *Vorgefühle*, they are emphasized in the formulation of the "key," as I have said, in both the second and fifth pieces; and the principal motive of *Farben* (m. 229) is composed of them. In the latter two instances (and pieces) the rhythm as well derives from the first measure of Ex. 1.

Ex. 3

Much of the remaining substance of the piece is contained in nucleus in Ex. 3, which is derived, in turn and as follows, from Ex. 1: mm. 7-8 from mm. 1-2; mm. 4, top line, from mm. 1-2; the last beat of m. 5, by diminution from m. 1. The last measure of Ex. 3 reappears in the body of the piece as an independent motive. So does m. 9, which is a mere extension of the preceding measure, but which, inverted and exploiting a hemiola effect, becomes a motive in its own right.

Ex. 4

The new motive's own extension, or consequent, yields, in turn, still another motive (Ex. 5), whose genealogy reaches back to m. 4 and mm. 7-8.

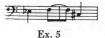

Ex. 5

Fashioned into a new figure, with note values four times as fast, the music of Ex. 5 acts as a bridge between the introduction and the main development. The next example is a compendium of motivic and intervallic material to date.

Ex. 6

But I must backtrack to collect one other motive (Ex. 7), the beginning of which is derived from an inversion of m. 1 and the last three notes of m. 9.

Ex. 7

These graftings form a new unit, nevertheless, and one that turns up again, in longer note-values but echoed four times as fast, as a principal voice (m. 100). From m. 26, the hesitations and fragmentations, the pauses and the sudden and frequent changes of tempo, give way to a continuing development in a steady rhythm (Ex. 8), which settles into an *ostinato* figure (Ex. 9) now recognized as the circled notes in Ex. 6, as well as an inversion of the intervals in mm. 7-8. Example 8 is derived from m. 4 and the augmented triad of Ex. 1.

(meas. 26-28)

Ex. 8

Ex. 9

But enough. From this point to the end of the piece the listener should be able to relate every event to the excerpts already quoted, or combinations of them. The newness of the new material is only apparent. Thus, the bass figure (m. 64; Ex. 10) is a rhythmic variant of the pedal harmony in Ex. 2. And thus the celesta, trumpet, and flute motive (Ex. 11) is an abstract of Exx. 1 and 2.

8ᵛᵉ basso

Ex. 10

Ex. 11

In spite of the *ostinato*, the movement of ideas is no less intense in the "very fast" development section. Repeated hearings[6] will reveal further motivic and rhythmic relationships, and at deeper levels, but I must turn to some general aspects of the music.

1. Few composers since the first of the B's have shown such prodigal variety in the use of augmentation, diminution, *stretto*. At the climax of the movement (m. 79), music from Ex. 8 is played in octaves against itself in both doubled and quadrupled note values (trombones and trumpets, respectively), as well as in canon at the rhythmic distance of a quarter-note (second violins and violas). The canon soon spreads to four voices, each one entering at the metric distance of an eighth-note; which is why the conductor should beat full measures (the largest unit of the augmentation), but show the groupings of measures rather than individual units.

2. The beginning is in triple meter, but the basic rhythmic unit of the development section (from m. 26) is a pattern of four notes to the measure (Exx. 8 and 9). Throughout most of the piece, from m. 36, the threes of the beginning return superimposed on the fours,

---

[6] These remarks were originally intended for a record album.

a relationship also expressed as 6's *vs.* 2's. This amounts to the discovery of a new rhythmic domain; a new continent, in fact, one often sighted and even previously explored, but never annexed by European music. Nor have all of the implications been pursued even today, experimentation in rhythm having concerned itself primarily with the loosening of metrical controls and with ever more mechanical subdivisions of the beat.

Phrase structures are equally new and complex, but a proper analysis would have to begin at a very elementary level. Webern's grouping of the phrase units from m. 26 gives a good example of the asymmetry: 3 measures, again 3, then 2, 1, 4, 5, 1, 3, 6.

3. Instrumentation. The "new effects"—the fluttertongue of the muted tuba in its lowest register, the trombone glissandos—are audible, obvious, and in no need of cataloguing, but two no less obvious general points might be worth making. One is the bestowing of the soloist's mantle on every individual in the orchestra (even including individual string basses), and the combining of soloists in new ways, both among themselves and with orchestral combinations, also new. The other is that the instrumentation pursues the progressive tradition of expanding and exploiting extremes of range. Thus, the strings move upward, basses to former cello territory, cellos to heights heretofore considered rarefied even for violas (large portions of Schoenberg's Cello Concerto are well suited, in range, to the violin), violas to violin registers, and violins to the stratospheres of the *flauto piccolo*. The old instrumental traits are extended and transformed with this shift, of course, and new intensities and color spectrums brought into commerce.

4. The dynamic range is also radically extended and quickened. The instant fluctuations from crisis to crisis in this music hardly seem to date from the same decade as the slowly piled-up climaxes in *Ein Heldenleben*. Moreover, the greater concentration is present in every fiber and dimension of the score. All of this ranting of mine has been provoked by barely two minutes of music! Small wonder the timescale of the next two pieces is progressively and greatly slower.

Vergangenes

> *The composer did not compose those smallest component parts; rather, he composed the whole piece. But when one takes it apart, the piece consists of component parts only.—Schoenberg*

If new listeners find this the most attractive and accessible movement, part of the reason is because, as the title suggests, the music is a look into the past. It is, in fact, more overtly anchored in the D-minor "key" than *Vorgefühle*, and it depends hardly less strongly on *ostinato* devices. As in *Vorgefühle*, too, the thematic, rhythmic, and harmonic fundamentals are exposed at the beginning. But rather than attempt to trace their development, I will outline the sonata-type form.

The standard alphabetical diagram must in this instance be modified to ab(a)C(abc), with "a" representing the introduction, "b" the exposition, "C" the main development, and the parentheses the telescoped returns. As the example shows, the *Vorgefühle* "key" is held over, but the recitative-like melody, with chordal punctuation, appears to be new. The "b" segment (m. 10 of the example) is moored to F♯; at the end of it (mm. 16-17), that F♯ is overlapped by G♯, the ultimate note of the principal melody and the pivot for the return—in a surprisingly literal way for Schoenberg—to the beginning of the piece. Intervallically speaking, "b" derives entirely from the introduction. In the first parenthesized version of "a," the bass line from mm. 2 and 3, now in longer note-values, leads to a cadence with an E-major triad in the torso of the chord and a D-sixth in the bass; *I*, at any rate, hear the chord in this compartmented way, but it is a different matter at the piano from the orchestra.

"C" is distinguished by a faster tempo, a change to 3/8 meter, and a melody in a four-rhythm (against the three) high on a solo viola's A-string (a color and intensity that Schoenberg exploited again in *Pierrot lunaire*). But for all its air of newness[7] this viola melody has been assembled and launched from components of "a" and "b." A flute imitates the viola melody but extends it differently, and in so doing reveals the derivation from mm. 10 and 11 of Ex. 12. Both forms, flute and viola, are developed polyphonically.

The 4 *vs.* 3 idea is developed, too, and a step beyond the application of the same idea in *Vorgefühle*, in that the two units are now alternated as well as superimposed. This amounts to the equivalent of a change of tempo or beat; and in fact the conductor *should* beat the first measure of the 3/8 in three and the second measure in two. (Curiously enough—and I whisper the observation—the possibilities discovered here have remained fallow ever since the *Five Pieces*.) The 3's and 4's are subdivided (to 6's and 12's), and the resulting complexity of rhythmic substructures at the apex of the movement (m. 194) nearly dissipates the isochronous accents.

Section "C"'s "salient" events are most quickly and compactly identified by the instrumentation. They are, first, the *stretto* at m.

---

[7] It reappears in m. 240, Act I, Scene 2, of *Wozzeck*.

173, with the clarinet motive from "b" now in the violins; second, the conjunction of an *ostinato* canon at the octave, in sixteenth-notes, played by celesta, and of a triplet-figure *ostinato* by two flutes; this is, of course, another manifestation of the 4 *vs.* 3 idea; and, third, the appearance of a new motive (actually derived from the second clarinet part in m. 156 by reversing the direction of the intervals) in the bassoon. The first two notes of the new motive are imitated in nine canonic parts, eight of them—in as many as four speeds of augmentation—at the same pitch,[8] and the ninth purely rhythmic (the triangle and cymbal). The same figure subsequently serves as an *ostinato* accompaniment to a further development of the viola melody, continuing in that capacity until the return of "a" (in, of course, the D-minor "key").

The celesta and two-flute *ostinati* reappear in the section of shortened returns, but with changes and accretions. The flute figure, now a major second lower and underpinned by the pedal F♯ (English horn) from section "b," is accompanied by a *flauto piccolo* repeating the F♯ and G♯ axial notes of section "b." The four principal motives make distant, figmental reappearances, too, in the manner of a cyclical symphony, the "a" and "b" themes persisting in their four rhythm in the three-meter context. Almost all of the recurrences of these materials are at original pitch.

The recapitulation of "C"—three statements of the viola melody, now in longer note-values—leads to a dazzling ending which I will not pick apart except to expose some of the interrelating machinery: the arpeggio of the celesta in the D-minor "key," connecting to the piccolo, which then repeats the first melodic interval of the piece in the original 4-meter (here *vs.* 3); and the last three clarinet notes, which are a fragment of the viola melody (see Ex. 12, upper line, four measures from the end), as well as the first three notes of *Vorgefühle* in reverse order. These three notes are brought into relief both harmonically—the first two being delays, or false resolutions—and rhythmically: four against the general three.

Farben[9]

I cannot unreservedly agree with the distinction between color and pitch. I find that a note is perceived by its color, one of whose dimensions is pitch. Color, then, is the great realm, pitch

---

[8] The alto clef is missing in the viola part at m. 184 in the 1949 score.
[9] Renamed "Morning by a Lake" in the 1949 score, though apparently Schoenberg

> *one of its provinces. . . . If the ear could discriminate between*
> *differences of color, it might be feasible to invent melodies that*
> *are built of colors* (klangfarbenmelodien). *But who dares to*
> *develop such theories.* —Schoenberg, Harmonielehre (*1911*)

The speed of Schoenberg's music of fifty-five years ago, meaning not the rapidity of the beat, of course, but the pace of the musical thought, is difficult to follow even today. Trained listeners are at least as rare as trained performers, and listeners whose training was acquired at subscription concerts are rarely exposed to music of the concentration of the *Five Pieces*. But *Farben* is an exception, not only in the *Five Pieces*, where it acts as a necessary brake, but in all of Schoenberg's music.

The form depends, nevertheless, on an arc-shaped plan of movement, quickening toward the middle with increasing rhythmic and motivic activity, dynamic pressure, harmonic change; and sloping from the climax at the center back to the comparatively motionless beginning. The form is a *crescendo-diminuendo* of movement, in fact, a further expression of the return idea, cognate with the melodic-harmonic returns in *Vergangenes*. And the formal construction is the most remarkable attribute of the piece, more so than the timbres or instrumental novelties[10] for which it is famous. The idea of ever-changing colors—so-called *klangfarben*—is employed in the other pieces as well, after all: at the end of *Das Obligate Rezitativ*, for instance, where the same chord is filtered through three different overlapping combinations. (A more rudimentary example is found in *Vergangenes*, mm. 4-7 of Ex. 12.) But *Farben* differs from the other pieces, in that the deployment of orchestral timbres is the chief accessory of the form, the means with which the "changing chord" is sustained.

---

had always called it that privately (see Wellesz, *Schoenberg*, Dent, 1925), even identifying a "jumping fish" motive:

[10] Which is the main reason, together with non-performance, why its instrumental pallette has still not faded, and why its colors have not yet been turned into technicolor. The more solid a structure the more difficult to burgle even its outward attractions.

II.

Ex. 12

Ex. 12 (cont'd)

The harmony is stationary at first.

Ex. 13

As in all of the pieces, the initial unit is the source of the whole. Instead of attempting to describe its growth, however, I will confine my remarks to some other aspects of the composition. The repeated and, later, gradually changing (one note at a time) chord[11] of the example is overlapped and therefore blended with itself in different instrumental combinations. Thus a canonic effect is established, in the upper notes of the chord at the distance of two beats, and in the bass note at the distance of one beat. This bass note, bandied between a single viola on the strong beats and at the lower limit of its range, and a single bass on the weak beats and in its first octave—in other words, between *solo* strings and *groups* of winds—is the most strikingly original feature of the instrumentation,[12] more so than any of the *ponticello* and string harmonic effects.

Schoenberg describes the music as a composition of chords and colors, without thematic development, or "motives to be brought out." But the thematic and motivic structure is precisely what saves it from the fate of a one-time-only experiment. The form divides into four sections. The first, which is eleven slow-tempo measures long and which ends in absolute stasis, reduces to the following thematic essence:

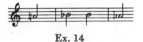

Ex. 14

[11] "The color of a sustained chord keeps changing," writes Erwin Stein (*The Elements of Musical Form*), but in fact the pitches of the chord change, too, whereas the color does not "keep" changing, at least not at the outset, but is limited to two regularly alternating and overlapping combinations.

[12] The solo bass is undoubtedly the source of the bass solo in the snoring scene of *Wozzeck*.

The A♮ and A♭, the before and after, are several times repeated, but the B♭ is found only in one measure, as in the extract. One other event occurs in this section, a two-note motive which, on repetition, sprouts parallel fifths above and below.

The second section, mm. 12-19, is marked by harmonic relocation, by upward-edging of the pitch range, and by a new application of the *klangfarben* idea: a different instrument, or combination of instruments, articulates and sustains each note of an arpeggiated chord, spreading out the chord melodically first, so to speak. The same idea is used with great dramatic effect in the final scene of *Erwartung* (mm. 382-84), as well as in the stabbing scene of *Wozzeck*.

In part three, mm. 20-30, more and more events are joined in increasing movement until, in the ebb of the climactic phrase itself, the beats are fragmented into three, four, and even six parts. In correspondence to the rhythmic flux the color turns to confetti, the individual particles succeeding, combining with, and overlapping each other more rapidly than the ear can analyze except as—and this is what Schoenberg's picture becomes here—Impressionism. The "leaping fish" motive is introduced in this section. It may be worth remarking in connection with the so-called tonal perspectives of the *Five Pieces*, that all six "leaps," in this and the final section, are described by the same pitches (with octave displacement).

In the mounting movement, Ex. 14 becomes:

Ex. 15

Ex. 16

At its zenith the progression of the three pitches originally embedded in eleven measures is compressed to:

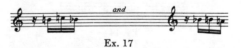

Ex. 17

The close of the third section is defined by a return to stasis.

The final section, initiated by a motive in triplet-rhythm fashioned from Ex. 15, is the least agitated in the piece with, at first, no movement at all on the second and fourth beats. The ending is a return to the beginning.

IV

Peripetia

Peripetia, a sudden change of fortune, a sudden change of direction. —Rudolf Kassner

Ex. 18

The beginning of the motive is from *Vergangenes* (at m. 165), whereas the D-minor, and the augmented triad in the upper part of the chord,[13] refer to the first piece. A trumpet "smear," consisting of seven augmented triads, devolves from the same chord, and as it returns at the end of the piece must be considered part of its frame. As in the preceding pieces, the first statement is a principal source for the whole, but in *Peripetia* the basic thematic materials succeed each other according to an obvious plan of rotation. The following motive (Ex. 19), for instance, reappears several times, not counting purely melodic imitations, and its first (and last) chord is part of the concluding harmonic structure.

Ex. 19

But the architecture is more evident, I think, than that of the other pieces, for which reason I will turn to a wayside matter. This is that identification in music operates through a number of associative means besides tonality. Item: the clarinet solo that follows Ex. 19, imitates the rhythm and to some extent the contour, but not the pitches or the intervals, of the motive quoted in Ex. 18:

Ex. 20

13 The 1949 score misprints D for C in the bass part.

The resemblance, nevertheless, is immediate to every ear in the house. And to confirm the same thing from another aspect, when the strings reiterate this melody, with the "F" transposed up to "G," the alteration is recognized, consciously or unconsciously, by everyone with reasonably tuned-up auditory equipment. The effect (an impossible one, incidentally, within the fixed-interval procedure of early twelve-tone music), is a marvelously dramatic and economical measurement of the form. But I should have noted, to begin with, that Schoenberg consistently recalls the motives or themes of *Peripetia* at the same pitch; a roundabout course, one would think, for anyone bent on destroying tonality.

Among the features of the piece are many ingenious uses of diminution; for example, the sounding of the principal motive in short note-values in treble (i.e., fast) instruments and, no less reasonably, in long note-values in bass (i.e., slow) instruments. While mentioning rhythm, I should also remark the ever-changing speeds and *rubato* character of the music. Both are in contrast to the quasi-motionless *Farben* and the even-keeled *Das Obligate Rezitativ*, which is the neighbor on the later side.

Finally, two high-points: the ending; and an episode at the heart of the piece (mm. 283-99) in which six themes, all of them in a high state of intrigue, are developed simultaneously. The ending is a musical juggling feat. Three canonic pairs twirl in continuous motion over three other parts, all swarming to a tremendous crash (the loudest contributor to which is a whistle produced by a cello bow drawn across the rim of a large cymbal—like rubbing the rim of a partly full drinking glass). But the catastrophe is not the end. A bass chord—the *coup de grâce*—follows it, and a final gurgle in the clarinets.

V

Das Obligate Rezitativ

I have come across six identical descriptions of this piece—such is the *vis inertiae* of music commentators (and the *taedium vitae* of their readers)—but failed to learn any more from them than that the listener is faced with an "example of the free chromatic idiom"; as if there were anything free about it, and as if idioms for this sort of thing were to be found lying about ready-made. But I can do little better myself; and I am running out of those escape clauses which are making my account of the music read like an insurance policy. I lack the tools to verbalize the logic which I have no trouble in following with my ears; and I confess that the verbalizing of music, the jargon of musical analysis, is to me the ugliest language in existence; words like "diminution" give me a very strong physical pain. Nor will the creaking tonal-system explanatory apparati dredged up in connection with the other pieces serve me here, apart from fragments that are local in effect, and ambiguous, by which I mean those so-called "passing polytonalities" which are frequently no more than the harmonizing of inner voices in thirds, a feature not only of *Das Obligate Rezitativ*, but also of *Erwartung* and the *Three Pieces for Piano* (cf. mm. 51-52 of No. 3). If the first four pieces can be labeled as examples of "extended tonality" (they have been), then *Das Obligate Rezitativ*, on the same (meaningless) terms, will have to be described as overextended. Schoenberg himself ridiculed (and defied) the attempts of academic theory to explain this music through traditional tonal analysis, but at the same time acknowledged the survival of tonal-system interval-pull in, for example, the tonal tendency of leading-tones.

Unlike the other pieces, the arguments of *Das Obligate Rezitativ* make no use of pedal-points and *ostinati*; reflect no plan of classical symmetry; do not compartmentalize into exposition, development, recapitulation; avoid, in their continuous melodic development, exact repetitions and unvaried return; and move through the orchestra always speaking in a different voice. *Like* the others, the thematic—intervallic and rhythmic—ideas are contained in the first measures:

Ex. 21

The reader will note that: a) the first three pitches, top line, are a return of the viola melody from the middle section of *Vergangenes*; b) the augmented triads (treble part) and "key frame" (bass part), in the second measure are referents to the very beginning of the *Five Pieces*; c) the figure ♫ in the second measure is reversed in the third and fourth measures; d) the close chromatic movement is relieved by wide leaps, both methods of progress being normal voca-bles of Schoenberg's melodic speech, of course; e) the intervallic and rhythmic design of the sixteenth-notes, A and G#, is imitated in two other voices in eighth-notes; in the top line in quarter-notes; and again in sixteenths but with the pitches in reverse order: the development of the piece depends on these and similar imitative devices.

I might add that the student of Schoenberg's music as a whole will be struck by close resemblances to the beginning of the third of the piano pieces of Opus 11.

The example does not identify instrumentation. Let us say of it, here and throughout, that it is far more complex than in the other pieces, if only because the polyphony it delineates is more complex and hence the voicing and balancing more intricate. One might add, though to the surprise of no one, that solo instruments and groups are newly combined, and in new ranges. Thus, in the third measure of the example the viola line is beneath the cello line; and thus the lis-tener's association of the string basses with, invariably, the lowest line of all, can no longer be automatic. In the final *tutti*, the climax of all of the *Five Pieces* from a recording engineer's point of view (but not only), the bass line is maintained by trombones and tuba, while the basses themselves are applied to a middle voice.[14]

The four-, five-, and six-part counterpoint at the beginning spreads at moments to seven and even eight parts, with, of course, chord structures becoming correspondingly dense. Linear relief is provided in quiet contexts. But to relieve and support principal lines in the saturating chromaticism and harmonic opacity of the *tutti*, octave doublings are employed; and this is the last instance, in this phase of his development, of the composer's willingness to incur their harmonic priority.

It is too late by many years to be talking about the *Five Pieces* and time, high time, that our orchestras were regularly performing them. As for my own performance (in words), I can say only that I have stuck to two of my resolves. The first was to avoid the hindsight of the "twelve-tone system" (not because I consider the direction of the view invalid but because Schoenberg uses it himself in his analysis of the *Four Orchestral Songs*). The second was not to hide my convic-tion that the *Five Pieces* are one of this century's richest musical experiences.

[14] The clef is wrong in the bass part, 1949 score, at m. 440.

ANALYSIS OF THE FOUR
ORCHESTRAL SONGS OPUS 22*

ARNOLD SCHOENBERG

In the recently published *Letters* (edited by Erwin Stein; London, 1964), the circumstances attendant upon the first performance of the Op. 22 Songs are clearly revealed. Schoenberg had been compelled by ill health to move to the south of Europe, and by October, 1931 had settled in Barcelona. There he worked on Act II of *Moses und Aron.* During January, 1932, he received Rosbaud's invitation to deliver a lecture in connection with the prospective performance of the Op. 22 Songs over the Frankfurt radio. Schoenberg was anxious to accept—and curious, of course, to hear his Op. 22 for the first time—but had severe misgivings about the effect that the trip northward might have on his illness. The three published letters to Rosbaud from this time (dated January 19, January 30, and February 13, 1932) are full of vacillations, hoping in one sentence that he might yet take the trip, and realizing in the next that he cannot go. Schoenberg says, also, that the Frankfurt station cannot be heard in Barcelona. In the letter of January 30, Schoenberg tries rather desperately to find a way to comply with Rosbaud's request, but he does not have the music of Op. 22 with him, and he writes a tabulation of possible dates on which return letters, music, and confirming telegrams might be sent and received, as well as the date on which the lecture might be finished. He proposes to travel on the 16th. . . . "But shall I then be in time for the rehearsals in Frankfurt? Shall we risk it?" The next letter is very downcast, and there is hardly any hope for the trip: "Snow has been falling here for

---

*NOTE: It should be borne in mind that this essay was specifically written to be *heard* rather than *read*. The disposition of paragraphs has therefore been left intact, so as to permit the reader to 'hear' the natural pacing of the speaker's voice.

Of all 75 musical illustrations called for in the text, nearly half were intended for actual performance by an orchestra and a singer. Since it would obviously be too cumbersome to provide these orchestral illustrations in full by having them printed, they will instead be referred to, in their appropriate locations, by mention of page and measure numbers in the commercially available score of Op. 22. Such references will appear in the left-hand margins.

The remaining illustrations, mainly for piano with or without the singer, are included in exactly the same manner as in Schoenberg's manuscript, and are placed in the center of the page.

three days, to the utter amazement of the population. . . ." Schoenberg therefore suggests that either Rosbaud himself, or Wiesengrund-Adorno, or a gentleman connected with Radio Frankfurt deliver the lecture. He adds that it took him over a week to write it. The title-page of the manuscript contains the following note: "read by Rosbaud, 21 February 1932".

Schoenberg had to forego the trip; he did not return to Germany until June of that year. Act II of *Moses und Aron* was completed on March 10. In the volume of *Letters* there is no further mention of the Op. 22 Songs. Subsequent letters to Rosbaud do not refer to their first performance. However, Radio Frankfurt made a recording for Schoenberg's private use. It is possible, furthermore, that he may have heard an actual performance of Op. 22 between July 1932 and the end of that year.

Late in life, Schoenberg expressed doubts regarding any performance possibilities, in view of the unusual requirements of the Songs' instrumentation and their great difficulty.

Claudio Spies

I COMPOSED the Orchestral Songs Opus 22 in 1915. Their style may best be characterized if I briefly describe the development leading up to and beyond them. About 1908 I had taken the first steps—also with songs—into that domain of composition which is falsely called atonal, and whose distinguishing characteristic is the abandonment both of a tonal center and of the methods of dissonance-treatment that had been customary up to that time. It was this latter feature, as I subsequently ascertained, that occurred if the perception of a dissonance could be ideally equated to that of a consonance.

Yet, indeed, only ideally!—since, in fact, the conscious and unconscious inhibitions in the perception of dissonance existed then and continue still, to a certain degree, to exist not only for the listener, but for the composer as well. Furthermore, while the use of consonances had fulfilled, as it were, the function of shaping form and context, their avoidance was bound to lead to stringent precautionary measures and to require a variety of safeguards.

One of the most important aids to comprehension is clarity of design. *Brevity* facilitates a grasp of the whole; it furthers clarity and it encourages comprehension. Unwittingly, I wrote *unusually short* pieces of music at that time.

Ladies and gentlemen, you have, no doubt, heard that I am a constructor; and I shall not contradict this, since it flatters me—at any rate, it flatters me more to be called a "brain musician" than if I were to be called a blockhead. For I have unwittingly done a number of other right things. There are, of course, various means of different value with which to produce formal cohesion within a piece of music. One of these means, tonal harmony, with its emphasis on tonal centers, guaranteed not only cohesion, but also made for clarity of design by articulating the constituent parts. By not using this device in the new direction that my music had taken, I was compelled, in the first place, to renounce not only the construction of larger forms, but to avoid the employment of larger melodies—as well as all formal musical elements dependent upon the frequent repetition of motifs. It seemed at first impossible to find pertinent substitutes for these through musical means. Unwittingly, and therefore rightly, I found help where music always finds it when it has reached a crucial point in its development. *This, and this alone,* is the origin of what is called Expressionism: a piece of music does not create its formal appearance out of the logic of its *own* material, but, guided by the feeling for internal and external processes, and in *bringing these to expression,* it supports itself on their logic and builds upon that. No new procedure in the history of music!—at each renewal or increase of musical materials, it is assisted by feelings, insights, occurrences, impressions and the like, mainly in the form of poetry—whether it be in the period of the first operas, of the *lied,* or of program music.

At the time that I wrote these Songs, I had overcome the initial difficulties of the new style to a certain extent, even though it was only through composition with 12 tones that the formal possibilities of an absolute music were unleashed and broke through, freed from all admixture of extra-musical elements.

Still, I continued to prefer composing music for texts, and I was still dependent purely upon my feeling for form. And I had to say to myself—and was perhaps entitled to do so—that my feeling for form, modeled on the great masters, and my musical logic, which had been proved in so and so many cases, must guarantee that what I write is formally and logically correct, even if I do not realize it. This consideration, as well as one other, increase the difficulty in making a formal analysis of these Songs.

As always during the first decades of a new style of composing, music theory has in this case not progressed nearly far enough. The other consideration, however, is that compositions for texts are inclined to allow the poem to determine, at least outwardly, their form. To be sure, this tendency can generally be noted less in songs than in dramatic or choral music. Yet here, in my Opus 22, it appears conspicuously, for the abovementioned reasons.

It is not feasible, therefore, in the first place, to present an analysis in the older sense by citing the main theme, subsidiary theme, development sections, repetitions, etc. . . . However, I can show you several other things which are very significant in regard to the essence of musical logic.

We present to you the first 18 measures—the instrumental introduction —of the first song, "Seraphita" by Ernest Dowson, translated by Stefan George. The opening 10 measures contain a melody for clarinets.

No. 1: Orch.
(Clarinets alone),
p. 5, mm. 1–10

This is followed by a phrase played by divided violins:

No. 2: Orch.
(Violins alone),
p. 5, mm. 10–16

I should like also to show you a few measures of the celli accompanying the clarinet melody, because several things that occur here will be heard again further on.

No. 3: Orch.
(Vlc.),
p. 5, mm. 1–4

Taken as a whole, the introduction sounds as follows—and I want to draw your attention to the figured accompaniments in the violin measures:

No. 4: Orch.
(Tutti),
p. 5, mm. 1–18

I do not know if it is possible, even after repeated hearings, to perceive this passage as melody, in the absence of those repetitions that are usually requisite to such perception. However, let the following demonstrate the unconscious sway of musical logic. The clarinet melody

No. 5 (at the piano, first phrase)

consists of a series of minor seconds

No. 6 (Piano)

to which an ascending minor third is appended.

No. 7 (Piano)

In the ensuing phrase the minor third and second are combined to yield the following shape (*Gestalt*):

No. 8 (Piano)

And similarly in the third phrase.

No. 9 (Piano)

Here, both times, the minor third led to the minor second; by the fifth phrase this order has already been reversed.

No. 10 (Piano)

The half-step A-G♯ comes first; the minor third G♯-B follows.

A G♯   G♯ B

No. 11a (Piano)

However, there has been an additional development: the minor second B-C

B   C

No. 11b

has turned into a major seventh B-C,

No. 11c

a new shape which turns up again immediately in the fifth phrase as B♭-B♮, with its appended minor third B-D.

No. 12 (Piano)

A different method for connecting is used in the sixth phrase

No. 13a (Piano)

which again takes up the rhythm

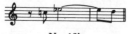

No. 13b

of the second phrase.

No. 13c

Further, the ninth phrase is of interest,

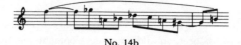

No. 14a (Piano)

as it represents a distinct variation of the beginning.

No. 14b

In the passage for violins, following the clarinet measures, it has perhaps struck you that the first and second phrases are merely variations of the preceding,

No. 15 (Piano)

and that, furthermore, a small phrase makes its appearance twice in succession at the end, in the accompaniment for celli:

No. 16a (Vlc. m. 16)   No. 16b (Vlc. m. 17)

The first three notes are once again in the sequence of minor second and third that we have heard before. It is to play an important role in what follows. Thus, the vocal part, which consists of 4 sections separated from one another by interludes, begins the first of these sections with that little phrase. We will now present this section to you. Notice that the three notes constitute a fixed motivic unit which occurs most frequently at the beginning of text lines, but which also plays a part in the remaining portions of phrases. Besides, this figure is varied and developed in manifold ways, as I will show further on. Perhaps you may also notice the accompaniment to the words "Lebens wilder See" and "sei meine Fahrt auch voll von finster Sturm und Weh."[1]

No. 17: Orch.,
p. 6, mm. 18–28

You heard the above-mentioned motif first in eighth-notes and then in sixteenths.

No. 18

And so on ... , in connection with which the rhythm of this figure will develop into an independent shape that will appear, moreover, clad with other intervals. I hope I may not have in vain called your attention to a place in the text, for in this regard there are some not unimportant matters of principle to be adduced.

"Wilde See," "Fahrt," "Finstrer Sturm," "Weh"[2]—: these are words whose representational impact hardly any composer from Bach to Strauss could have resisted—words which could not simply glide past without being reflected by some musical symbol. And yet this place affords a very telling example of a new way to deal with such images. I may say that I

---

[1] "life's passionate sea"; "Troublous and dark and stormy though my passage be" (Dowson).
[2] "passionate sea," "passage," "dark storm," "woe."

was the first to have proceeded in this new manner; the others who imitated it under a misapprehension have, for the most part, concealed this fact—yet, thanks to that very misunderstanding, I am pleased to acquiesce .... It had apparently been thought that I took no notice *whatever* of texts, since with me they no longer give rise to sounds like a storm or swords clashing or sardonic laughter. This impression was exaggerated to such a degree that music was composed to *no* text, or at best to a text *other* than the one which was actually being sung. My music, however, took representational words into account in the same way as abstract ones: it furthered the immediate, vivid rendering of the whole and of its parts, according to the measure of their meaning within the whole. Now, if a performer speaks of a passionate sea in a different tone of voice than he might use for a calm sea, my music does nothing else than to provide him with the opportunity to do so, and to support him. The music will not be as agitated as the sea, but it will be *differently* so, as, indeed, the performer will be. Even a painting does not reproduce its whole subject matter; it merely states a motionless condition. Likewise, a word describes an object and its state; a film reproduces it without color, and a color film would reproduce it without organic life. Only music, however, can bestow this last gift, and that is why music may impose a limit on its capacity to imitate—by *placing* the object and its being *before the mind's* eye, through performance.

In the second section the voice repeatedly employs the three-note motif in a variety of ways. For example, at the words "laute Angst,"

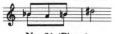

No. 19 (Piano)

or at "in deines Ruheortes"

No. 20 (Piano)

where, to be sure, changes have become evident, so that

No. 21 (Piano)

attests to the original shape

No. 22 (Piano)

—if one disregards the ornamental half-step—

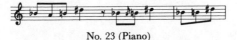

No. 23 (Piano)

and where the minor third has become a major third. To this will be added a further transformation; the minor second likewise becomes major.

No. 24 (Piano)

This enlargement of intervals clearly prepares for the even larger intervals of the third section by introducing them, for the present, in conjunction with the same basic rhythm. We will now play you this second section.

No. 25: Orch. &
Voice,
p. 6, mm. 26–44

We have also played the measures that introduce the more agitated middle section, during which you heard the violin figures:

No. 26: Orch.
(Violins),
p. 7, mm. 41–43

whose large intervals are in the rhythm of the first figure. But there is an additional connection: by stressing the top notes in the first phrase,

No. 27 (Piano)

you will obtain the first figure.

No. 28 (Piano)

The first measures of this section are taken up with this agitated figure, both in the orchestra and in the vocal part. The motif structure returns to an approximation of the primary shape in the last measures—for instance, in the clarinets.

No. 29: Orch.
(Clarinets a 6),
p. 8, mm. 48–49

Here the accompaniment also brings to mind the beginning.

No. 30: Orch.
(Vlc.),
p. 8, mm. 48–50

We will now demonstrate this whole section for you.

No. 31: Voice &
Orch.,
p. 7, mm. 39–54

I would not have you believe, ladies and gentlemen, that with this analysis all aspects of this section have been elucidated. And it can only be a consolation for me that I may be spared from using those elegant but hypocritical turns of phrase with which it is customary, in analyzing, to gloss over the inexplicable. I state what I see, as far as I am able to express it. Yet in the end, this is still a path on which one must feel one's way, step by step, with the tip of one's toes.

From the final section and its orchestral conclusion, I would like first to show you that the initial motif returns in the voice in the form of a chain of motifs.

No. 32a (Piano)

The motif is included six times:

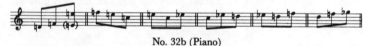

No. 32b (Piano)

One might be led to believe that this is a coincidence, especially since this motif is not in itself a striking one, and could therefore appear elsewhere without any particular significance—let alone the circumstance that changes do occur in the size and the direction of its intervals. In fact, it plays a not altogether negligible role in the second of these songs, and this merely proves the well-known point that with only one motif it is possible to fashion an unlimited number of pieces, all of them totally different from one another; that in this context the motif need be nothing more than a building-stone, and that the only thing that matters in this respect is the manner of its structuring. Even so, it is not quite immaterial that such a changeable shape should exhibit a certain trait which will circumscribe its use. By the same token, one would not want to build a fortress with playing cards, or make a hayloft of ashlar-stone, or use bricks for a house of cards—to say nothing of a castle in the air.

Let me now show you a clarinet melody from the accompaniment to the afore-mentioned vocal part:

No. 33: Orch.
(all clarinets),
p. 8, mm. 54–59

and from the orchestral conclusion, the *Hauptstimme* in the violins:

No. 34: Orch.
(all violins),
p. 9, mm. 74–84

And now the entire final section.

No. 35: Voice &
Orch.,
p. 8, mm. 53 to
the end.

The second song, "Alle, welche dich suchen" from "Das Stundenbuch" by Rainer Maria Rilke, contains the same motif from the first song, as I have already mentioned—but maybe that is no more than a coincidence? —in several places. Nevertheless, I could perhaps point out that here the real connection is another one. That, however, would lead us too far afield, and it would not be worthwhile because the result could hardly be in keeping with a piece such as this song. It is an extraordinarily short song: only 25 measures long. Now, according to my observations, the conditions pertaining to the construction of short pieces are the following: one must be wary of setting up materials that may call for development, since it is unfeasible to grant them any extensive development in only a few measures; besides, one must provide each tiniest element—as in an aphorism, or in lyric poetry—with such a wealth of relationships to all other component elements, that the smallest reciprocal change of position will bring forth as many new shapes as might elsewhere be found in the richest development sections. The various shapes will then be as in a hall of mirrors—continually visible from all sides, and displaying their mutual connection in every possible way. Naturally, I can only show you a fraction of the relationships that I am able to see for myself. But first, a few instances of the above-mentioned motif from the first song; for example, in the voice:

No. 36a (Piano and Voice)

—actually, rather often:

No. 36b (Piano alone)

But also in the accompaniment; for instance, in the celli:

No. 37a (Piano)

or in the flutes:

No. 37b

Yet, as I say, there are other guide lines. The shape

No. 38 (Piano)

at the outset of the vocal part appears at once in the second and third measures of the accompaniment—first in the flute and the second time in the clarinet. Please try to remember this clarinet and the ensuing rapid figure in the flutes; we will come across them again.

No. 39: Voice &
Orchestra,
p. 10, beginning
to m. 6

You may have heard this motif appearing frequently in the voice, as for instance at "so dich finden, binden dich/an Bild und Gebärde"

No. 40a (Piano)

No. 40b

Our search will be even more fruitful if its object is two consecutive thirds, for they are to be found almost everywhere and may well be considered as the "common denominator" of all shapes in this piece. They already appear in the opening phrase, "Alle, welche dich . . ."

No. 41a (Piano)

"versuchen dich . . ."

No. 41b

"und die, so dich finden . . . ."

No. 41c

Likewise, in the second segment:

No. 42a (Voice and Piano)

No. 42b (Piano)

Now listen to this entire second segment:

No. 43: Voice &
Orch.,
p. 10, mm. 6–12

The third segment emerges as a middle section whose typical formal peculiarities make allowances for the continued use of the original motifs, in their strict basic forms, to be somewhat relaxed. Nevertheless, in the voice you hear

Ich   weiss,   dass die Zeit   an - ders heisst   als du,

No. 44 (Piano)

as well as

The consecutive thirds   and the opening motif

No. 45 (Piano)

Furthermore, consider the part for contrabassoon and double-bass which is built on the succession of thirds.

No. 46: Voice &
Orch.,
p. 10, mm. 12–19

In the fourth segment, which acts as a "third part of a ternary structure," there is again a closer approximation to the primary shapes. Above all, I should like to remind you of the figure in the clarinet (m. 3) and the flutes (m. 4)

No. 47 (Piano)

which now appears, but little changed, in another instrumental context, with the cello part using the motif in thirds.

No. 48: Orch.
alone,
p. 11, mm. 20–21

It is even possible to discern the opening motif on its original pitches in the vocal phrase: "Gib deinen Gesetzen recht,/die von Geschlecht . . ."

No. 49a (Piano)   No. 49b

and, further, in the flutes, directly thereafter:

No. 50 (Piano)

We shall now play the end of the song

No. 51: Voice &
Orch.,
p. 11, mm. 20–25

The third and fourth songs afford their analysis far greater difficulties. I would not, however, want to act as if I were withholding this analysis from you merely because I cannot take for granted so thorough an acquaintance with technical notions as might be desirable. Yet, in fact, this *is* the case, as I will prove to you through an example. Nevertheless, the reason is not that—on the contrary, I believe I could almost be tempted to try to present this difficult matter to you in such a way as to allow it to be grasped readily. But in actual fact I cannot do so. I know that these songs do not dispense with logic—but I cannot prove it. That is why I will adopt a different course and touch on something that I have not yet mentioned. But first I must redeem my promise to indicate which complex processes I would have to explain were I to undertake a thoroughly technical analysis.

We will begin by playing for you the first of the three sections into which the third song, "Mach mich zum Wächter deiner Weiten," from "Das Stundenbuch" by Rainer Maria Rilke, is divided.

No. 52: Orch. &
Voice,
p. 12, mm. 1–14

In analyzing, one cannot simply go by the look of the notes on the page. *I*, at any rate, hardly ever discover relationships by means of the eye; however, I *hear* them. Only in this way is it possible to perceive that the first bar of the orchestral introduction and the first bar of the voice part are alike almost to the point of identity—after which one may also see this correspondence in the notes. Listen first to the orchestral passage, played on the piano:

No. 53 (Piano)

· 39 ·

and now listen to the vocal part:

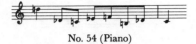

No. 54 (Piano)

and once more, to both of them:

No. 55

and again. (The same thing [Nos. 53–54] repeated several times.)

You may, by now, be aware of the great resemblance between both these elements. In part it is because their first three notes are the same: D, D♭, C

No. 56a (Piano)

But the continuation is E-F in one

No. 56b

and E♭-F in the other.

No. 56c

In the first, however, the E♭ is "delayed" in an upper part. Both then proceed, in different ways, toward B-C.

No. 56d   No. 56e

and again

No. 56d   No. 56e

It can be pronounced a law of music that it is possible to recognize (i.e., to perceive) not only the regular rearrangements of musical shapes, but, given favorable conditions, irregular ones as well, provided only that enough will remain constant, once the intervals have been exchanged. The effect will therefore be of repeating or of making a variant, and its purpose could be for transition, introduction, resolution or, simply, for the sake of variety. Here, however, there is another matter, and it is this that I should like to explain to you, insofar as the present scope will permit.

Since Richard Wagner, the treatment of texts in German music has diverged from that of the folksong, as well as from the music of Southern people—for example, of the Italians. Even Schubert does not set off words singly in any marked fashion, according to the weight of their meaning. Rather, by means of a comprehensive melody, he may pass over a salient textual feature, even when it is most important in regard to content and poetic substance. It should not be surprising, then, that a genuine melody will arise relatively seldom from a procedure which strongly emphasizes the text. After all, a melody of that sort would require a good deal of regularity, besides repetitions, concision, etc., so that all these demands could hardly ever be met completely in following the course that an idea may impose upon words, their rhythm and their sound. In these songs I am in the preliminary stages of a procedure which is essentially different both from the Italians and from Wagner. I am myself not yet quite able to say how far this may apply to my most recent works. At any rate, I am aware that it is mainly a concern with the art of variation, which allows for a motif to be a constant basis while, at the same time, doing justice to the subtlest nuance in the text. Here, however, at this preliminary stage, I have not yet carried it so far. As yet, there is no distinctive motif to be varied; nor did I yet understand how to work out so *binding* a shape, as a motif must be, in such a novel way. (One cannot work out shapes that are not binding.) But there is another factor that underlies all this: something imperfect, unfinished, a scaffolding, a skeleton which is clothed only when notes are hung on it, and only then assumes a shape; a succession of tones in a changeable rhythm. That succession of tones will now give rise to the new shapes which will adapt themselves—in their capacity as principal notes—to the words by surrounding themselves with subsidiary, ornamental notes. With this method of variation, which presumably also plays a part in my later works, I found myself on a path that was altogether right, as the following reflection will prove.

Richard Wagner tells of Spontini, the celebrated Italian opera composer, that he had declared himself, as inventor of the "appoggiatura to the sixth"

No. 57

—which I cannot quite understand—to be the last musician who had anything of consequence to say, since it would be impossible ever to surpass this invention. However wrongly Spontini may, by this curious assertion, have judged the magnitude of his alleged invention, his feeling for the importance of the appoggiatura to a composer who writes music to words was nevertheless right.

I find, in fact, that one may draw the following conclusion from this. During fairly expressive speaking, the voice moves between changing pitches. But at no time does one remain on any one particular pitch, as in singing. Now, in the endeavor to gain a sung melody from the natural intonation of the words in spoken melody, it is obvious that one will have to evade the principal notes in singing, as much as one will avoid the fixed pitches in speaking. If, in the former, one slips away from them, so in the latter case one will surround principal notes with embellishments. Indeed, perhaps it is this which imbued the recitatives in older operas with their liveliness—this embellishment named appoggiatura. If this interpretation is acceptable, light will be shed on many aspects of my works from this period, which might otherwise be difficult to understand. You will then be able to admit that, in fact, both the places that I designated as being practically the same, actually are so:

No. 58 (Piano)

Furthermore, you will then perhaps be able to hear that the three segments which make up the second part all begin with this sort of ornamented figure.

The first:

No. 59a (Piano and Voice)

the second:

No. 59b

the third:

No. 59c

And now, the whole middle section:

No. 60: Voice &
Orch.,
p. 13, mm. 15–27

It will not be necessary to stress that the same thing may also be found in the third section. Please listen to it:

No. 61: Voice &
Orch.,
p. 14, mm. 27 to
the end.

The fourth song, "Vorgefühl" by Rainer Maria Rilke:

I have taken care to discuss a particular aspect of each of these songs, since a purely scholarly analysis would take up much too much time. Now I should like to bring up a few references to the orchestration, because so far I have not mentioned it at all. My orchestration is preponderantly soloistic and, despite the frequently high number of parts, it is mostly *transparent*. Listen, for example, to the orchestral introduction. In the first measure there are three parts, violins I & II and celli; in m. 2 the violins are accompanied *singly* by English horn, clarinet and flute.

No. 62: Orch.,
p. 15, mm. 1–4

For a typical example of how I combine, and make an entity out of, heterogeneous elements, listen to the *first quarter of m. 5.*

No. 63: Orch.

Or the second and third quarters of m. 6.

No. 64: Orch.

This kind of scoring does not, of course, arise from any affectation, but from the desire to lend color to each part so that it may assert itself among the other participating parts. I think that in this way I achieve a very clear, if slightly sharp, sound which complies with my principle that everything that is written must also be audible. Again, listen to the third quarter of m. 8, in which violins, violas and celli make an odd mixture.

No. 65: Orch.

I also think that the voice part can unfold to its advantage in such surroundings. Let us listen to a portion of it.

No. 66: Voice &
Orch.,
p. 15, mm. 1 to
first quarter of
10

In the last measure the vocal part was unusually low for a soprano. Yet a rather rich orchestral accompaniment did not succeed in covering it. But notice how delicately the accompaniment is articulated in the following place:

No. 67: Orch.
alone,
p. 15, mm. 10–11

Moreover, you may gather from the text[3] that although the voice must provide a "prescient" expression, it must remain calm in doing so:

No. 68: Voice &
Orch.,
p. 15, mm. 10–14

There is an interesting sound which I would like to demonstrate by itself; listen to the colorfulness that is possible even in the low register:

No. 69: Orch.,
p. 16, m. 15

---

[3]"Die Türen schliessen noch sanft, und in den Kaminen ist Stille;/die Fenster zittern noch nicht, und der Staub ist noch schwer." (The doors still close softly, and there is stillness in the hearths;/the windows do not yet shake. and the dust is still heavy.)

It is not easy to provide a good accompaniment to places in the singer's part where the vocal registers change through big, rapid leaps—especially if the expression is also to be underlined. Such was the case in the following:

und bin er - regt   wie das Meer

No. 70 (Voice and Piano)

Notice, please, how carefully the orchestra is gauged in this place—transparent, yet at the same time lending support:

No. 71: Orch.
alone,
p. 16, mm. 17–18

Listen now to the section in which all of this happens, beginning with the low-register sounds that we had shown you a moment ago.

No. 72: Voice &
Orch.,
p. 16, mm. 15–18

In m. 20, the voice goes from its middle to its lowest register, in rapid notes:

fal - le   in mich hi-nein

No. 73 (Voice and Piano)

I should like to cite the accompaniment to this place as an example of how, with me, the necessity to accompany such a critical place gently and simply is corroborated not only by the instrumentation, but by the compositional means as well.

No. 74: Orch.
alone,
p. 16, m. 20

And now we will show you the end of this song, with which my lecture and analysis will be concluded.

No. 75: Voice &
Orch.,
m. 15, with upbeat
for the voice, to
the end.

—Translated and annotated by Claudio Spies.

THREE ESSAYS ON SCHOENBERG

MILTON BABBITT

CONCERTO FOR VIOLIN & ORCHESTRA, OP. 36

SCHOENBERG'S only violin concerto, completed in 1936, dedicated to Anton Webern and unperformed until 1940—when it was presented by Louis Krasner with The Philadelphia Orchestra under Leopold Stokowski—has since that time become one of the most widely studied, taught and analyzed source works of twelve-tone composition by the creator of twelve-tone composition, while it has entered the repertory of few violinists and few orchestras; performances, particularly in the United States, have been rare to a degree sadly unbefitting one of the most influential compositions of our time. Certainly, it is a difficult work. For the violinist, it is a virtuoso work demanding a mastery of his instrument that includes new extensions of virtuosity and, above all, an organic virtuosity that must take into account the compositional materials of the work and the total sound ensemble. The elements of virtuosity are never separable from compositional considerations, and are therefore never to be achieved as isolated instrumental accomplishments, nor is the virtuoso separable from the other sound sources, for he must collaborate in the most intricate and delicate of rhythmic, articulative and sonic ensembles with the manifold combinations of other instruments, while ever remaining the soloist. For the orchestra, also, the difficulties of the work often reside in areas where difficulties sometimes remain unrecognized and unrealized; the orchestral player in the concerto may not encounter extraordinary demands of sheer dexterity and facility, but there are the most subtle demands of phrasing, intonation, dynamic control, rhythmic precision and coordination, and mode of tone production, if he is to fulfill adequately his role in the constantly exposed, ever-changing texture of which he is a component. Some of this difficulty stems from the absence of any octave or multiple-octave instrumental duplication—so-called "octave doubling." This principle, applied in Schoenberg's previous twelve-tone works but not in his next twelve-tone orchestral work—the Piano Concerto of 1944—of necessity places great emphasis upon accuracy of unison duplication, that most critical of duplications in its demands of intonation, balance and temporal coordination.

For the listener, the most efficient and revelatory first step towards acquiring familiarity with and comprehension of this, or any other twelve-tone work, is that of identifying and examining the composition's twelve-tone set, that ordering of the familiar twelve chromatic pitch-classes, which, in its—at most—forty-eight transformations arrived at by transposition, inversion, retrogression and the combinations of these, supplies the total pitch material of the composition and so endows the composition not merely with its local sonic characteristics but with its structural properties at every stage and level of compositional unfolding. The following table presents these forty-eight sets of the concerto:

	I											
	1	2	3	4	5	6	7	8	9	10	11	12
1	A	Bb	Eb	B	E	F#	C	C#	G	Ab	D	F
2	Ab	A	D	Bb	Eb	F	B	C	F#	G	C#	E
3	Eb	E	A	F	Bb	C	F#	G	C#	D	Ab	B
4	G	Ab	C#	A	D	E	Bb	B	F	F#	C	Eb
5	D	Eb	Ab	E	A	B	F	F#	C	C#	G	Bb
6	C	C#	F#	D	G	A	Eb	E	Bb	B	F	Ab
7	F#	G	C	Ab	C#	Eb	A	Bb	E	F	B	D
8	F	F#	B	G	C	D	Ab	A	Eb	E	Bb	C#
9	B	C	F	C#	F#	Ab	D	Eb	A	Bb	E	G
10	Bb	B	E	C	F	G	C#	D	Ab	A	Eb	F#
11	E	F	Bb	F#	B	C#	G	Ab	D	Eb	A	C
12	C#	D	G	Eb	Ab	Bb	E	F	B	C	F#	A

S ———————————————————— R

RI

The rows, read from left to right, present the names of the pitch-classes of the transpositions of the set (designated S), and—therefore—from right to left, those of the retrograde forms (R); the columns present—from top to bottom—the inverted forms (1), and —therefore—from bottom to top, the retrograde—inversions (R1); the order numbers associated with each row and column are combined with the designatory initials to identify any set form or element.

The set S1 (the set occupying the first row) is the form presented at the opening of the work by the conjunction of solo violin and cellos. The rhythmic character of this presentation most strikingly articulates—by a rest—the set into two halves, two disjunct hexachords, and immediately suggests the fundamental role of hexachords in the set, and so in the work (and incidentally explains the presence of the dividing lines in the table). The set has that hexachordal property common to almost all of Schoenberg's sets; the (unordered) content of the two disjunct hexachords is inversionally equivalent. Therefore, associated with every set is an inversionally related set whose corresponding hexachords have no pitch-classes in common with the original set; corresponding hexachords together produce an aggregate, a collection of all twelve pitch-classes. S1 and I11 are so related, and the opening of the concerto explicitly discloses this relationship: after the mentioned statement of S1, I11 is presented, similarly articulated by a rest, into its two hexachords and identically orchestrated. The statement also exemplifies the principle of the preservation of set-defined order within registrally and/or instrumentally delineated parts, but not necessarily between such parts. These successive statements most obviously effect an identification of the second hexachord of S1 with the first I11, from the standpoint of pitch content and the other properties of identification and complementation than can be inferred immediately. They scarcely need be, for Schoenberg himself next presents the sets simultaneously, assigning S1 to the solo violin and I11 to the bassoon, violas, and cellos, thus compositionally displaying their aggregate forming capacity and presenting these aggregates by simply continuing to articulate the component hexachords.

Two such related sets, together with their retrograde forms, create a complex of sets so hexachordally related; at no point in the concerto are two sets stated simultaneously which are not so related, and such complexes dominate exclusively large sections of the composition. For example, the four sets so associated with S1 (S1, I11, R1, RI11) are the only sets employed during the first fifty-eight measures of the concerto, and the area thus delineated is normatively closely analogous to a functional phonal area. And when, at measure 59, a new hexachordal area is introduced, it is associated with new thematic materials. The new area is that defined by the hexachords S11, a transposition by a perfect fifth of S1. This transpositional relation may suggest a parallel with the dominant region of tonal "second subjects," but—be that pertinent or not—this particular transposed form (and, naturally, its complement the perfect fourth) has a singular hexachordal relation to S1, in that it preserves the greatest number of pitches (four) between corresponding hexachords of any set not in the initial complex. In other words, S11 is that set which, by a traditionally tested and reasonable criterion of relatedness, carries the work away from the opening area to the most closely related area, and this relatedness is determined completely by the structure— the intervallic structure—of the hexachords of the set.

Schoenberg's concern with thematically structured composition, with thematic formation, dissolution, and reformation, which often results in a "theme and accompaniment" texture, and the need to differentiate linear and vertical events, is particularly well accommodated to the technique of aggregate construction through hexachords. For that interval (or intervals) which is most characteristic of, in the sense of occurring most frequently in, the constituent hexachords, is necessarily the least characteristic of the intervals formed between the hexachords, and vice versa. So, whereas in the tonal system those triadic intervals characteristic of simultaneities, and those intervals of scale adjacencies characteristic of linear succession, are independent of the individual works, in aggregate formations the so characteristic intervals depend upon the nature of the particular set. In the Violin Concerto, the most characteristic interval of the hexachord is the perfect fifth (or fourth), while the characteristic intervals between hexachords are the major second (or minor seventh), and the major and minor thirds (or sixths). To account for striking occurrences of apparent recurrence in the work, it should be observed that corresponding to each set is an inverted form which preserves the content of the four disjunct trichords. Corresponding to S1, for instance, is I8; the contents of the first and third trichords map into each other, while those of the second and fourth map into themselves. Each set in a complex consisting of two so related sets and their retrogrades is constructed of the same pitch trichords, with the order of pitches within a given trichord—in general—permuted differently in each set. The short range pitch identification which maintains among such sets makes them particularly useful in securing pitch-related compositional sections less literal than repetition. Schoenberg's Fourth String Quartet, completed in the same year as the Concerto, is based on a set with similar trichordal structure.

Those listeners who depend on surface similitudes, particularly thematic ones, to provide continuity and association in the first stages of their acquaintance with a work, will find numerous and strategic examples in this composition. The opening figure of the solo violin returns, not only at the end of the first movement, but in the cadenza near the conclusion of the final movement. The solo violin theme at the opening of the middle movement is a representation of S11 (the set of the first movement's second theme), while its final statement is a representation of S1. The violin opens the final movement with I11, and the movement ends with the combination of S1 and I11 with which the work began.

DAS BUCH DER HÄNGENDEN GÄRTEN
OPUS 15 FOR VOICE AND PIANO

In the history of music, the George-Lieder—Schoenberg's most extended composition for voice and piano—must be accorded a position with the song cycles of Beethoven, Schubert, and Schumann as one of the source works for this medium. In the history of Schoenberg's creative development, the George-Lieder occupy a crucial position as one of the works that initiated and defined the compositional procedures of his "second period," during which the structural role of functional tonality is superseded gradually by that of more singularly internal, contextual means of securing musical continuity and design. On the occasion of the work's first performance, over a half century ago, Schoenberg wrote: "With the George-Lieder I have succeeded for the first time in approaching an expressive and formal ideal which has hovered before me for years."

The work was composed between the end of 1907 and early 1909, and its composition apparently overlapped that of the first two piano pieces of Opus 11, which more commonly are regarded as the first of Schoenberg's "non-tonal" works, and immediately preceded that of the Five Orchestral Pieces, Opus 16, the only purely orchestral work of this period.

This song cycle, in the breadth and wealth of its variety, is a compendium of techniques for the treatment of a medium which is inherently materially limited in that it combines the registrally most restrictive instrument with the—in many respects—timbrally most restrictive instrument. But even a first hearing will reveal methods of securing extraordinary diversity. In the voice, the almost recitative, characteristically mezzo registered second song, whose vocal range extends over but a major ninth up from low "a," is followed by a song whose range is characteristically pure soprano, from "d" to the "a flat," a diminished twelfth above; short range repetitions of pitch and vowel sound duplications are avoided, thus obtaining the greatest possible timbral contrast within the vocal sound. In the piano, for example, the simple chordal texture of the fifth song is followed immediately, in the sixth song, by a succession of quickly changing pianistic texture, creating a rhythmic variety such that only three measures of the total of eighteen are rhythmic repetitions of earlier measures. In the relation of voice to piano, one need but observe the independent development of each from the motive presented by both in unison in the opening measure of the third song, and the rhythmically diversified effects of intermittent and patterned conjunction in, for example, the seventh and eleventh songs. The flexibility of phrase length, always a primary rhythmic concern in Schoenberg's music, is all the more remarkable in that the terminal rhymes of the verse lines are scrupulously articulated, but the articulative methods rest more on associative similitude than on duplication of metrical position, of pitch, or of harmony.

No one can fail to observe aurally the consistency of the associative harmony in, say, the thirteenth song, whose initial simultaneity returns, an octave lower, at the song's conclusion, where it is approached as it was originally departed from; the encompassing motion between these two harmonies is achieved entirely through the redisposition of the intervallic content of these harmonies, together with the iteration of different octave representations of a fixed pitch "f." It is from but these two fundamental premises, the invariance of pitch identification with regard to time, and the invariance of interval identification with regard to transposition, that Schoenberg's unique and intricate structural principles derive. The closing six measures of the fifth song provide a striking, immediately perceptible instance of the application of these procedures: the pitches "e flat" and "a" are heard in the first event of this section on the piano, in the second measure between the voice and the piano bass, in the fourth and fifth measures as exposed dyads between the voice and piano, and—in the final measure—the two notes are stated successively in the voice, ending the song. At the same time, such explicitly stable elements are in constant interaction with the forces of large scale motion, which are reflected most obviously in such results as that in not one of the songs does the voice begin and end on the same pitch.

Yet, as one immediate means of endowing the cycle with continuity and connection, Schoenberg repeats a pitch or pitches from the piano or voice parts from the end of one song to the beginning of the next in all but one case, and this one case is between the seventh and eighth songs. The eighth song provides the point of greatest contrast within the cycle: it is the only genuinely fast song, and makes the greatest demands of virtuosity upon the performers, individually and—above all—as a collective ensemble.

On the surface, the George-Lieder no longer may sound "advanced" or "problematical," but the conceptions of musical coherence which they embody beneath this surface are certain to be a source of discovery and suggestion for, at least, another half century.

MOSES AND AARON

In 1941, Arnold Schoenberg, surveying retrospectively his compositional development toward and in the twelve-tone system, observed: "I discovered . . . I could even base a whole opera, *Moses and Aaron*, solely on one [twelve-tone] set. . ." If we today, with the wisdom of hindsight, are surprised to learn that this represented a discovery to the creator of the twelve-tone system, to the composer who—when he began the composition of *Moses and Aaron*—already had composed the Variations for Orchestra (a veritable "Art of the Fugue" of early twelve-tone technique) and the one-act *opera buffa Von heute auf morgen*, it is probably because of our inclination to forget that each composition fulfilled a uniquely innovatory stage in Schoenberg's voyage of musical discovery, and that therefore *Moses and Aaron*—as the most extended of all his works—constituted a particularly significant and personal validation of the compositional possibilities of the twelve-tone system. Schoenberg's musical career, so revolutionary in its implications and effects, was—for him—a gradual, considered evolution along "the harder road" on which the "Supreme Commander" had "ordered" him. We may, without embarrassment, regard the figure of the "Supreme Commander" as a metaphor embodying the most concrete principle of artistic conduct: the obligation of the responsible artist to do that which he is convinced must be done, and which others apparently are unable or unwilling to do.

If now Schoenberg's creative career appears easily susceptible to periodization, it is only that when one approaches a frontier, there is always the single step that carries one over the border. Throughout each of Schoenberg's "periods" we can discern clearly the path that led him to the next. As an example of the early "tonal period," we need but consider the familiar First String Quartet to observe the characteristics of and motivations for the next, "contextual" (unfortunately, commonly termed "atonal"), period. And such remarkable and still mysterious products of the second period as *Erwartung*, *Pierrot Lunaire*, and the Four Orchestral Songs nevertheless reveal the inherent limitations and problems of "contextual" composition, however singular and satisfactory individual instances may be. We may assume that it was an awareness of this, and, therefore, the need to solve these problems and transcend these limitations that led Schoenberg, "after many unsuccessful attempts during a period of approximately twelve years," to the composition of, and the formulation of the conceptions of, twelve-tone music.

The twelve-tone system, like any formal system, can be characterized by the elements employed, the stipulated relationships among the elements, and the operations defined upon them. In the twelve-tone system, the elements are those of the usual equal-tempered chromatic scale, with membership in twelve pitch classes determined by the familiar criterion of octave equivalence. The relations, of pitch and interval, among these pitch classes is defined for each composition by a total ordering of the classes, each class appearing once and only once. This ordering defines a twelve-tone "set" (sometimes termed "row" or "series"), with no specification of the registral[1] member of the pitch class, or of duration, dynamic level, or timbre, all of which properties are, of course, associated with any compositional representation of the set. It is assumed that this ordering can be inferred from a genuinely twelve-tone work, but not necessarily from any one compositional representation of the set in the work.

The stipulated operations upon the so-specified "prime" set are the three independent ones of transposition, inversion, and retrogression, and of all combinations of these. The "justification" for the incorporation of these operations into the system resides in those unique musical invariants associated with each of them, that is, those characteristics of a set which are preserved under such a transformation, and those relations between a set and its transformed version which are inevitably and universally determined by the transformation. Thus, transposition (which, for present purposes, may be regarded in its usual sense, with the important stipulation that the transposition is performed on pitch classes, not necessarily on registrally specified elements of these classes) preserves, for example, the intervallic succession of a set. Inversion (which, again, is not necessarily the customary contour-interval inversion, but structural inversion of pitch classes) determines, for example, the symmetric property for dyads.[2] Retrogression preserves the interval succession, in reverse, of the inverted set; the set resulting from the successive applications of the operations of retrogression and inversion preserves the intervallic succession of the prime set.

These are but the simplest instances of the multitude of invariants preserved under these operations, and—it must be added—these operations themselves must be and easily can be defined more rigorously than is appropriate or possible here.

In almost all of Schoenberg's twelve-tone works (including *Moses and Aaron*) sets possessing a specific property (that is, one not possessed by all sets) are employed. This property is founded upon the relation between the content of the two discrete hexachords of the set, so that at least one transpositional relationship (and, in the set of *Moses and Aaron*, at only one) each set form can be paired with an inversionally related set whose first hexachord is identical in content

[1] *registral*: differentiated by register from all other members of the same pitch class.
[2] *dyad*: a unit comprising two pitch classes.

(not necessarily in ordered content) with the second hexachord of the original set, and vice versa. Thus, the first hexachords taken together contain all twelve pitch classes, as must—then—the second hexachords, also. Such an arrived-at collection of the twelve pitch classes is termed an "aggregate," not a "set," for it is not necessarily totally ordered, since the order relationship between elements belonging to different set segments is only transitive. It also follows, from the structure of such a set, that retrograde-inversionally related forms of the set can form such an aggregate from a combination of the first hexachord of one and the second hexachord of the other, while a succession of such related forms creates a "secondary set" between the second hexachord of the first such set, and the first hexachord of the second set. Two set forms so related as to make possible the formation of aggregates or secondary sets are "combinatorially" related. The structural use and utility of this property is demonstrated strikingly throughout *Moses and Aaron*.

The identification of the "prime" set in a given composition is not a meaningful task, since the property of "primeness" is not an immanent one, but a relational one; thus, the designation of a particular set form at a specific transpositional level as "prime" is, analytically, usually determined by temporal priority or emphasis, since the closure and symmetry properties of the system assure that the musical relationships remain unaltered, regardless of the choice of the "prime" from the, normally, forty-eight possible compositional sets.

In *Moses and Aaron*, it appears most logical to designate as the "prime" that set a representation of which is sung by Aaron on his first appearance in the opera, in Act I, Scene 2. On this basis, the following table contains the twelve-tone source material of the work:

	I	II	III	IV	V	VI	VII	VIII	IX	X	XI	XII
1	C♯	D	G♯	F♯	G	F	B	A	B♭	C	E♭	E
2	C	C♯	G	F	F♯	E	B♭	G♯	A	B	D	E♭
3	F♯	G	C♯	B	C	B♭	E	D	E♭	F	G♯	A
4	G♯	A	E♭	C♯	D	C	F♯	E	F	G	B♭	B
5	G	G♯	D	C	C♯	B	F	E♭	E	F♯	A	B♭
6	A	B♭	E	D	E♭	C♯	G	F	F♯	G♯	B	C
7	E♭	E	B♭	G♯	A	G	C♯	B	C	D	F	F♯
8	F	F♯	C	B♭	B	A	E♭	C♯	D	E	G	G♯
9	E	F	B	A	B♭	G♯	D	C	C♯	E♭	F♯	G
10	D	E♭	A	G	G♯	F♯	C	B♭	B	C♯	E	F
11	B	C	F♯	E	F	E♭	A	G	G♯	B♭	C♯	D
12	B♭	B	F	E♭	E	D	G♯	F♯	G	A	C	C♯

(Each row of this table, read from left to right, contains one of the twelve transpositions of the prime set, and, read from right to left, one of the twelve transpositions of the retrograde form of the set. Each column, read from top to bottom, contains one of the twelve transpositions of the inverted form of the set, and, read from bottom to top, one of the twelve transpositions of the retrograde-inverted form of the set. For purposes of identification, the prime forms will be designated by the corresponding arabic numerals, and the retrograde forms by the corresponding arabic numerals followed by the letter R; the inverted and retrograde-inverted forms will be identified respectively by the corresponding roman numerals, and the roman numerals followed by the letter R. It is understood that enharmonic substitutions are always possible in the actual composition.)

The designation of 1 as the prime set of the opera is, first of all, logical from a standpoint of musico-dramatic emphasis, for, as has been mentioned above, it is stated explicitly at the entrance of that one of the two protagonists of the opera whose vocal expression is pitch-determined. Then, Aaron's vocal part immediately follows with statements of XII, 1R, and XIIR, the combinatorially determined transpositions of the other three set forms. At no other point in the opera is there such a vocal succession of set form statements, a succession which is characteristic of other of Schoenberg's works, including the statement of the theme in the earlier Variations for Orchestra (the set of which, incidentally, has the same total content within the discrete hexachords as that of *Moses and Aaron*), and the openings of the later Fourth String Quartet and Piano Concerto. Indeed, the order of presentation of set forms here is identical with that of the opening of the Fourth String Quartet. This particular succession has the effect of creating a secondary set only at the hexachordal midpoint, between the second hexachord of XII and the first hexachord of 1R, an effect which is made easily audible by Schoenberg's procedure of following the statement of 1 with a three-beat rest, 1R with a two-beat rest, but XII with only a half-beat rest. The 1 and XII sets together assume the character of a single unit, with regard to which the following 1R and XIIR together assume the character of a total retrograde inversion, an interpretation justified in the large by the frequent formal function of retrograde inversion in the opera, and reflected in the small in the structure of the set itself, since its second and third discrete trichords[3] are retrograde inversions of one another.

Further, Aaron's statement of these set forms is accompanied in the orchestra by the aggregate forming combinatorial complements, with Aaron's statement of 1 divided by an eighth rest into its two hexachords, further clarifying the structural significance of the hexachordal sub-unit.

Moses is permitted to desert his *Sprechstimme* (precisely

[3] *trichord*: a unit comprising three pitch classes.

rhythmed, contour-determined speech) and pure speech for sung pitches at only one point in the opera (Act I, Scene 2, at the words "Reinige dein Denken"), and the succession of twelve pitches granted such privileged treatment is a representation of II.

The combinatorial association of unique pairs of sets is the predominant criterion of simultaneity and succession of set statements in the opera. The particular ordering within the hexachords of the set yields other useful musical characteristics in association with such pairs, such as that of preserving the pitch adjacencies of discrete dyads. Considering 1 and XII, for example: the first discrete dyad of 1 is the sixth of XII, the second of 1 is the fourth of XII, etc.

Relationships between combinatorially unrelated forms are determined primarily by the total pitch identity of other sub-units. For instance, the chorus ends Act I, Scene 3, with set 2, and opens Act I, Scene 4, with set II, immediate continuity and association being effected through the identification of the middle tetrachords of the two set forms, whose middle hexachords are identical. Set forms are associated also through the mutual identification of the pitch levels of the two tritones in the set; this consideration associates, for example, 2,3,6,7,II,III,VI, and VII. Similarly, the second and third trichords associate, for example, 1,6,VII, XI, and 1,8, XI, V. The opera employs these, and a myriad of comparable, often more extensive, relationships.

At this late date, it is perhaps unnecessary to emphasize the fact that a set representation is employed by no means necessarily in an explicitly melodically, motivically, or thematically delineated manner. In *Moses and Aaron* such use is a significant rarity (as at Aaron's first appearance); rather, the set and aggregate function as matricial units of progression, both vertically and horizontally, from which motivic and thematic elements are drawn and constructed and in which their unfolding is imbedded. As a result, the immediate musical continuity is perceived most easily through the structure (not necessarily the ordered structure) of the discrete hexachords, as an element of set statement or aggregate statement. In the later stages of 'the opera, particularly, there are deviations from the established order within the hexachord (in Schoenberg's words: "when the set had already become familiar to the ear"), arising most often from the temporal redistribution of previously established thematic elements, which, in themselves, do preserve the defined ordering.

Among any events in the opera coherence and continuity are effected through set forms, transpositional levels, melodic, harmonic, and rhythmic motivic elements, individual and composite rhythms, timbre, texture, and the interrelation of all these factors with the ideational and sonic structure of the text. So complex a unity can be indicated only by a lengthy and—in its own way—equally complex analysis. What follows is but a cursory indication of some of the aspects of the more strategic and easily identifiable points in the work.

Act I, Scene 1. There is no orchestral "overture" or "prelude," but merely a brief (six measure) introduction in which the ensemble of six solo voices (seated in the orchestra, and always doubled by a fixed group of six solo instruments) and orchestra present 6 and X. Moses' entrance is accompanied by the succession of IR and 5, arranged in the form of six four-part chords, thus allowing the upper voice (English horn) to state the middle hexachord of 6, which form returns explicitly (again, in association with X) in the solo ensemble and orchestra. The following alternations of Moses' *Sprechstimme* (accompanied by the orchestral adumbration of motivic elements which are to acquire extended significance throughout the later course of the opera) and the simultaneously singing and speaking chorus lead back, at the close of the scene, to the musical materials of the introduction.

Act I, Scene 2. The orchestrally light introduction to this scene becomes the accompaniment to Aaron's first appearance (also the first of a solo singing voice) with the musical material discussed above. This scene is vocally unique in the opera in its restriction to two solo voices: that of Aaron's (sung) and Moses' (*Sprechstimme*). After the statement of the four set forms, Aaron participates in the presentation of a passage in triple counterpoint, compounded from a simultaneous statement, at the outset, of V and 9. (Actually, there is also a fourth part of repeated note pairs, which—however—always plays a subordinate role in this scene.) This passage is repeated ("Auserwähltes Volk") with textural and rhythmic variation, and with Aaron now singing a second of the three original contrapuntal elements. Eventually ("Du strafst die Sünden") he states the third of these elements, followed by Moses' "Reinige dein Denken," with its unique privilege to be sung. After a return to a varied form of the "triple counterpoint" section, the scene closes with the orchestral statement of the music of "Reinige dein Denken" accompanying Aaron.

Act I, Scene 3. This extended scene complements the preceding by omitting Moses and Aaron, eschewing solo *Sprechstimme*, and containing enormous variety of choral and solo vocal expression. The first voice heard is the first solo female voice of the opera, that of the Young Girl, presenting 10R (accompanied by VIR) in a characteristic manner, with phrases consisting of the first four notes, then the first five notes, then the total first hexachord of the set; the second hexachord is presented similarly. The Young Man follows with VIIR unfolded analogously, thus in strict inversion to the Young Girl's solo. The music of these two solos, together with that following in the voice of Another Man, constitutes the most important musical substance of the scene, reassigned through various solo and choral parts, and combined simultaneously in the trio of the Young Girl, the Young Man, and Another Man, preceding the final choral section.

Act I, Scene 4, follows the preceding immediately and is, likewise, musically connected immediately by the chorus, as mentioned above. All types of vocal expression are juxtaposed and combined in this scene, which is, in many respects, a cumulative combination of the elements of the preceding scenes. By-now-familiar musical materials or clear derivations from them are shaped into an intricate formal mosaic of cross references to preceding events, and within the scene itself. The return of the chorus of six solo voices (for the first time since Scene 1) with the word "Aaron" set to the identical music (compounded of the initial and terminal trichords of 8 and III) of that point in Scene 1 where Aaron's name is first mentioned is an emphatic indication of the focal role played by Aaron in this scene. Likewise, there are varied but unmistakable returns to the music of his entrance in Scene 2, most importantly at the words: "In Moses Hand"; "Erkennet die Macht"; "Seht, Moses Hand"; "Jetzt aber wohnt in Moses Busen"; "Erkennet euch auch darin"; ". . . und der Ewige." The triple counterpoint section of Scene 2 returns with "Es ist euer Blut," and it is with this music in the orchestra that the scene closes.

The Interlude begins with a statement of VIII, and thus refers to Moses' last utterance in Act I, as support to the chorally spoken "Moses." Employing only the orchestra (at a dynamic level of ppp) and chorus, this Interlude states motivic material of the following scene, by selection from Act I material.

Act II, Scene 1, contains only male voices, those of the Priest, the individual Elders, Aaron, and the unison chorus of Elders. Aaron's single solo is formed from a new concatenation and orientation of elements from his music in Act I, Scene 2, and is followed immediately in the orchestra by a significant reference to his first appearance in the opera, in the form of a statement of 1.

Act II, Scene 2, follows immediately. After the choral opening, the chorus of Elders returns to the opening material of this act. In this scene Aaron's is the only solo part; at the end of the first of his two vocal statements, he quotes (at the words: "Es ist ein strenger Gott") his vocal line from the end of Act I, Scene 2, which associates it, in turn, with Moses' "Reinige dein Denken." The music of Aaron's second solo, continuing with choral accompaniment, is founded entirely on the "prime" combinatorially related sets of Aaron's first appearance, while the specific motivic disposition is repeated, with rhythmic compression, at the opening of

Act II, Scene 3, after which the orchestra presents the material which dominates and formally delineates this climactic scene. The primary motives are statements of the first three notes of 1, and its inversion at the combinatorially determined transposition level, the first three notes of XII. Each of these motives is accompanied by the simultaneous linear statements of the remaining three trichords of the appropriate set. The following orchestral sections are founded on lucid techniques of motivic extraction and development, which, however, often result in "liberties" of ordering within the total set form, but set defined ordering is adhered to within each of the individual, so-delineated motives. The music of the "bringing of the sacrifice" begins with the extraction of an "accompaniment figure" of fifths from 6; the "Butcher's Dance" with the extraction of minor and major triads from 11R and IIR, etc. The second phase of the scene begins with (backstage) trombones stating the orchestral motives of the scene's opening; recapitulation and reminiscence of earlier material continues, such as that of the Young Man and the Young Girl of Act I, Scene 3, between whose appearances the third stage of the scene begins, at the "Alla Marcia." After the extraordinary culmination of this, "The Dance around the Golden Calf," the music returns to a simple presentation of materials from the very opening of the opera.

Aaron does not participate in the main body of this scene, and the absence of the two protagonists is but the most obvious of many reasons for regarding this scene as an extended, intensified parallel of Act I, Scene 3.

Act II, Scene 4. This extremely brief scene leads to a return, in the orchestra accompanying Moses' single utterance, of the prime set level.

Act II, Scene 5, opens with the final dialogue between Moses and Aaron, and, therefore, is founded on material from Act I, Scene 2. As Moses was, in that scene, granted the privilege of song, so here Aaron (at the words "Umschreibend, ohne auszusprechen") is granted the privilege of speech. The chorus enters with the "theme" of the "chosen people" (first stated by the chorus of solo voices in Act I, Scene 1), and the act ends with Moses speaking against the single line instrumental statement of IVR.

MOSES UND ARON:
SOME GENERAL REMARKS, AND
ANALYTIC NOTES FOR ACT I, SCENE 1

DAVID LEWIN

———————————————————■■■■■■■———————————————————

General Remarks

THE DRAMATIC idea of the work hinges on the paradoxical nature of God: the *Unvorstellbares* that commands itself to be *vorgestellt*. The musical metaphor that reflects (or better defines) the dramatic idea is the nature of the twelve-tone row and system as "musical idea" in Schoenberg's terminology. "The row" or "the musical idea" is not a concrete and specific musical subject or object to be presented for once and for all as referential in sounds and time; it is, rather, an abstraction that manifests itself everywhere ("allgegenwaertiger") in the work. And yet it can only be perceived, or realized, by means of an aggregation of specific *Vorstellungen,* even *Darstellungen.* Or, more exactly, the *composer* may perceive it as a sort of resonant abstraction, but it remains unrealized and unfulfilled until it is manifested through performance and communicated to an audience by means of material sounds, representing the idea in all its manifold potentialities.

In this connection, the multiple proportion—God: Moses: Aron: Volk equals "the idea" (row): composer (Schoenberg): performer: audience—is suggestive. Moses, like Schoenberg, perceives directly and intuitively a sense of divine ("pre-compositional") order. He cannot communicate this sense directly, however. As he suggests in Act I, Scene 1, he would much prefer to spend his life in simple contemplation of this order. But God commands him to communicate it ("Verkuende!") and he is powerless to resist.

God demands that His order be communicated to the Volk. Yet how can they be taught to love and understand the immaterial and *Unvorstellbares* (the true musical experience)? They will likely mistake this or that specific material manifestation of it (especially when brilliantly performed by Aron) for the idea itself. In fact, this is exactly what happens. To make matters worse, Moses is no performer, he cannot communicate directly to the Volk. As it turns out, he cannot even make himself understood by Aron, his sympathetic performer. This state of affairs is symbolized, of course, by Moses's Sprechstimme as opposed to Aron's coloratura tenor.

In sum, the following dramatic relationships are set up:

God loves the Volk (more than He loves Moses, as we gather from Act I, Scene 1) but cannot communicate with them directly, and they do not know or love Him.

Moses knows and loves God; he does not love the Volk, nor they him, though they fear him; he cannot communicate with the Volk.

Aron does not know God, but wants to love Him; he loves the Volk and is loved by them. Note that, in his love for the Volk, Aron is more like God than is Moses. He communicates easily with them.

Moses and Aron (the crucial link) love each other and think they know each other; as it turns out, they do not. The link breaks down, with tragic consequence.

Aron has dual allegiance: to Moses, whom he respects and tries, at first, to obey; and to the Volk, by which he gets carried away (just as the performer gets carried away by the audience even while intending to concentrate on the composer's wishes). Ultimately his infatuation with the Volk wins out. (And we must recall that, in his love for the Volk, Aron is closer to God than is Moses in feeling, if not in understanding. Note his "Israels Bestehn bezeuge den Gedanken des Ewigen!" in II.5, mm. 1007ff.)

To what extent the tragic breakdown is due to Moses's inability to communicate clearly enough to Aron, or to Aron's inability to suspect and resist his natural affection for the Volk—this remains an open question at the end of Act II. Schoenberg evidently meant to decide this question, in the third act, in Moses's favor. But the libretto is unconvincing to me. The problem posed by the drama is not whether Moses or Aron is "right," but rather how God can be brought to the Volk. If the triple-play combination of God to Moses to Aron to Volk has broken down between Moses and Aron, and if the Moses-Aron link cannot be repaired, then the catastrophe of the philosophical tragedy has occurred in Act II and the drama is over. If there is a personal tragedy involved, it is surely that of Moses, and he, as well as or instead of Aron, should be the one to die (which in a sense he does at the end of Act II).

Remarks on the Singing-and/or-Speaking Chorus, in General, and in I. 1

By opening the opera with the bush scene, Schoenberg first presents the singing-and/or-speaking vocal ensemble as the voice of God. It is important for us to have made this association *before* we encounter the Volk, who will constitute the same sort of vocal mass—singing or speaking or both together. The effect is to bind God and the Volk together in a special way which, so to speak, includes both Aron (singing) and Moses (speaking). *Both* Moses and Aron are necessary to realize God's plan. God's voice is a mixed speaking-and-singing mass, hence He seeks the Volk, who can realize the *Klangideal*. Neither Moses nor Aron, both being individuals rather than masses and vocally restricted to only speaking or only singing, is of real interest or importance to God except as "a tool," a means of focusing the two paradoxically coexistent facets of His nature. The speaking facet is identified with the "unvorstellbar" nature of God, the singing facet with His demand to be "verkuendet." (Note the absence of the Sprechchor under the text "verkuende" at m. 15 of the opening scene, and again at the end of the scene.)

Aron, the singer, is necessary for the "Verkuendigung," then. He can, for instance, pick up the tune of "Dieses Volk ist auserwaehlt..." (m. 71 of I. 1), without even having heard it, at the end of Act I (m. 898) and feed it to the Volk for a triumphal reprise of the *sung* part of "Dieses Volk" (mm. 919ff.). But he is unaware of the overwhelmingly powerful *spoken* element going with the sung chorus at m. 71. From the point where Aron takes over from Moses (m. 838), there is no speaking to the end of the act. This reflects Aron's unawareness of the "unvorstellbar" part of God, and the Volk's consequent lack of understanding of it. Aron's text from m. 838 on is a compendium of *material* ideas and promises; his *mis*-reading of the text of mm. 71ff. is also symptomatic and disastrous:

Voice of God, mm. 71ff.	*Aron, mm. 898ff.*
Dieses Volk ist auserwaehlt, vor allen Voelkern,	Er hat euch auserwaehlt, vor allen Voelkern
das Volk des einzigen Gottes zu sein,	das Volk des einzigen Gottes zu sein,
	ihm allein zu dienen,
dass es ihn erkenne	keines andern Knecht!
und sich ihm allein ganz widme;	Ihr werdet frei sein
dass es alle Pruefungen bestehe	von Fron und Plage! (!)
denen in Jahrtausenden der Gedanke ausgesetzt ist.	
Und das verheisse ich dir:	Das gelobt er euch:
Ich will euch dorthin fuehren	Er wird euch fuehren
wo ihr mit dem Ewigen einig	in das Land wo Milch und Honig fliesst, und ihr sollt geniessen
und allen Voelkern ein Vorbild werdet.	leiblich was euren Vaetern verheissen geistig. (!)
	(But cf. Exodus 3:17 ... ! !)
	(following sung Volk chorus to the same text)

Aron here is surely the virtuoso performer, carried away in front of his audience, adding, as he thinks, expressive embellishments and "interpretation" to a piece he "knows"! Moses is, of course, the writhing composer in the audience at the concert.

In contrast, we immediately identify Moses, in I.1, with the speaking, "unvorstellbar" aspect of God. From a purely theatrical point of view, this involves our understanding those parts of I.1 in which the Sprechchor predominates over the solo singers as particularly intense for Moses. Thus: "Du muss dein Volk befrein" (m. 26) and the entire prophecy (mm. 67–85). It will be noted that these sections are those most crucially involving Moses's duty with respect to God's love for the Volk.

In I.1, Schoenberg uses a variety of means to shift the focus between the solo singers and the Sprechchor, most notably (i) relative dynamics, (ii) entry time with respect to text (who leads off, who follows), (iii) completeness vs. hocketness of text presentation.

Dramatic Structure of I.1

The scene glosses into four dramatic sections:

α): EXPOSITION (1–28). Moses encounters the bush. God commands him: "Verkuende!" (not yet specifically mentioning the Volk). Moses wants to demur, but God tells him he is not free to do so, and more specifically and forcefully commands "Du muss dein Volk befrein!"

β): AGON (29–66). Moses offers a series of objections, God counters them.

γ): THE PROPHECY (67–85) for the Volk.

δ): CODA (86–end). Transition back to the immediate situation, and "Verkuende!"

Serial Background for I.1

Example 1 shows the row and its hexachordally related inversion, S_0 and I_0. Hexachords, hexachordal "areas" will be denoted as follows: H_0 is the first (unordered) hexachord of S_0, the second of I_0; h_0 is the first of I_0, the second of S_0. A passage is "in A_0" when the hexachords involved appear as H_0 and h_0, or when rows used are S_0, I_0, R_0, RI_0, or when X and Y ideas (see below) appear at levels derived from S_0 and/or I_0, etc. A_1, A_2, etc. denote the corresponding transpositions of the entire complex A_0.

Ex. 1

S_0 and I_0 have the same dyadic segments; also, the chromatic tetrachord 3-4-5-6 of S_0 is the same as 7-8-9-10, reordered, of I_0. Textures reflecting these segmental structures emerge in the scene.

Schoenberg does *not* state any complete row-form in I.1 in a melodic linear way. The first such statement in the opera is reserved for Aron's entrance in I.2. At the prophecy, in I.1, we do get linear melodic statements of hexachords, at 0 level, and with periodic musical construction.

Up to that point, the principal thematic intervallic ideas are those indicated by Exx. 2 and 3. Example 2 is the chordal progression X_0 from the first to the last three notes of the row, with answering rx_0. As first presented, the relation sounds more variational than (retrograde) inversional. Later in the scene, as we shall note, when X appears against x rather than rx, Schoenberg makes the inversional relation aurally clear. In the sequel, I will speak of X chords or Xx textures, etc. pretty loosely. It will be noted that any X chord is sufficient to define the row and area in which it appears. This is aurally very helpful in the scene.

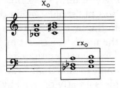

Ex. 2

Example 3 shows the melodic idea Y_0, notes 4 through 9 of S_0. The thematic idea has a preferred contour (as in Ex. 3) and rhythm, but is subject to some variation in these respects. It can also be split, symmetrically, in half. Note that y_0 (4 through 9 of I_0) is the same, linearly, as rY_1; analogously, $Y_0 = ry_{11}$. These relations can be used to pivot between areas related by 1-or-11 interval, and Schoenberg makes use of the property to do so in the scene (mm. 50 1/2–53 1/2, mm. 67–70, m. 85). In the passages just cited, A_0 is "inflected," in this way, by both A_1 and A_{11}; A_8 is inflected by A_7 ... (presumably).

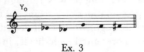

Ex. 3

The reason for "presumably" is that, although there is only one occurrence of $Y_8 = ry_7$ (so that it is not intrinsically clear which is accessory to the other), the area A_8 is very clearly one of the important secondary areas in the scene, and it is frequently preceded or followed by A_7 or A_9 (without the use of the Y-pivot).

It will be noted that both the X and Y ideas contradict the hexachordal, dyadic and 3-4-5-6 vs. 7-8-9-10 articulations of the row. This abstract "tension of textures" is realized in the scene by the use of musical textures in the chorus that reflect the abstract one. Of course, the X and Y ideas are not only compatible, but serially complementary with each other, and are so employed in the music to a great extent. In the course of the scene, the chorus moves from X texture (with Y obbligato, representing Moses, in the orchestra) at the opening of the scene, to more dyadic textures approaching the prophecy, to linear hexachord statements with fairly dyadic accompaniment at the prophecy, and then returns to its original X texture in the coda.

Analysis of α Section (Exposition)

The chorus sings in A_0 up to the end of the section, where it breaks loose violently into A_5 at "Du muss dein Volk befrein!" (m. 26), generating energy for the following section. The Xx chords belong to the singers. They sing nothing else until "so kannst du nicht anders mehr" (m. 25), where we get a sort of "serial *Zug*" in the women's voices (passing through the row from the first X_0 chord to the second one), and x_0 linearized against y_0 in the men's voices. At m. 26, the singers return to X chords, but in A_5. Here x, rather than rx, is presented against X, bringing out the inversional rather than "variational" relation, as the A_0 area is left. (But all this is greatly covered by the Sprechchor dynamically and in the text-setting.)

The chorus is thus essentially a *static* musical element until the end of the section. This reflects its dramatic position. It is *Moses* who introduces tension into the scene. Correspondingly, Moses's music is very active in the section. He is never accompanied by A_0 row forms here, and he is very modulatory.

(We do not hear the Sprechchor until after we hear Moses speak. This may symbolize the notion that God is not "unvorstellbar" when He is singing to Himself, but only to *human beings*.)

The Y idea belongs to Moses. The characteristic slow, uneven, trudging rhythm laboriously wending its way through small intervals that is generally imposed on presentations of Y seems apt to depict musically the character that appears through Moses's self-descriptions. At Moses's first speech (mm. 8–10), Y_0 is presented melodically in the upper notes of the chords, arhythmic but with its characteristic contour. It is harmonized by 4-note chords from RI_1 and S_{10}. The function of neither the texture nor the row-forms is clear to me, but they certainly do introduce contrast, while presenting a melody which will "go with" the serial area of the chorus.

The melody is, in fact, picked up immediately by the orchestra, in A_0, as obbligato to the following choral statement; presumably this represents Moses listening to the bush.

The local connections into and out of Moses's first speech are smooth, hinging on the tritone E-B$\flat$: that tritone plus D pivots from m. 7 to m. 8; the tritone plus A pivots from m. 10 to m. 11. Contrast, but little tension yet, as the text indicates.

However, Moses is much disturbed by "Verkuende." He launches into his longest and most structured speech of the scene, with very sharp harmonic contrast and quick "harmonic rhythm" (total-chromatic turnover). As we shall see at the end of this paper, the serial structure of this speech can quite suggestively be regarded as generating the large structure of the whole remainder of the scene; at any rate, it certainly introduces important areas and area relations that will figure later on.

This speech falls into two parts, dividing at m. 21 ("Ich bin alt"). The first part is, rhetorically, in form aba′b′, with the apostrophising of God articulating the a and a′:

a: "Gott meiner Vaeter . . ."
b: "der du ihrem Gedanken . . ."
a′: "mein Gott,"
b′: "noetige mich nicht . . ."

That form is supported by the music. a and a′ correspond in texture. For a, we get a quick run-through of I_9 and R_8, coming to rest in A_5 at b, with a clear thematic texture, X and Y. At a′, we get an analogous quick run-through of I_2, followed at b′ by a return to A_5 in which the serial texture clears up again, this time into dyads in m. 20. In sum, Moses's gesture here is a twofold modulatory excursion, coming to rest in A_5 both times, first with X and Y texture, then with dyad texture.

(A nice psychological touch is provided by the "groaning" modulatory X chords alternating with awful, squashy-noise chords at the 9, 8, and 2 areas, depicting Moses's reaction to the implacable static A_0 X-chords of the chorus.)

N.B.: It will become clear later on that A_8 and A_5 are the two principal secondary areas of the scene, and that A_9 is "supposed" to inflect A_8 via the 1-relation of areas. Hence, the area progression: $9\ 8 \rightarrow 5,\ 2 \rightarrow 5$ may be "reduced," intellectually, to: $8 \rightarrow 5,\ 2 \rightarrow 5$. Thence it will be noted that there is an inversional balance which "motivates" the choice of A_2 to balance A_8 about A_5, "tonicizing" A_5. This idea seems to go nicely with all the previous analysis of the passage, and the actual rows involved, RI_8 and S_2, do have a harmonically inversional relation. Whether one is actually aware of this, or to what extent one is, at m. 16 3/4 and m. 19, is somewhat hazy, to say the least, but possible to my ear.

DAVID LEWIN

There is still a bit of "smooth" connection from m. 15 to 16: the texture hints at picking up the oscillating A and B from the chorus melody into the agitated opening of m. 16; these notes recurring as a harmonic pair at the bar-line of m. 17, and finally vanishing in effect as the 5-area sets in.

The second part of Moses's speech ("Ich bin alt . . .") begins with a distorted X and Y texture applied to S_8, and proceeds, in m. 22, to a straight run-through of I_9 and RI_9. Measure 21 picks up the F♯-C-F chord of S_8 from the second beat of m. 17, creating an aural link between the two 8-forms. Here, A_8 is the clearly and thematically textured area, just as A_5 was in the first part of the speech; important, since these will become the two principal secondary areas of the scene.

The pickup of the chorus at m. 23 is definitely "smooth," in view of the preparation of the C-F-B in m. 22 (see Ex. 4). The C-F appears to refer back to m. 21 also: while several elements carry over harmonically from m. 20 to 21, the striking sense of harmonic change (and local arrival) at m. 21 seems most strongly created by the conjunct move from the melodic E-B-F♯ of m. 20 to the chordal F♯-F-C of m. 21; thus the fourth C-F is what is moved to at that point. To this extent, Moses is setting up the chorus entrance (unconsciously?) at m. 23—or perhaps they are showing him that he can't escape.

Ex. 4

The turn of the chorus to A_5 at m. 26, then, picks up that area from the first part of Moses's preceding speech. Perhaps Moses had a premonition of this most unwelcome command, or perhaps they are hitting him in his vulnerable area. At mm. 26–27, Y and y forms appear in the orchestra as before, but now greatly distorted in contour (mirrorwise, as are the X chords in the chorus)—probably reflecting Moses's agonized reaction to the chorus's command.

Analysis of β Section (Agon)

Dramatically, the section divides in two at 48 1/2 ("Ich kann denken . . ."). Throughout, the chorus becomes very active in all respects (modulation, new textures, initiative for same). Up to 48 1/2, Moses becomes more and more passive, musically as well as dramatically: here he is not so much raising real problems as offering excuses and evasions. His speeches become shorter and shorter. At 35 1/2, 40 1/2, and 47 1/2, he accepts whatever serial area the chorus has left off on, and the chorus changes area with their replies (this serial situation is quite audible).

At 48 1/2, though, Moses finally articulates a real insight and problem: "Ich kann denken, aber nicht reden." Here, Moses becomes active again musically also. He returns to the original area A_0 "all by himself" (that is, from his own preceding A_9, which he had picked up from the chorus, rather than in response to any immediately preceding nudge from the chorus). The serial return is supported by a sort of reprise of mm. 11ff. This finally gives the chorus some pause; it has to stop and think during the modulatory orchestral interlude that follows. The remainder of section β consists of the chorus's answer to this real objection of Moses: first, they bolster his faith and reassure him ("Wie auf diesem Dornbusch . . ."), then they come up with a practical solution ("Aron soll dein Mund sein . . ."). The latter, of course, sets up the central problem of the drama.

(As later metric analysis will attempt to show, "Aron soll dein Mund sein . . ." carries a very big stress; it will be analyzed as *the* big A_8 arrival of the scene. In this respect, it is perhaps of note that when Aron enters, in I.2, he is singing in A_4, an area which is *antipodal* to A_8 with respect to A_0!)

While Moses soon becomes passive after the opening of section β, he is still musically active at m. 29. (Nevertheless, his speech covers only two measures, as opposed to his previous three-with-fermate and five-measure speeches.) Texturally, the gesture of m. 29 is similar to that of m. 19. The trail-off into quintuplets is a familiar aspect of Moses's complaints by now, and the I_9 form at m. 29 1/2 can be heard, to some extent, as recalling the I_9 of m. 22.

"On paper," the preceding S_7 (m. 29) balances the I_9 about the A_8 coming up in the chorus at m. 31. As will become clear in the sequel, this relation is "supposed to be" functional, as are the 1-and-11 area relations between 7-and-8 and 9-and-8.

An aspect of m. 29 that is very audible to me is the emergence of the 3-note chromatic "half-of-Y" motive as a musical carrier *across* an articulation, from mm. 26–28 *into* m. 29. (Ex. 5 shows what I mean.) Likewise, the same motive carries the B-C♯ trill of m. 30 into the middle C of m. 31, across an articulation. While there are also some binding common-tone relations involved at these moments, we are used to that situation; the *kinetic* use of the 3-note motive is new, very effective, and goes well with the activation of the Moses-chorus agon.

The speech of the chorus at mm. 31–35 sits in A_8. As noted above, this is the "balance point" for Moses's previous S_7 and I_9. A_8, of course, picks up the other main area Moses had already exposed, in the second

Ex. 5

part of his long speech in section α. In fact, the chord on the last beat of
m. 30 can be heard to pick up the relevant chords from that earlier section (2nd beat of m. 17, first half of m. 21).

The chorus now begins to sing the "inversional" X-against-x (as opposed to the "variational" X-against-rx), just as they did in A_5 ("Du
muss dein Volk . . ."), and as they did *not* do in A_0. They do not complete the Xx idea though; instead, they become very active serially, running through hexachords, Y motives, etc. in more or less mirror fashion.

Moses's next question (m. 35 1/2) is supported by only one chord, a
vertical h_8. While he appears to be taking the initiative rhetorically, by
asking a question, the musical and serial treatment make it clear that
he is really simply treading water, taking his cue from the chorus.

As before in section β, there is a strong kinetic sense about the inter-
changes between Moses and the chorus here. Moses's chord in m. 35 1/2
sounds "passing," via the Bb-Ab-F♯ in the upper register, mm. 35–37.
(The serial rationale of the three whole-tones is not clear to me.) Also
there is a 3-note chromatic carrier from the E-Eb within Moses's chord
to the F-E in the men's voices at m. 36.

The chorus calms down at 36–40. (Why? There seems to be some sense
of return to the texture preceding m. 8 here. I can't figure out what the
idea might be.) They return to simple Xx chords in A_7. The Xx relation is inversional, as it always has been in secondary areas, rather than
variational as in A_0.

The Ab of Moses's "passing" chord in m. 35 1/2 returns as neighbor
to the F♯ of m. 37, and this relation is prolonged in register through
Moses's subsequent extension of the chorus's A_7 area (again, in spite of
his rhetorical "initiative"), up to another local stress (like m. 36 1/2) at
m. 41 1/2. There, the chorus lands again on an X-chord, changing area
back to A_5. Intensifying the situation of m. 30 3/4, we get here only a
mere hint of "X-ness" before other serial textures set in.

The longish choral speech that follows is modulatory, from the familiar A_5 through A_8 (orchestra, m. 43), through A_3 and A_9 (mm. 44, 46).
Two features seem to stand out strongly.

First, the chorus begins to pick up dyadic and chromatic-tetrachord
(3-4-5-6 and 7-8-9-10 of the row) textures more and more. (N.B. already

the line of the chorus bass from m. 36 to 42.) As pointed out in the "serial background" portion of this paper, these textures are incompatible with the X texture, and we may note again that (except for the mysterious sitting on that texture in mm. 36–40) there has been a progressive liquidation of X sounds in the chorus going on (noted in connection with the amount of X-reference at m. 30 1/4 and m. 41 1/2). There is some hint of X-sound in the female voices at mm. 44–45, but by 46 they have very definitely yielded to the dyads and chromatic tetrachords. This seems to have to do with God's turning to thinking about the Volk.

The second feature that stands out strongly in the chorus passage under discussion is that the $B\flat$-$A\flat$-$F\sharp$ idea which was introduced in mm. 35–37 gets picked up and developed here into $E(38)$-$D(41\ 1/2)$-$C(42)$-$[C$-$B\flat$-$B]$-$C(44)$-$D(45)$-$E(46\ 1/2)$. The medial C-$B\flat$-B is, of course, our friend the 3-note "half-of-Y" motive. As I said before, I can't find any serial rationale for this three-whole-steps idea, but it does seem more than fortuitous in the music.

At m. 47 1/2, Moses begins another stock excuse, continuing the chorus area, as he did earlier at m. 35 1/2 and m. 40 1/2. (We might note that the three areas, in order, are A_8, A_7, and A_9. This might be viewed as a composing out of the already cited use of 7 and 9 areas as balanced "accessories" to the 8-area, noted in connection with mm. 29–31. Perhaps both of these are supposed to compose out the "half-of-Y" motive?) His opening chord and quintuplet texture recall the old story of his earlier I_9 statements as m. 22 and m. 29 1/2. But here we are in an *antecedent,* not a *consequent* part of his phrase, and there is a sudden and dramatic break texturally, dynamically, and serially, as he puts his finger on what is *really* troubling him: "Ich kann denken, aber nicht reden." The reprise here has already been mentioned. One notes also that Moses picks up the X and Y ideas that have just been abandoned by the chorus in favor of the dyads and chromatic tetrachords. If we recall that the latter gesture of the chorus was tied up with God's thinking on the Volk, the dramatic appropriateness of Moses's gesture here is clear, though hard to put into words. His X-chords make a particularly strong color contrast after the chords in m. 47 and the first half of m. 48.

There follows a modulatory orchestral interlude (mm. 50 1/2–53 1/2), involving extended chromatic wiggling à la "half-of-Y" or chromatic-tetrachord. The motion is from I_0 (RI_0?) to S_1 (R_1?), demonstrating $Y_1 = ry_0$ for the first time, and thence sequentially through I_7 and S_8, demonstrating the analogous relation $Y_8 = ry_7$. This suggests yet another rationale for the 7-and-9-surrounding-8 area relations already discussed: that it will be an analogous tonicization of the principal secondary area A_8 to the tonicization of A_0 surrounded by A_1 and A_{11} (and Schoenberg will make the latter very clear in the sequel, via the appropriate Y/y symmetries). In this connection, since mm. 52–53 is the only passage in the scene which explicitly links A_8 with A_7 or A_9 via a Y-symmetry, we might note that the X-chords that appeared in the chorus S_8 at m. 31 and I_7 at 36 1/4 are picked up in mm. 52-53. (Measures 31 and 36 1/2 were clearly paired by the text, recalling in both cases Moses's original "Einziger, ewiger . . ."—although Moses did not use those areas at that time.)

As mentioned before, the last choral speech of section β divides in two: bolstering Moses's faith (mm. 53 2/3–59 1/2) in A_5; then solving the practical problem via Aron (mm. 59 1/2–67) in A_8, inflected by RI_9 and R_7. A_5 and A_8 are, of course, the two principal secondary areas of the scene, originally exposed in Moses's speech at mm. 16–22. And the RI_9 and R_7 inflection of A_8 is by now an old acquaintance. The A_5 and A_8 of this chorus should be taken as the definitive "answer" to Moses's early speech, for Moses does not speak again, and, after this point, everything is very clearly in a basic A_0 (although the chorus does return to A_5 for a bit to begin its coda).

After an initial run-through of S_5, the remainder of the A_5 part of this choral passage is completely based on the dyads of A_5. (In fact the run-through itself is pretty dyadic, especially as accompanied.) All the more striking, then, is the return to inversional Xx chords for the A_8 section at m. 59 1/2. The G♭-C-F of the female voices is a familiar tag for recognizing A_8 (cf. 17 1/4, 21, 31, 43?, 52 3/4?); the chord is restated at m. 62, where we get overlapping presentations in run-through form of S_8, RI_9, R_7, and I_8. The powerful inversional Xx at m. 59 1/2 is the last time we shall hear such a clear X texture until the coda. Because of the great power of the inversional feeling at 59 1/2, and the symmetrical formal arrangement of rows in mm. 62–65, the chances of our hearing the RI_9 and R_7 as balanced inversionally about A_8 seem pretty good here, in spite of (or maybe to some extent even because of) the dense texture.

Analysis of Section γ (the Prophecy)

The prophecy is articulated musically, as in the text, into two parts, each beginning with a preliminary announcement of upbeat character: mm. 67, 71, 79, 81. Each part builds to a climax at its end. The second part is much more intense than the first in all musical respects.

I have a very clear sense of m. 81 being the "big downbeat" of the scene, rather than m. 71. I can't find any "tonal" reason for this. Other factors seem to indicate that 81 is a more crucial metric articulation than 71. For instance, the setting of "Und das verheisse ich dir" that precedes 81 is such as to make the text, with its built-in strong upbeat character, very clear. The rest that begins m. 81 and the purity and clarity of the sung sound in m. 81, after all the speaking static and noise preceding, create for me an enormous (negative) accent. Probably, too, factors of large-scale metric consistency are operative in my hearing here: as we shall see later, "Aron soll dein Mund sein," "Dieses Volk ist auserwaehlt . . . ," and "Ich will euch dorthin fuehren . . ." (mm. 59 1/2, 71, and 81) are metric articulations on the same level to my hearing, and I certainly hear "Aron soll . . ." as a *bigger* stress than "Dieses Volk . . . ," which is of course consistent with hearing "Ich will . . ." as also more stressed than "Dieses Volk. . . ." The drama supports the latter readings, I think. "Aron soll . . ." is the release (downbeat) for all the accumulated tension of the problem of Moses involving his inability to communicate. "Dieses Volk . . ." involves vision, but not action or decision, and the section has the character of God taking a very deep breath to come out with a decisive statement of resolve at "Ich will. . . ."

Measures 67–68 present A_0 with a complex texture: in the orchestra, we have X_0 progression in whole notes, Y_0 theme obbligato, and dyads from A_0. The chorus sings the dyads, but only one note from each of the X_0 chords. (As mentioned earlier, the chorus will not return to clear X_0 sound until the coda.) Measures 69–70 are in "sequence" with mm. 67–68, in A_{11}, displaying $ry_{11} = Y_0$ (and thus balancing the earlier A_0-A_1 relation at mm. 50 1/2–51, just as A_7 and A_9 have been balanced about A_8. An analogous A_0-A_1 will, in fact, return later.)

The connection from the orchestral I_8 at m. 66 to the choral opening at m. 67 involves not only the carry-over of the G in the bass, but also, to some extent, the common-tone function of the chromatic tetrachord D♯-C♯-D-E between m. 66 and m. 67. The latter relation is noteworthy, since it demonstrates, for the first time, a *segmental* (hence intrinsic serial) relation between I_8 and I_0 (also S_0); this provides a "natural" serial basis for a link between A_0 and the important secondary area A_8. (Cf. the dyads of A_0 that open I.2 and the segment G♯-F♯-G-F of S_4 at Aron's entrance—more specifically, m. 98 1/2 et al. and Aron's part at mm. 125 3/4–126. The analogous relation functions here between A_0 and S_4.)

The chromatic tetrachord is also used to slide kinetically into m. 71: F♯·E going to G-F at the bar-line in the orchestra.

The emergence of linear hexachords in the Hauptstimmen from mm. 71–76 was noted earlier; it seems to be the big serial event of the scene, after all the play with X textures, dyads, and chromatic tetrachords in the chorus textures. We are evidently getting close to "the idea," and, logically enough in terms of the sonorous metaphor of the opera, the Sprechchor begins to get very noisy and to take over the lead in presenting the text. The orchestra makes it clear that the accompanying voices are basically derived from a dyadic texture, though various other hints occur, notably of X-chords at "wrong" levels in the choral bass part at mm. 71 and 74, and in the alto at m. 75.

At mm. 77–78, the serial texture is liquidated, hexachords alone more or less taking over, reflecting the change of character in the text.

Measures 79–80 make another big textual upbeat, with analogous texture to mm. 67–68 and mm. 69–70.

Measures 81–84 in the sung chorus and orchestra are basically an intensification of the texture of mm. 71–76. The relative dynamics of singers and orchestra versus (reinforced!) Sprechchor are disturbing here, but Schoenberg's conception is consistent, in terms of the musical metaphors: As the tonal texture becomes more and more complex, revealing and suggesting infinitely complicated relationships which one would have to strain to sort out under the most favorable conditions, the "unvorstellbar" static rises in a great swell to block Moses's (and our) perception of it.

As the Sprechchor drops out at m. 85, the area shifts to A_1, with mm. 67–68-type texture. The orchestral Hauptstimme demonstrates $rY_1 = y_0$, balancing the events of 69–70, which demonstrated $ry_{11} = Y_0$. The soprano link B-C, A-B♭ over the bar-line into m. 85 is very neat: these are the sevenths associated with the rX_0 progression, and here they are demonstrated as combining to form a chromatic tetrachord!

Analysis of δ Section (Coda)

After having whipped itself into a frenzy of sublimity, the chorus suddenly remembers Moses, who is standing there, doubtless open-mouthed and utterly clobbered. It returns abruptly, without smooth tonal connection, to its misterioso pianissimo texture, to X-chords and then dyads, in A_5. Measure 86 evidently refers back specifically to 36 1/2, 87 3/4 to 41 1/2, and 88 1/2–89 to 55 (and thence 20), all of these being earlier A_5 moments. The idea is, I think, that the chorus is reminding Moses that all his objections were answered in section β.

I don't know exactly what the A_{10} is doing in m. 90—it certainly provides a fresh kind of contrast for the last return of A_0 at m. 91. A_{10} was used once (and only once) before: this preceding the first return to A_0 (m. 11). The analogy is intellectually attractive, but musically pretty thorny; the texture preceding m. 11 was so different (in fact, unique in the scene, and the 4-note chord texture does not reappear until the equally "unique" m. 208 of the second scene: "Reinige dein Denken . . ."). Nevertheless, there may be something in the fact that the common-tone transition from m. 10 to m. 11 was E-B♭-plus-A, and that the same sonority appears at the return to A_0 in m. 91. (However, it is not conspicuous in m. 90.)

The concluding A_0 passage (mm. 91–97) presents X-chords and liquidates the Y-motive. I.e. the bush remains, *sicut erat in principio;* Moses leaves. Interesting are the harmonic tritones formed of the sixth and seventh notes of the rows that appear as a result of the Y liquidation in mm. 95 and 96. These tritones *bridge* the hexachords, and perhaps, in terms of the textures we have had so far in the scene, this has something to do with their pertinence as cadential sonorities.

Further Remarks on Some of the Textures

The X-texture seems to be generally associated with God as a mystery, as drawn into Himself. (This is not to be confused with His "unvorstellbar" aspect, which involves human reaction to Him and is pretty clearly identified with speech, rather than with any tonal idea.)

One can make a good case for the dyadic texture as going with God's desire to be "verkuendet," and His thinking of the Volk (which is essentially the same phenomenon). Thus, the first dyadic texture we encounter is at m. 20, under Moses's text: ". . . ihn zu verkuenden." The accompaniment textures for the prophecy (to the extent they are audible) are basically more dyadic than anything else, and here God is certainly thinking of the Volk. Similarly, the dyadic bias of the textures at mm. 43ff. appears to go with God's imagining Moses before the Volk. The opening of scene two, with its veritable orgy of dyads, seems suggestive here, as heralding and accompanying Aron, who is to accomplish the "Verkuendigung."

But here we run into trouble and inconsistency in our symbolism. For the *most* dyadic chorus texture certainly appears at mm. 53–58, where God is thinking about Himself communicating to Moses, not about Moses or Aron communicating to the Volk. And, along with this, we have the spectacular contrast of the X-texture, and *not* dyads, immediately following, at "Aron soll dein Mund sein . . . ." According to the reading of the previous paragraph, this seems completely, even perversely, inconsistent.

In sum, I can't make consistent symbolic sense out of the use of the textures. But it's a problem of interpretation that is certainly worth grappling with, since Schoenberg handles these textures so carefully and dynamically in the scene.

Summary and Speculative Metric Analysis of the Scene

The chart on page 17 attempts, first, to make sense of the area-structure of the scene, assuming that A_8 and A_5 are the main secondary areas (which is very clear), that A_1 and A_{11} are inversionally balanced accessories to A_0 (which also seems clear) and that A_9 and A_7 are analogous accessories to A_8 (which is at least intellectually convincing, in light of our preceding labors).

DAVID LEWIN

The A_2 at m. 19 makes good intellectual sense, as mentioned earlier, if it is regarded as balancing A_8 about A_5, "tonicizing" A_5. The 1 and 10 areas at mm. 8–10 remain a puzzle (as does the passage itself—A_1 is certainly "accessory" to A_0 here only by a real stretch of the imagination). This is not too disturbing, since the melodic Y_0 at that point serves to prolong A_0. The 3 area at m. 44 and the 10 area at m. 90 also don't "fit in"; otherwise the area chart seems quite logical.

Additionally, I have attempted, largely "by ear," to articulate the scene into commensurate metric units at a fairly large level; I have indicated these articulations, which overlap the Greek-letter formal divisions of the scene, by dotted lines on the chart.

This metric reading seems by and large convincing and suggestive to me. It supports Moses's entries at m. 8 and m. 16, and then indicates how God takes over the important stresses up to Moses's articulation of his "real" problems at 48 1/2. Also, the reading seems to work well, in other respects, with the dramatic kinesis of the scene, and with the importance of A_5 and A_8 as secondary areas. (The mysterious areas at m. 8 and m. 90 are made more mysterious by the metric reading, but this, too, seems appropriate.)

Even a larger metric reading still seems suggestive: taking m. 81 as *the* big downbeat (as discussed earlier), the reading:

1 | 8 16 | 23 31 | 41 3/8 48 1/2 | 59 1/2 71 | 81 90

appears logical, and stimulates thought. Thus, after the anacrustic A_0 of m. 1, the big measure | 8 16 | is dominated by Moses and his tension against A_0. Measure 23 then provides the first A_0 big downbeat, releasing this tension, as God takes over.

The foreground push from A_0 to A_5 that God then introduces with "Du muss dein Volk befrein . . ." is covered with speech static locally, but works itself out in the large progression from A_0 at m. 23 to A_5 at m. 41 3/8 (the next "big big bar-line") through a subsidiary A_8 at m. 31. And this motion, from A_0 to A_5 through A_8, seems also to augment the progression of the opening of Moses's long speech (mm. 16–19, after the preceding choral A_0).

Moses's "Ich kann denken . . ." at 48 1/2 is an A_0 upbeat, on this metric level, to God's downbeat A_8 answer at m. 59 1/2, "Aron soll dein Mund sein." The latter, and the relative stresses at m. 71 and 81, were discussed earlier.

Thus, from the first A_0 big-big downbeat at m. 23, we have the following:

| 0́ 8̆ | 5́ 0̆ | 8́ 0̆ | 0́ ⌐ |
| 23 31 | 41 3/8 48 1/2 | 59 1/2 71 | 81 90 |

and, reducing this, we get:

| 0 | 5 | 8 | 0 |
| 23 | 41 3/8 | 59 1/2 | 81 |

And this big progression makes excellent sense as an expansion of Moses's long early speech (mm. 16–22, together with the preceding A_0 and the following A_0 downbeat at m. 23).

It probably would be helpful to read over the analysis again at this point, following the chart.

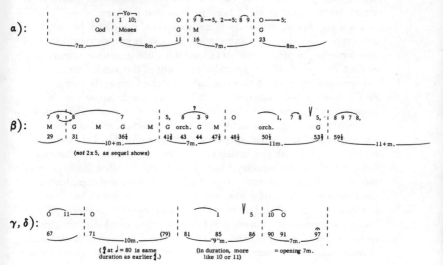

A STUDY OF HEXACHORD
LEVELS IN SCHOENBERG'S
VIOLIN FANTASY

DAVID LEWIN

I N T H E following study I shall examine Schoenberg's choices of hexa-chord transpositions in his Violin Fantasy Op. 47. These should be of structural importance, and I hope to show that they are.

I am *not* offering my study as an analysis of the piece. In fact, I do not even claim that the examination of hexachord transpositions and row-forms in the piece would entail anything like a complete description of even the specifically structural component of this work. Our theoreti-cal terminology at this point has only scratched the surface of Schoen-berg's musical thought; that we can say as much as we can in this respect is largely due to Babbitt's inspired theoretical work. The virtually universal sense of unfulfillment with which musicians are left after read-ing any technical discussion of Schoenberg's music (as, I should think, will be the case with this article) is not due to the failure of the music, George Perle to the contrary,[1] but rather to the manifest inadequacy of our theoretical equipment to cope with its richness and complexity. To say that the equipment is inadequate, of course, is not to say that it is irrelevant or useless—far from it. "Roman numeral" and thorough-bass harmony as understood in the first half of the nineteenth century seem to us today woefully inadequate concepts for the discussion of Beethoven's symphonies; yet they are appropriate, and a perceptive critic such as Berlioz could present quite valid and interesting insights through them.

What I do wish to accomplish is to engage the structure of the piece significantly in my discussion, to the extent that the reader will be sen-sitized to its presence and its interaction with other formal components of the work.

In the sequel, I shall denote:

by H_0 the (*un*-ordered) hexachord: [F-G-A-B♭-B-C♯];
by h_0 its (un-ordered) complement: [C-D-D♯-E-F♯-G♯];
by S_0 the 12-tone row of Ex. 1.

[1] "Babbitt, Lewin, and Schoenberg: A Critique," PERSPECTIVES OF NEW MUSIC, Vol. 2, No. 1, pp. 120–27.

Ex. 1

S_0 consists of a certain ordering of H_0 followed by a certain ordering of h_0. I shall denote these *ordered* hexachords by $H_0{}^a$ and $h_0{}^c$ (as shown in Exx. 2 and 3).

Ex. 2 $H_0{}^a$ Ex. 3 $h_0{}^c$

[The superscripts "a" and "c" denote "antecedent" and "consequent," a terminology employed by Schoenberg.]

I shall denote I_0 the 12-tone row of Ex. 4.

Ex. 4

I_0 consists of an ordering, $h_0{}^a$, of h_0; followed by an ordering, $H_0{}^c$, of H_0. (See Exx. 5 and 6.)

Ex. 5 $h_0{}^a$ Ex. 6 $H_0{}^c$

For each integer i between 0 and 11 inclusive, I shall denote by H_i the unordered hexachord obtained by transposing H_0 through the pitch-class interval i, by h_i the corresponding transposition of h_0, by S_i and I_i the corresponding transpositions of S_0 and I_0; $H_i{}^a$, $h_i{}^a$, $H_i{}^c$, and $h_i{}^c$, will be the corresponding ordered hexachords. ·

When the hexachords H_i and h_i are being employed in a given section of the piece, I shall say that that section is in the area A_i. Such areas are often (but not always!) strongly associated with obvious formal articulations in Schoenberg's hexachordal pieces (such as changes of texture, tempo, thematic material, et al.). I intend to demonstrate here their specifically structural role in the piece.

Now, it is possible to compose using hexachordally determined "areas" without necessarily writing serially (as via Hauer's method of composing with tropes), and Schoenberg often does so. I shall call such a texture (or, better, a lack of serial texture) *tropic*. One of the most characteristic features of the Fantasy is that through most of it the violin part is serial while the piano part is conspicuously more tropic. The subtitle, ". . . for violin with piano accompaniment" (*not* "for violin and piano"), is perti-

DAVID LEWIN

nent in this respect. I hope to show, again, that while the structure of
the piece is, to some extent, blocked out in the large by the relations of
the areas to one another, the choice of these relations is determined by
serial considerations (intimately related, in Schoenberg's musical idiom,
to thematic and motivic ones). There would then be an interesting analogy between the construction of this piece and that of a tonal piece with
a melody-and-accompaniment texture, in which the accompaniment
blocks out the harmonic structure of the piece, while the choice of that
structure is determined by the implications of the melodic line.

A chart showing the areas used in the piece is shown below. The
numbers underneath show the measures where the areas change; the
integers above denote the intervals of transposition from each area to
the next.

$$A_0 \; {}^{9}_{21} \, 1/2 \; A_9 \; {}^{9}_{25} \, 1/2 \; A_6 \; {}^{5}_{26} \; A_{11} \; {}^{4}_{27} \, 1/2 \; A_3 \; {}^{8}_{29} \, 1/2 \; A_{11} \; {}^{1}_{32} \; A_0$$

$$A_0 \; {}^{5}_{34} \; A_5 \; {}^{9}_{52} \; A_2 \; {}^{8}_{60} \; A_{10} \; {}^{9}_{77} \; A_7 \; {}^{9}_{85} \; A_4 \; {}^{9}_{102} \; A_1 \; {}^{8}_{110} \; A_9 \; {}^{9}_{117} \; A_6 \; {}^{9}_{135} \; A_3 \; {}^{9}_{143} \; A_0$$

$$A_0 \; {}^{5}_{161} \, 1/2 \; A_5 \; {}^{7}_{162} \, 1/2 \; A_0$$

I have divided the piece into three sections. The bases for this division
are, provisionally, simply the returns to the original area A_0. It will be
noted that the change of area at m. 32 corresponds to an obvious major
formal articulation of the piece, and that the A_0 area between m. 143
and m. 161 1/2 contains a formal "reprise" [m. 154].

(The reader who is not familiar with the piece might well go through
it at this point, verifying the chart for himself and forming some
acquaintance with the music; he will then feel much less at sea during
the ensuing discussion.)

Let us now turn to the music.

One of the most striking features of the piece is that until m. 10 only
the antecedent forms of the hexachords, H_0^a and h_0^a, and their retrogrades, are employed. Thus, up to m. 10 the listener either 1) thinks the
row of the piece is symmetrical (i.e. consists of H_0^a and h_0^a) or 2) recognizing the inversional relation between H_0^a and h_0^a, realizes that he has
not yet heard the complete row of the piece. In either case, the entrance
of the consequent forms H_0^c and h_0^c at m. 10 is a most striking event.

It is made even more striking by the augmented triads, which are a
new sonority in the piece. Note, however, a result which will turn out to
be of considerable importance: by the *coup* of 12-tone technique, and by
the striking entrance of the new sonority, Schoenberg manages to *distract*
the attention of the listener from the fact that the last three notes of the

row, as a group, [D, E♭, F♯], form a transposition of the first three notes of the row, as a group: [A, B♭, C♯]. The interval of transposition being 5, we see that S_5 will have the same 3-note group at its beginning as S_0 has at its end. (See Exx. 7 and 8.)

Ex. 7　S_0

Ex. 8　S_5

Likewise, I_0 will have the same 3-note group at its beginning as I_5 has at its end. (See Exx. 9 and 10.)

Ex. 9　I_5

Ex. 10　I_0

Naturally, the same relations, *mutatis mutandis,* will occur between any transposition (S_i, I_i) of the row-and-its-inversion and the transposition five semitones "higher"—in particular, between (S_7, I_7) and (S_0, I_0).

As we have seen, however, Schoenberg in m. 10 draws the listener's attention away from this conspicuous property of the row. The distraction is reinforced by his sustaining the augmented triad [A, D♭, F] through the next measure, while he "gets over" this touchy property.

Why the [A, D♭, F] augmented triad rather that the [C, E, A♭] one? First, because it is in the piano, which has been more "discursive" (i.e. tropic) than the violin. But there is another possible value in choosing the [A, D♭, F] triad which we shall soon notice.

Since the first change of area in the piece is from A_0 to A_9 at m. 21 1/2, let us examine the relations between the rows (S_0, I_0) and the rows (S_9, I_9) of Ex. 11.

The augmented triad [A, D♭, F], which occurs at the beginning of $H_0{}^c$, also appears at the beginning of $h_9{}^c$; the [C, E, A♭] in $h_0{}^c$, however, is replaced, in $H_9{}^c$, by [F♯, B♭, D]. Thus it is plausible that [A, D♭, F], which may be regarded as a potential "pivot chord" in the "modulation" to come, should be given priority over [C, E, A♭] in mm. 10–11.

Ex. 11

However, looking at mm. 21 1/2–25 1/2 (the A_9 area to come), we see that this potentiality is *not* exploited (although the [A, D♭, F] obviously will have a certain aural effect, considering its conspicuousness through page 4 of the piece).

Instead, the "modulation" from A_0 to A_9 is effected by enlarging the 3-note group [G, B♭, B] (= the end of I_0) to the 4-note group [F♯, G, B♭, B], and then extracting from this 4-note group the 3-note group [F♯, G, B♭] (= the beginning of S_9). Thus the real "pivot sonority" of the "modulation" is [F♯, G, B♭, B]. Note its preparation through mm. 15–16 (still within A_0). Then, at the moment of change of area (m. 21 1/2), it "bridges" the two areas (violin part, m. 21). Finally, note its appearance in m. 24 as a cadential sonority (now completely within A_9). (N. B. the position here of the indication "molto rit.")

Thus, the 3-note motive that begins and ends the row is used to "modulate," not to A_5 or A_7, as one might "expect," but to A_9![2] In mm. 10–11, where one would "expect" the 3-note motive to be exploited, the augmented triads were stressed. And here, where one might "expect" the [A, D♭, F] to be exploited, Schoenberg "modulates" by means of a 4-note group embedding the 3-note cells. The effect strikes me as most dramatic.

This 4-note group should also be considered in the light of a structural property which Babbitt has pointed out as operative quite often in Schoenberg's choices of area change. Referring back to the diagram showing (S_0, I_0) and (S_9, I_9), the reader will note that the inversion which takes the row S_0 into the row I_0 has as one of its "centers of inversion" the pitch-class pair (G-F♯). (That is, this inversion exchanges G ↔ F♯, A♭ ↔ F, A ↔ E, B♭ ↔ E♭, etc.) And the dyad (G-F♯), which is a center of inversion between S_0 and I_0, also appears as incipit for S_9. As Schoenberg's use of the dyad in its latter capacity is hardly in doubt (violin part, m. 21 1/2, cadence in m. 24), we should devote some attention to his treatment of it as an inversional "center" between S_0 and I_0.

There is overwhelming evidence in Schoenberg's hexachordal music that he heard centers of pitch-class inversions as structurally powerful.

---

[2] The fifth-relation associated with this motive is suggested, however: cf. the violin part in the first half of m. 21 to the violin part in the last quarter of m. 8 and the first quarter of m. 9.

One can observe this particularly clearly in his use of *pitch* mirrors. There are many more sophisticated examples at hand than the opening of the Orchestral Variations; m. 1 of the String Trio, for instance, where the sforzato on the (C-A) pair coincides with the breaking of the "mirror" registration. (See mm. 253 1/2–255 of that piece for a "structural reprise" of the idea.)

To return to the Fantasy in this connection, the opening measure presents H_0^a in the violin against its pitch-class inversion h_0^a in the piano. A center of this pitch-class inversion is (G-F$\sharp$). Now Schoenberg actually presents the *pitches* of this measure (in register!) as inversionally symmetrically mirrored (about middle C and C$\sharp$) with the *exception* of the final pair: G in the violin and G$\flat$ in the piano, which "breaks the mirror." The coincidence of this event (at the entrance of the piano's G$\flat$) with the completion of the total chromatic, and the attainment of the final low goal of the downward-plummeting accompaniment figuration (N.B.: to "mirror" the violin's low G, the G$\flat$ would have to be the G$\flat$ *above* middle C, and thus *higher* than any previous tone in the piano, instead of *lower*), puts, to my ear, a quite extraordinary emphasis on the pair (G-F$\sharp$).

We should then consider the pivotal use of the 4-note group between A_0 and A_9 as structurally significant not only in that it embeds the 3-note cells, but also because it carries with it the transformation of the (G-F$\sharp$) dyad from center of inversion to linear incipit. In the subsequent course of this piece, Schoenberg will several times again avail himself very clearly of the 4-note pivot and/or dyad-transformation resource in changing area by 9: for instance: from A_7 to A_4 into m. 85 (4-note group [F, D, F$\sharp$, C$\sharp$]), from A_4 to A_1 into m. 102 (4-note group [D, E$\flat$, B, B$\flat$], violin part mm. 99ff.), from A_9 to A_6 into m. 117 (inversional dyad [E$\flat$-E] at m. 110 and mm. 115–16 becomes incipit dyad at m. 117). But he does not *invariably* use these resources in changing area by 9: although perhaps latent, they are not so easy to spot at, say, the change from A_6 to A_3 at m. 135 or the change from A_3 to A_0 at m. 143.

(Naturally, I would not conclude from this that Schoenberg should be accused of "inconsistency"; in general, the fact that we may not always be able to formulate an intellectualized description of what Schoenberg was doing is not *prima facie* evidence that he wasn't doing anything; in particular, this specific accusation would, to my thinking, be analogous to asserting that if the composer of a tonal piece modulates once from, say, G major to e minor using G:II = e:IV as a pivot, he is thereafter under some restrictive obligation to use the same pivotal relation every time he wishes to modulate from some major key to its relative minor in the piece.)

Going on: in the first half of m. 25, h_9^a and H_9^c in the violin are accompanied by $H_9{}^c$ and $h_9{}^a$ in the piano (*not* by $H_9{}^a$ and $h_9{}^c$). This gives rise to "imitation" between the instruments; i.e. the violin in the second quarter of the measure "imitates" what the piano played in the first quarter, and vice versa.

The area then changes, again by 9 semitones (going to A_6). This time a connection *is* made via the augmented triad in common [B♭, F♯, D]. Now in this second half of the measure, the retrograde of I_6 is accompanied, *not* by the retrogrades of $h_6{}^a$ and $H_6{}^c$ (as would be analogous to the first half of the measure), but by the retrograde of S_6. Thus there are no "imitations" *within* the second half of the measure. This increases the aural significance of the augmented triad link; it will also increase the significance of a link to come at m. 26.

Possibly, another device of continuity between the two halves of m. 25 may be the relation of the [A♭, A, C] on the third beat (the beginning of the A_6 area) to the [C, D♭, A] in the violin at the beginning of the measure (and in the piano on the second beat). The relation of [A♭, A, C] to [C, D♭, A] is the same as the relation of [F♯, G, B♭] to [B♭, B, G] involved in the "modulation" at m. 21.

At any rate, the [A♭, A, C] group quickly assumes significance at the beginning of m. 26, where it is used climactically as a "pivot chord," changing the area by 5 semitones. Such, as we noted above, is the most "natural" serial use of this 3-note group, given the row of this piece, and this is the first time that it has been so employed in the work. Schoenberg stresses this important serial event: at the beginning of m. 26 he directs the violinist to play the A on the D-string. The result is that the three notes resound simultaneously (which would not be the case if the A were open). The association with the third beat of m. 25 is thus strengthened. The dynamics and the melodic contour of the violin part, leading to this climax, enhance the effect.

Note, however, the speed with which all this happens in the piece, compared to the more deliberate pace at which we have hitherto progressed. This speed succeeds in continuing to withhold from the listener the full savor of the important serial relation, which Schoenberg is, as it were, still reserving for the right moment, dramatically speaking.

I must admit that I do not find any cogent motivations for the changes of area at m. 27 1/2 and at m. 29 1/2. It is clear, however, upon inspecting the chart of areas, that Schoenberg's "plan" in the first section of the piece is to "move through the diminished seventh chord": $A_0 \rightarrow A_9 \rightarrow A_6 \rightarrow A_3 \rightarrow A_0$ by consecutive intervals of nine, interrupting this process by two intrusions of the area A_{11}.

The question arises: is not this "moving through the diminished seventh chord," which, N. B., occurs twice again in the piece (mm. 60–110; mm. 110–161 1/2), only a "plan on paper" with no musical cogency? I feel it would be irresponsible to dismiss, a priori, any evidence of Schoenberg's musical thought processes. Schoenberg's technique of "moving through the diminished seventh chord" must, then, I think, be carefully examined.[3] I do not think that the question of the nature of its musical relevance can be definitely answered at this point in musical history; I propose to show, however, that the problem *can* be stated in a musically relevant way.

Consider the Consolation No. 3 (D♭) of Liszt. Although this piece is everywhere *locally* tonal (and, indeed, largely diatonic), I would not consider it tonal *as a whole*. This is because the structure of the piece is determined by the motion of the piece "through an augmented triad" (D♭ → F → A → C♯ = D♭). The relations of the areas of F and A to the tonal functions of the key of D♭ are not elaborated structurally in the piece; these relations are used only in the most local contexts, to provide smooth "modulations"; the piece as a whole is certainly *not* an elaboration of tonal relations associated with the key of D♭. The listener who hears the "areas" of D♭, F, and A in this piece as "keys" will be frustrated.

The same remarks, if generalized, hold true for many of Liszt's works: he organizes his material into "areas," often diatonic; the structure of his pieces is largely determined by the way in which he transposes one of these "areas" into another. At times his transpositions outline a motive of the piece; sometimes they "fill in" an important interval chromatically, diatonically, or through a whole-tone scale; and sometimes they "move through" a whole-tone scale, diminished seventh chord, or augmented triad.

Liszt's procedures, in this respect, were adapted by (among others) both Wagner and Debussy to their own idioms. These composers tended to use such techniques on smaller structural levels, albeit still structurally. Wagner used them dialectically, contending with simultaneous tonal functionality; Debussy experimented with extending them to work with less "tonal"-sounding "areas" than those of Liszt (whether more chromatic or "modal"). Looked at from this point of view, Schoenberg's practice merely amounts to extending the same methods to "areas" determined by hexachords. Thus the question we are really asking about Schoenberg is: is this extension musically legitimate?

To examine this problem would take us into a very fundamental and involved discussion of the nature of transposition itself; we obviously have not the time to do so here. It seems to me, however, that to discredit Schoenberg's use of the technique on a priori grounds would certainly involve discrediting Liszt's, and quite possibly Debussy's as well.

Even giving Schoenberg the benefit of the doubt a priori, we may still

---

[3] The technique is not confined to this piece. Cf. the first section of the slow movement of the Fourth Quartet, various episodes in the String Trio, passages in the last movement of the Violin Concerto, et al.

ask whether his use of the technique makes sense in the context of the present piece. Let us reconsider the work from the beginning through m. 25. So far, the areas have been $A_0 \rightarrow A_9 \rightarrow A_6$. As we have noted, both these transpositions of area had serial and compositional justification. Now let us construct a Lisztean prototype of this situation, i.e. a piece in which we have moved (for presumedly good reasons) from the area of C to the area of A to the area of F♯. In the idiom, we would certainly conclude that there is an expectation on the listener's part of the area of E♭—an expectation which could be exploited compositionally. Analogously, Schoenberg might argue, in this piece there is an expectation of A_3 which he can legitimately exploit (by interrupting the "diminished seventh chord" with A_{11}). Whether or not one agrees with him, I think it must be admitted that his procedure here is not capricious, in light of the above discussion.

Why the reappearance of the area A_{11} at m. 29 1/2? I would suspect that Schoenberg does not want to return to A_0 directly from A_3 (via the interval of 9); he is reserving this return for a later moment (m. 143). The result of the reappearance, of course, is to strengthen the relation between A_3 and A_{11}, a serendipity the value of which will become manifest in the second section of the piece.

We might now make a somewhat more elaborate chart of the areas in the first section of the piece. The dotted lines indicate transpositional relations between noncontiguous areas which we may nevertheless presume to be functional.

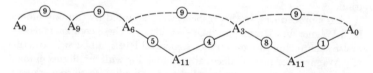

Before leaving the first section, let us note that from m. 21 1/2 (where we first leave the A_0 area) on, the violin plays complete forms of the rows, rather than forms of (ordered) hexachords. This state of affairs will continue up to m. 102.

Going on to the second section of the piece, we note that at m. 34 the change from A_0 to A_5 via the 3-note motive [E♭, F♯, D] is made very explicit (violin part, mm. 32 3/5–35). This is exactly the very obvious serial relation whose savor Schoenberg worked to obscure in the first section. Its exploitation here, therefore, marks a point of great structural catharsis (or, to be more elegant, *Entspannung*). Note also that the hexachord h_5: [F, G, G♯, A, B, C♯] has five notes in common with the hexachord H_0: [F, G, A, B♭, B, C♯]; likewise H_5 has five notes in common with h_0. Since two different hexachords cannot have *more* than five notes in common, the areas A_0 and A_5 are of maximal "closeness" to each other in sonority.[4] This closeness of sonority has the effect of enhancing the feeling of relaxation after the *Entspannung;* it also helps to establish the "modulation" (cf. piano part, first half of m. 32, to violin part, m. 34). Another aspect of "relaxation" at this point is the "harmonic rhythm" in the large (i.e. rate of change of area): whereas, between m. 21 1/2 and m. 34, in 12 1/2 measures (9 of them at faster than original tempo) we have had six changes of area, now, from m. 34, we remain in A_5 up to m. 52, that is, for 18 measures (12 of them at slower than original tempo). That is, in fact, roughly the same amount of time as was spent in A_0 from the beginning of the piece to m. 21 1/2; and these 18 measures cover a variety of episodes and textures. In sum then, while through the first section of the piece strong compositional resources were used to play down the natural serial relation between A_0 and A_5, at m. 34 strong resources are used to *emphasize* that relation.

We go now to m. 52, where the next area change occurs. At the risk of becoming tedious, I must remind the reader again at this point that I am examining *only* the area changes in the piece, and matters of immediately evident relevance; I do not claim to be making a complete analysis or even an exhaustive *structural* analysis. Thus I am ignoring all formal events (thematic changes, phrase-building, ABA patterns, variations, et al.) that do not exercise a direct and immediately obvious effect upon area changes.

At m. 52, then, the area changes from A_5 to A_2, via the 9-relation. The change is emphasized compositionally by the caesura, the radical change of texture and tempo, and the rhythmic and contour association to the opening of the piece. The change by 9 is certainly the natural one to use here: in the "exposition," after a lot of A_0, we finally moved away by 9 (m. 21 1/2); now, in the "development," after a lot of A_5, we again move away by 9. An assumption Schoenberg seems to make here is that the listener can, at this point in the piece, recognize something characteristic about a change of area by 9. I think that the events of the first section of the piece make such an assumption plausible. (As listener, I happen to find it aurally convincing, also—this is just my personal reaction, of course. Nevertheless my strongest association connecting these areas is that of the violin part in m. 55 (within A_2) to the violin part of m. 34, an association which does not directly involve the structural relations hitherto considered in connection with area changes by 9.)

So far then, the middle section has moved: $(A_0) \rightarrow A_5 \rightarrow A_2$. Now,

4 Cf. the diatonic "areas" of C and G (or C and F) in a Lisztean prototype: the fact that these areas have six out of seven notes in common can often be more significant, in such a piece, than the fifth-relation between them. Of course, since h_5 has only *one* note in common with h_0, the areas are simultaneously of maximal "distance"; these terms are likely to be deceptive if not used carefully. However, it is the "closeness" which Schoenberg actually exploits here, especially in the violin part.

considering the plan of the first section, one obvious plan to complete the middle section would be simply to finish off the new "diminished seventh chord" that has just been started: $(A_0) \rightarrow A_5 \rightarrow A_2 \rightarrow A_{11} \rightarrow A_8 (\rightarrow A_0)$. This plan makes perfectly good sense: it has the advantage of including the A_{11} which was left hanging at the end of the first section, and the return from A_8 to A_0 would fit very nicely with the $A_{11} \leftrightarrow A_3$ relation of the first section.

There are nevertheless two serious objections to it, given Schoenberg's mentality: 1) it leaves the whole "other diminished seventh chord" of areas A_{10}, A_7, A_4, A_1 unused, and 2) it is dramatically rather tame, especially in comparison with the first section. Although this is certainly biographical conjecture, I feel that the rationale of the change of area to A_{10} at m. 60 is motivated by such considerations.

The *grazioso* section falls into a thematic and textural ABA pattern, the first closed thematic construction as yet in the piece; the A_{10} area slides in very naturally at the return of the "A" part. This, in some sense, "links over" the interruption of the $A_5 \rightarrow A_2 \rightarrow$ etc. . . . . motion.

Looking back at the chart of areas, we see that Schoenberg, having arrived at A_{10}, is going to move right through the "diminished seventh chord": $A_{10} \rightarrow A_7 \rightarrow A_4 \rightarrow A_1$.

During its stay in A_7, the piece comes to its climax (mm. 82–85). The texture of the violin part in these measures associates quite clearly with mm. 56–60. In fact, comparing the beginning of m. 56 with the beginning of m. 82 (violin part), we see that the 3-note motive (in this case, [E, F, G♯]) is exploited. This brings out the interval of 5 between the area of A_2 (m. 56) and the area of A_7 (m. 82); thus the A_2 area, which had been left hanging structurally, is now picked up, albeit in an unostentatious way.

In addition, does not this reminder of the 5-relation, coming here, bring forcibly to our attention the fact that, if he wanted to, Schoenberg could use that relation to get directly from A_7 back to A_0? This would be extremely easy: cf. violin, last quarter of m. 82 and first of m. 83 with violin, m. 6. Or, N. B., the [G, B♭, B] group by means of which we first "modulated" to A_9 in the piece (violin, second quarter, m. 83; first quarter, m. 84). And H_7 has five notes in common with h_0, as does h_7 with H_0 (*vide* relevant remarks preceding and including footnote 4). Schoenberg's dramatic idea here is, I think, unmistakable. He builds up the expectation of a strong return $A_7 \rightarrow A_0$, and fools us by making the weak continuation $A_7 \rightarrow A_4$ instead (m. 85). The weakness is, of course, emphasized by the change in texture and tempo.

The "diminished seventh chord" is then completed by the motion to A_1 at m. 102. Here a significant serial event occurs: the violin, which has been playing complete forms of the rows since m. 21 1/2, starts playing in hexachords again ($H_1{}^a$ in mm. 102–105 1/2; retrograde of $h_1{}^a$ in mm. 105 1/2–110).

Having moved through the "diminished seventh chord" $A_{10} \rightarrow A_7 \rightarrow A_4 \rightarrow A_1$, Schoenberg leaves it at m. 110 via the interval of eight, the same way he entered it (m. 60). We have now had the following motions of eight in the piece: $A_3 \rightarrow A_{11}$ (m. 29 1/2), $A_2 \rightarrow A_{10}$ (m. 60), $A_1 \rightarrow A_9$ (m. 110). Thus, each "diminished seventh chord of areas"—0 9 6 3, 1 10 7 4, and 2 11 8 5 (the last functioning only *in posse* in the work)—has been left by eight and approached by eight.

The A_9 area (mm. 110–17) is characterized by more hexachordal prestidigitation, e.g. the violin part (See Ex. 12).

Ex. 12

The rationale for the serial complications in these areas is probably 1) to recall and develop the "mirror" serial texture of the beginning of the piece, and 2) to maintain a certain level of complexity, now that the possibilities of area manipulation have been exhausted, as far as the piece is to exploit them.

Having arrived at A_9 in m. 110, Schoenberg effects the return to A_0 simply by passing through the diminished seventh chord once more: $A_9 \rightarrow (117) A_6 \rightarrow (135) A_3 \rightarrow (143) A_0$. In the A_6 area (117–35) he works again with complete rows; in the A_3 area (135–43), with hexachords again.

Here, then, is an elaborated chart of the area-structure of the middle section:

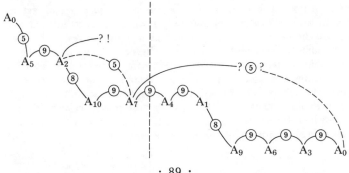

The third section of the piece is simple, as far as area changes go:

$$A_0 \rightarrow (161\ 1/2)\ A_5 \rightarrow (162\ 1/2)\ A_0$$

I feel it sheds interesting light on Schoenberg's personality to reflect, at this point, upon the consistency of his avoiding the area A_8 in the piece. Having chosen to construct his "development" section as he did, the presence of A_8 in the piece, together with the A_{11} of the first section and the interrupted $A_5 \rightarrow A_2 \rightarrow \cdots$ of the middle section, might demand some elaboration of this diminished chord of areas *qua* diminished seventh chord. This would have greatly increased the dimensions of the piece (it would probably mean, for instance, that at some point he would actually have to move explicitly through that diminished seventh chord of areas). The inclusion of A_8, subsuming the strong A_5 area into a diminished seventh chord, would correspondingly weaken that area, and it probably would also have been necessary for Schoenberg to exploit the $A_7 \rightarrow A_0$ relation more explicitly. This in turn would have involved more work with the diminished seventh chord containing A_7, etc., etc. In short, the piece would have begun to assume really large-scale proportions. One may thus presume the omission of A_8 to be connected with Schoenberg's conception of the work as relatively compact.

* * *

Although I have disclaimed any intention of analyzing this work, I should like to indicate the utility of the study I have undertaken here in approaching an analysis. It seems to me that the study throws into sharp relief certain seemingly paradoxical aspects of the piece ("seemingly," if we fall into the error of considering the structure of its area-relations as "its form"), and I believe this to be good evidence for the crucial significance of these aspects as manifestations of form in the work.

Among the most obvious problems that arise, one group concerns the treatment of the "reprise" in the work: the return of area A_0 occurs at m. 143, with different thematic material from that of the opening of the work; the thematic reprise is delayed until m. 154, after the A_0 area has been present for some time. The reprise at 154 is one of texture, rhythm, and (to *some* extent) contour, but the pitches are different, and the hexachordal contents of violin and piano parts are reversed.

Of course, from a stylistic point of view, it is well known that "Schoenberg avoids literal reprises" (if we conveniently overlook the String Trio), but I assume that no reader will be any more tolerant of that observation in this context than he would be if I were to assure him, in connection with mm. 398ff. in the Eroica, that Beethoven customarily *does* employ literal reprises. What we are concerned with is the way in which Schoenberg's treatment of the reprise is musically compelling in this piece.

I shall merely make a series of observations which seem relevant in this connection, without concluding that they "explain" the situation: the return to A_0 at m. 143 ushers in the first extended use of the *complete* rows S_0 and I_0 we have had (until now, the only statement of these rows *qua* rows was in m. 32). The hexachordal complications in the preceding A_1, A_9, and A_3 areas highlight the suddenly straightforward serial character of mm. 143ff. From this point until the end of the piece, the violin works entirely with complete rows. This being the case, it is impossible for Schoenberg to recapitulate more than m. 1 of the piece literally, since, at the beginning of the piece, he was working only with the hexachords H_0^a and h_0^a.

Since Schoenberg brings out the straightforward serial texture when he returns to A_0, he would probably not wish to recapitulate m. 1, with its hexachordal associations, at this point. The positive result of the variation he chooses at m. 154 is to stress the "incipit" dyads ($B\flat$-A) and ($E\flat$-E) of S_0 and I_0 at the expense of the inversional dyad (G-F$\sharp$). The ($B\flat$-A) double-stop in the violin appears at the moment analogous to the appearance of the low G of m. 1, and violently breaks the contour association to that measure. The low (E-$E\flat$) in the piano is in some sense analogous to the low $G\flat$ of m. 1. In sum, the structural focus has been shifted from the dyad (G-F$\sharp$) as center of inversion at m. 1 (to become incipit dyad for S_9 at m. 21 1/2) to the incipit dyads of S_0 and I_0 themselves.

The ($E\flat$-E) dyad seems to be prepared with special care. I think one can get some sense of its preparation as early as m. 110, picking it up at mm. 115–16 (as center-of-inversion dyad), and following it through m. 117 (as incipit dyad), through the cadence, in the violin part, at mm. 130 1/2–35, through its appearances in the subsequent section (mm. 139 1/2–41), and, already within A_0, through mm. 148–51.

Another seeming paradox arising from this study is the entrance of the "second theme" of the piece at m. 25, after a very conclusive cadence, but *without* a change of area.[5] To some extent, the difficulty arises simply because the concept of "area" is too crude to cope adequately with the structure of the work. That is, the cadence in m. 24 involves the [B, B$\flat$, F$\sharp$, G] group as cadential sonority, and this sonority is not present in the new "theme," which avoids even [B$\flat$, F$\sharp$, G] in the violin part, since Schoenberg employs I_9 here (for the first time in the violin part) rather than S_9. That is, the hexachordal relation between S_9 and I_9 provides him with a resource for continuity, but the cadential sonority of m. 24 has been liquidated. Even the crucial dyad (F$\sharp$-G) is relegated to the accompaniment, insofar as its power persists.

[5] My thanks to Seymour Shifrin for having pointed out this problematic aspect of the passage to me.

However, the fact that the area does not change at m. 25 is still interesting, for this is a rather exceptional treatment of area in the piece. I cannot help being reminded of m. 143, the other passage which is seemingly "in the wrong area," and upon comparison of the two passages other interesting similarities can be observed. In both cases, the thematic ideas begin with a motivic cell whose rhythm and contour are repeated exactly twice more, and in both cases that contour expands in range, beginning from a very close statement. In both cases, the tessitura rises with each repetition. These characteristics are all the more noticeable in the general rhetorical context of the piece.

Are we to consider m. 143, in some sense, the "reprise of the second theme?" Perhaps so, and yet I would be quite cautious about this sense. Personally, I have always felt uncomfortable about mm. 161 1/2ff.; they have, indeed, struck me as if redundant. And yet it is in exactly such matters that one must be very careful, for here I am in danger of accusing Schoenberg of not knowing what he was about, against which attitude I have been inveighing through this paper. I should prefer to conclude that *I* have not yet apprehended what Schoenberg was about.

SCHOENBERG AND THE ORGAN

GLENN E. WATKINS

SCHOENBERG IS GENERALLY thought to have turned his attention to the organ only once, in his Variations on a Recitative, Op. 40, as the result of a commission from the H. W. Gray Co. for their contemporary organ work series. He was, however, more concerned with the organ than this single work would suggest, as two sources hitherto little known will show. The first is an early essay (1904?) entitled "Die Zukunft der Orgel." The second is a sizeable fragment of a *Sonate* for organ dating from 1941. A study of these and of the Variations, Op. 40, a work neglected by even the most ardent Schoenbergians, should prove an interesting contribution to our knowledge of the composer.

Unfortunately, I have not been able to see the early essay itself, but Schoenberg commented on it in a letter written in 1949 to a Dr. David of Berlin. Mrs. Schoenberg has assured me that this letter contains everything in the essay, which she calls merely an "introduction." Its contents will make clear why in 1904 Schoenberg wrote *about* rather than *for* the organ.

> Actually, I have set down my views about the organ more than forty years ago in an article which I never finished and therefore never published. Among other things, I demanded that such a huge instrument should be playable by at least two to four players at once. Eventually, a second, third or fourth set of manuals could be added. Above all, the dynamics of the instrument were very important to me, for only dynamics make for clarity and this cannot be achieved on most organs.
>
> If one did not remember the splendid organ literature and the wonderful effect of this music in churches, one would have to say that the organ is an obsolete instrument today. No one—no musician and no layman—needs so many colours (in other words, so many registers) as the organ has. On the other hand, it would be very important to have the instrument capable of dynamically altering each single tone by itself (not just an entire octave-coupling)—from the softest pianissimo to the greatest forte.
>
> Therefore, I believe that the instrument of the future will be constructed as follows: there will not be 60 or 70 different colours, but only a very small number (perhaps 2 to 6 would certainly be enough for me) which would have to include the entire range (7-8 octaves) and a range of expression from the softest pianissimo to the greatest fortissimo, each for itself alone.
>
> The instrument of the future must not be more than, say, 1½ times as large as a portable typewriter. For one should not strike too many wrong keys on a typewriter either. Why should it not be possible for a musician, also, to type so accurately that no mistakes occur?
>
> I can imagine that, with such a portable instrument, musicians and music-lovers will get together in an evening in someone's home and play duos, trios and quartets; they will really be in a position to reproduce the idea-content of

all symphonies. This is, naturally, a fantasy of the future, but who knows if we are so far away from it now? If tones can be transmitted quite freely into one's home (much as the radio transmits tone now) all that will probably be possible.[1]

An organist would probably say that Schoenberg is not talking about the organ, but rather of some new invention; and this is largely true. He is dealing, however, with just those factors which have made most composers of this century hesitate to approach the organ. His affection for the instrument as it now exists is no greater than that of the host of composers who have left it alone. But he wishes to deal with what he sees as its faults and does so by this theoretical fantasy.

Basically, Schoenberg's desire for a few stops with great dynamic range, without recourse to the addition of layers of upper octaves, is in keeping with his almost lifelong obsession with the avoidance of octave doublings. A note appended to the H. W. Gray edition of the organ Variations is instructive in this regard:

> I write always the pitch which I want to hear. . . I am not very fond of unnecessary doublings in octaves. I realize that the organ to some extent can become louder only by addition of upper and/or lower octaves. I realize that one must allow an organist to do this if there is no better way of balancing the voices according to their structural importance. But I would like to have such doubling avoided if clearness and transparency can be achieved without addition of octaves.[2]

Oddly, he seems here to disregard what he surely knew as a master orchestrator: that to score piccolos above flutes, for example, not only increases the volume but intensifies the pitch. Loudness and intensity are not equatable, and Schoenberg, realizing this instinctively as a musician, seldom let his theories of doubling obstruct his practice as an orchestrator. His dissatisfaction with the organ must surely have sprung from the fact that, apart from the rather crude device of the "swell box," this "doubling" provides the only significant method of altering the dynamic level of the instrument. In a later moment of reflection, Schoenberg confessed to Leibowitz that his insistence upon the avoidance of octave doublings as a general principle had probably been overdone:

> In my *Harmonielehre,* on page 505, I speak very cautiously about tonal harmonies and their use among dissonant harmonies. At this time I was of course eager (perhaps too eager) to have my new works different in every respect from the past. Nevertheless, you find in all the works between 1906 and 1921 occasional doubling in octaves. That is also quite correct. The fear that it might produce similarity to tonal treatment proved to be an exaggeration, because very soon it became evident that it had—as a mere device of instrumentation—no influence upon the purposes of construction.[3]

---

[1] Josef Rufer, *Das Werk Arnold Schönbergs* (Kassel: Bärenreiter, 1959); English translation by Dika Newlin (London: Faber & Faber, 1962), p. 68. All references here are to the English edition.

[2] Arnold Schoenberg, Variations on a Recitative, Op. 40, Preface (New York: H. W. Gray, 1947).

[3] *Arnold Schoenberg Letters,* ed. Erwin Stein, trans. from the original German by Eithne Wilkins and Ernst Kaiser (London: Faber & Faber, 1964), p. 236.

His concern for clarity and lack of interest in the organ's colors is emphasized earlier in the same letter to Dr. David:

> I consider the organ, in the first place, as an instrument with keyboard, and I write for the hands in the way that they can be used at a keyboard. I am little interested in the instrument's colours—for me, the colours have a meaning only when they make the idea clear—the motivic and thematic idea, and eventually its expression and character.[4]

In a letter to Rufer a few months earlier, in which he deplores the edition prepared by Carl Weinrich for H. W. Gray, he reemphasizes the point:

> The organ does not need to be an American one. Through the registration of a Mr. Weinrich, who has an unusually large organ in Princeton, the whole picture of my music is so confused that most people cannot make it out; but Mr. Stein [the publisher?] has promised to give me a list which shows my original version. . . . If I were doing the registration, I should work it out only in such a way that all the voices come out clearly. But that seems to be impossible on the organ.[5]

Schoenberg again mentions his dissatisfaction at the end of the letter to Dr. David already cited:

> The registration of my Organ Variations is apparently designed for the Princeton University organ. This does not suit me at all and so many people have complained about it. I have asked my publisher to bring out an unregistered edition also, so that each player can make his own registration. For me, an edition in which the bass is often higher than the tenor is really unreadable. It seems unmusical to me, and, besides, I do not believe that a well-educated musician needs this.
>
> In my original draft, I included an occasional indication of sonority. But this is only to indicate whether something should be played tenderly and cantabile, or more roughly and staccato, or energetically—nothing more than that.[6]

In all fairness, it must be stated that every organist knows the meaning of Mr. Weinrich's suggestions. That they could not be easily duplicated on many other organs is apparent, the rather complex indications being nothing more than a rough guide. The instrument at Princeton is obviously of the large Romantic type and calls for layers of sound to be piled on top of one another in order to make marked variations in tone quality. That this does not represent a tonal ideal for Mr. Weinrich should be abundantly clear to those who know his Bach recordings on a fine Swedish instrument of much more modest size.

Schoenberg was understandably more alarmed by the long list of registers than an organist would have been. While Schoenberg admits that each performer usually "makes his own registration"—and in view of Weinrich's indications especially recommends it—he simultaneously reveals, perhaps subconsciously, the apprehensions of most composers today who, not wanting to abdicate their control

---

[4] Rufer, *loc. cit.*
[5] *Ibid.,* pp. 67–68.
[6] *Ibid.,* p. 68.

over the tonal spectrum to such a degree, have chosen to leave the organ alone. Furthermore, the average composer's knowledge of organ tone is limited in most cases to the Romantic monsters which have existed in the most significant churches and recital halls until the last decade. Fortunately, with the reemphasis on the tonal ideals of the Baroque organ, this does not represent the best thinking in organ design today, but too few instruments incorporating these principles are available anywhere in America. The "new vogue" (actually quite old in origin), then, is largely unknown to most serious composers through lack of examples. This was certainly the case twenty years ago with Schoenberg when he wrote the Variations on a Recitative.

Schoenberg's own indications for registration in the manuscript[7] version of Op. 40 are, it must be admitted, not very helpful. But, as we have seen in a quotation above, he intended them only as the most general guide. In fact, he gives only two markings: "col 8' & 16'," and "senza 8' & 16'." Even these sometimes occur in places where their execution is impossible without an assistant and often where the addition of 16' tone would make the manual writing unclear. Here Schoenberg's stated wishes for a transparent texture are more useful to us than such rather naïve indications.

Marilyn Mason, who played the work for Schoenberg in the summer of 1949, tells us that he did not care for a forte sound, except in certain intense, dramatic spots. He especially liked the brilliance of the reed choruses, and interestingly enough was partial to the flutes and strings, as he felt that these sounds pleased the ear. He said, "Whatever you do, choose a sound that is pleasing to the hearer." Finally, he urged the use of a strong basic 8' line, which he preferred to the sound of the organ mixture stops.[8]

It can be seen in the original manuscript that Schoenberg occasionally wrote passages which exceeded the compass of the organ. A great deal can be done through octave choices in organ registration, and Weinrich was able to save the day in most of these places. What apparently bothered Schoenberg most about Weinrich's edition—that the bass seemed to be playing above the tenor—was in most instances not actually so. For if a 16' sound is drawn (as, on the pedals, it most frequently is), the lowest sound will in fact be an octave lower than it is notated: hence the lowest bass sound and the tenor do not really cross. On the other hand, what would Schoenberg have the organist do but break back to a higher octave when he writes below the compass of the pedal board? The opening measures of Variation I in the pedal part as written in Schoenberg's original version and as they appeared in Mr. Weinrich's edition illustrate this point. With 16' and 8' pitches drawn, the D_1 in m. 11 of the original actually sounds, as published by Gray, and at the same time the last eighth-note of m. 15 (C) sounds below the tenor G as well as above it (Ex. 1).

---

[7] I am grateful to Mrs. Schoenberg for providing me with a photocopy of the original manuscript.

[8] Marilyn Mason, "An Organist Plays for Mr. Schönberg," *Organ Institute Quarterly*, 6:19 (Spring, 1956). See also in the same issue an article by Dika Newlin, "A Composer's View of Schönberg's Variations un a Recitative for Organ."

Ex. 1a. The original

Ex. 1b. The H. W. Gray edition

Adjustments of this sort, especially in the pedals, are made throughout this edition. And surely Schoenberg must have taken into account—even if subconsciously—these octave characteristics of standard registrations when he wrote such otherwise unplayable passages for the pedals as this (Ex. 2).

Ex. 2

Only once does he exceed the range of the manuals. In his preface, Weinrich offers a similar solution:

> In measure 92, the manuscript contains a C sharp above the compass of the organ keyboard. I have suggested that the passage leading up to this note be played an octave lower, but have kept the pitch desired by the composer by using stops above 8′ pitch only.

The Variations on a Recitative is a major work, the composer's most extensive work for any solo instrument. According to the manuscript, it was begun on August 25, 1941, and completed on October 12 of the same year. As Op. 40, it was written between his two original solo concerti, the one for violin, Op. 36 (1936) and the Piano Concerto, Op. 42 (1942). Unlike these strict twelve-tone compositions, however, the organ variations mark a return to a quasi-tonal basis (D minor), while the composer's characteristic predilection for contrapuntal artifice remains. Virgil Thomson has called this work "the most important organ work of the 20th century," while Schoenberg himself in a letter to Leibowitz referred to it as:

> . . . my "French and English Suites," or, if you wish, my Meistersinger-Quintet, my Tristan-duet, my fugue of Beethoven and Mozart (who were composers of homophonic melody); my "piece in olden style," similar to the Hungarian influence in Brahms. In other words, as I have already said so often: every composer of a new style has a feeling to return to the old style (as did Beethoven in the fugue). The harmonic language of the Organ-Variations fills in the space between my Chamber Symphony, op. 9, and the "dissonant" music. A great number of unutilized possibilities are to be found therein.[9]

Similar sentiments are to be found in the article "On revient toujours" (*Style and Idea*). One must remember, though, that this is Schoenberg speaking and not

[9] Arnold Schönberg, *Briefe*, ausgewählt und herausgegeben von Erwin Stein (Mainz: B. Schott's Söhne, 1958). Translation here is by the author.

expect too old-fashioned a sound. While triadic references abound, and a tonal
feeling can be grasped easily, the "return to the olden style" is not nearly so extreme as that in the Variations for Band, Op. 43. Stuckenschmidt is correct when
he observes that:

> The work is in D minor, but a D minor which has lost its original nature
> through intense chromaticism. In his instrumental treatment of the organ
> Schoenberg demonstrates the same lack of prejudice with which he approached
> all artistic tasks. Unusual registration, tremoli, contrasting effects of the extreme
> registers, these things cast a most curious light on the piece.[10]

But he is mistaken in his comparison of the two sets of variations: "The Organ
Variations are closely related to those for orchestra[11] in the technical sense; they
have the effect of a lighter parallel work, if not a study for them." For in every
respect, the organ variations show at least as fertile an imagination, a freer play
with tonal resources, and even more ingenious working out of the contrapuntal
texture.

There are ten variations, a cadenza and a fugue. The theme, called a recitative,
is monophonic, and its 36 notes include all 12 of the chromatic scale (Ex. 3). The

Ex. 3

theme is divided into seven phrases. Phrases B, C, D, E, and G each consist of six
notes, while the anticipatory phrases A and F consist of three notes each. Some have
seen in this arrangement a reflection of the hexachordal division of the twelve-tone
rows found in the serial works of Schoenberg's last period; it may be observed
additionally that none of the six-note phrases repeats any of its notes.[12] The
rhythmic symmetry suggested between the opening phrases A and B and the
closing phrases F and G recalls a similar approach to thematic formulation and
shaping in the Variations for Orchestra, Op. 31.[13]

It will be noticed that this theme proceeds mainly step-wise, and that its range
is that of a major seventh. More important, analysis of the phrasing discloses
numerous motifs which are suitable for variation. This potentiality is indeed fully
explored, but Schoenberg also exposes the original theme, *untransposed,* straight

[10] H. H. Stuckenschmidt, *Arnold Schönberg,* trans. by Edith Temple Roberts and Humphrey
Searle (New York: Grove Press, Inc., 1959), p. 128.

[11] *Ibid.,* p. 129. Stuckenschmidt obviously refers here to the orchestral version, Op. 43b, of
the Variations for Band, Op. 43, and not to the earlier Variations for Orchestra, Op. 31.

[12] Hans Keller, "Schoenberg's Op. 40," *Music Review,* 1:145 (May, 1955).

[13] Cf. Schoenberg's radio talk, "The Orchestral Variations, Op. 31," in *The Score,* 27
(1960), p. 32, where the phraseological similarity between opening and closing sections
is discussed.

through in every variation. If one considers the disposition, revealed in his serial compositions, to transpose even to the most distant intervals, this is perhaps unexpected. The use of the theme "in the tonic" might at first appear to define a tonality to a degree that Schoenberg would find undesirable, but the diverse tonal character of the theme itself is not sufficiently restrictive to pose any real problem in this regard. In addition, it must be remembered that Schoenberg favored this idea of untransposed thematic statement in his other works in variation form. The counterpart in a serial work to this use in Op. 40 is to be found in the earlier Variations for Orchestra, Op. 31. In both, the untransposed theme moves for long stretches in the same part, sometimes appearing as a migrant *cantus firmus* moving from one part to another in various rhythmic transformations against a counterpoint which always contains motivic derivations from the main theme.

There are three principle motifs used throughout the work. One of them (x), derived from the third phrase (C) of the theme, plays an important role in numerous variants, especially in the fugue, and notably in a form involving octave transposition (Ex. 4).

Ex. 4

A second motive (y), a lower auxiliary type of figure, recalls the fact that most phrases of the original theme end with a falling semitone (Ex. 5).

Ex. 5

It appears at the beginning of Variation I in the soprano, followed immediately by a statement in the alto at the dominant. (Cf. Ex. 1.)

The motive (z) (Ex. 6) is even more important but is not so easily recognized as a derivative of the main theme. It appears as early as the first variation where, in its basic and inverted forms, it constitutes the primary material for the pedal part for the entire variation.

Ex. 6

It appears at numerous other places, such as Variation II, mm. 23–25 (Ex. 7).

Ex. 7

This motif also is apparent at mm. 31–32 (Ex. 8).

Ex. 8

The motif (z) forms the basis for the entire center section of the cadenza (Ex. 9).

Ex. 9

And it constitutes one of the most important figures throughout the fugue, as will be noticed at mm. 155–156 (Ex. 10).

Ex. 10

This same motif appears incompletely at mm. 163–166, combined with (x) (Ex. 11).

Ex. 11

At mm. 172–174 it combines with (y) (Ex. 12).

Ex. 12

Ex. 12 (*Continued*)

And again at mm. 179–185 it appears with motifs (x) and (y) (Ex. 13).

Ex. 13

Ex. 13 (*Continued*)

Whence this motif (z)? It does not directly derive from any single phrase of the original theme. But if one takes the first note of *every other measure* (not phrase) of the original recitative and concludes with the final note of it, this motif is produced exactly. The intrinsic meaning of the bar lines, in an otherwise free and un-measured statement, is hereby revealed, and it is probably not risking too much to guess that Schoenberg was aware of this. If not, it must at least rank with some of the intuited shapes of which he became aware a posteriori in his *Kammersymphonie,* Op. 9, mentioned in his *Style and Idea* in the article "Composition with Twelve Tones."

Finally, it should be said that Schoenberg, in stating that this music "fills in the space between my Chamber Symphony, Op. 9, and the 'dissonant' music," has given us a clue to the significance of the language which he employs here, and suggests its importance in coming to any comprehensive view of Schoenberg's style.

The tantalizing prospect of another organ work by Schoenberg was first made generally known in Rufer's excellent index of Schoenberg's works, and Mrs. Gertrud Schoenberg has been kind enough to provide me with a photocopy of the original. This *Sonate,* the only composition so entitled in all of Schoenberg's works, was begun on August 7, 1941, about two and a half weeks before he began the Variations. Thus, we can assume that this work was the one originally intended to satisfy the H. W. Gray commission. Why he abandoned it in favor of the Variations, which he ultimately completed, would be interesting to know, but the radically different character of the two works will at least suggest some hypotheses.

The *Sonate* is strictly twelve-tone: the row is exposed at the beginning as a melodic statement in the right hand (Ex. 14).

Molto moderato (♩ = 96)

Ex. 14

The accompaniment is derived from the inversion at the fourth. The row is inversionally combinatorial at the fourth in a way which had been illustrated in virtually every major work of the Opus 30's. Thus, the accompaniment figure, at the outset, is derived from the same material as exposed in the right-hand melody but produces no pitch duplications (Ex. 15).

Ex. 15

A complete analysis of the row content of the entire piece would be out of order here. Perhaps more important, considering that he had not written for solo keyboard since Op. 33, are the types of keyboard figurations used in the *Sonate*. In general, it can be stated that the manuals receive the composer's primary attention, which is not surprising in light of Schoenberg's views cited earlier concerning his approach to the organ. The style is more akin to that of the Piano Concerto, which was written the following year, than to any of his previous keyboard works. Certain figures (Exx. 16 and 17) clearly foreshadow what was to come, both in their general style and their virtuoso character.

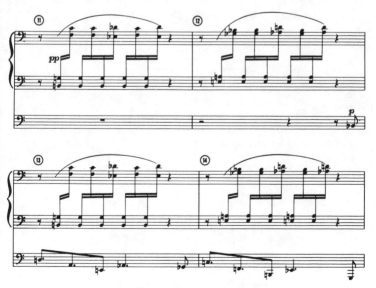

Ex. 16. *Sonate,* mm. 11–17

Ex. 16 (*Continued*)

Ex. 17. Piano Concerto, mm. 92–99

It will also be noticed that one rhythmic motif (Exx. 18 and 19), similar though not identical to an important one in the concerto, predominates throughout the work.

Ex. 18. *Sonate,* m. 22

Ex. 19. Piano Concerto, mm.313–14

The fragment ends with a series of alternating harmonic figures similar to those announced earlier in mm. 11–17 (Ex. 20).

Ex. 20. *Sonate,* mm. 46–50

The work breaks off here (m. 50), but as it appears to end abruptly in the middle of a developing musical figure, Schoenberg probably had sketched ideas past this point. Moreover, it can be seen in the manuscript that this is a fair copy on translucent paper and not a work sheet. However, as Schoenberg originally wished to write a short work, he probably planned only a one-movement sonata. Thus, the fragment may well constitute the major portion of the complete piece, and could be played quite convincingly in its present guise, with perhaps a simple conclusion added from an earlier passage (e.g., the last three chords of m. 47, and the first of m. 48). A few adjustments of the nature made by Weinrich in his edition of the Variations would also be required where the range of both the manual and pedal keyboards is exceeded. The *Sonate* has in fact been performed at a concert that included the *Jakobsleiter* premiere in Hamburg on December 1, 1958.

Gunther Schuller in an interview with Steuermann raised the question of pianistic problems in Schoenberg's music, particularly in its relation to the Romantic tradition. Steuermann replied, ". . . as far as style is concerned, the Brahms tradition (from which I also came) is the main influence on Schoenberg in the first piano works. Later, in Opus 23, Opus 25, and Opus 33a and b, the twelve-tone system brought a very different approach to the piano style. . . ."[14]

[14] Gunther Schuller, "Conversation with Steuermann" in PERSPECTIVES OF NEW MUSIC, Fall-Winter 1965 (Vol. 3, No. 1), pp. 33–34.

What might be added to this description, which is correct as far as it goes, is that in the early forties, Schoenberg reaffirmed his ties with Opus 11 and the virtuosic style of the past. In the Organ Variations, Op. 40, the Organ *Sonate,* the piano part of the *Ode to Napoleon,* Op. 41, and the Piano Concerto, Op. 42, we have a concentrated series of four works which discloses the intensity of this resubscription. Indeed, there are a considerably greater number of measures of keyboard writing in these works than in all of the music of Opp. 23, 25, and 33a and b, and no portrait of Schoenberg's musical personality would do well to ignore this fact.

In conclusion, we may cite a few remarks that Schoenberg made in a letter to Fritz Stiedry (written July 31, 1930)[15] about transcriptions he had made for orchestra of two chorale-preludes[16] for organ by Bach. They reveal a sentiment similar to that mentioned at the beginning of the article and reemphasize his basic lack of affection for the organ, or perhaps (more properly) they disclose a keen ear interested in clarity of texture above all. A great deal more is known now about the Bach organ than when Schoenberg wrote these remarks, and the ability of these instruments to do what he requires of them can be judged on a number of fine recordings. The letter to Stiedry is in the form of an outline, parts III through VII being the only ones particularly relevant here. Most organists today would disagree with Schoenberg concerning parts IV and V, and particularly the conclusion to part VII, in the light of some of the superb instruments built here and abroad in the past decade.

III. What the Bach organ was like, we barely know!

IV. How it was played, we do not know *at all!*

V. If we assume that the organ of today has, at least in some particulars, developed from the spirit of the Bach organ, the tremendous multiplication of registers cannot be entirely contradictory to this spirit. In that case, the organist who exploits his instrument not only *in pleno,* but also in a *differentiated* manner, must use all registers and change them frequently.

VI. Then you have a choice: do you prefer an interpretation by Straube or Ramin or any other organist to an arrangement by me?

VII. Our "sound-requirements" do not aim at "tasteful" colours. Rather, the purpose of the colours is to make the individual lines clearer, and that is very important in the contrapuntal web! Whether the Bach organ could achieve this, we do not know. Today's organists *cannot;* this I know (and it is one of my points of departure!).

---

[15] Rufer, *op. cit.,* p. 94.

[16] "Schmücke dich, o liebe Seele" and "Komm Gott, Schöpfer, Heiliger Geist." These transcriptions were made in 1922. In 1928, Schoenberg transcribed another Bach organ work for orchestra, the Prelude and Fugue in E♭ from the third part of the *Klavierübung.*

ARNOLD SCHOENBERG IN
SOVIET RUSSIA*

BORIS SCHWARZ

SOVIET HOSTILITY toward twelve-tone music borders on fanaticism. Time and again, prominent Russian composers have expressed their distaste for dodecaphony. In the opinion of Shostakovich, "the dogma of dodecaphony kills the composer's imagination and the living soul of music." Kabalevsky says, "Dodecaphony is an elaborate system of crutches for the composer." Khachaturian sees "danger when a young composer borrows the schemes of serial music." Khrennikov refers to "twelve-tone gimmicks." All this sounds ominous, as if there were an international conspiracy to contaminate the purity of Russian music. The verbal invectives against dodecaphony are matched by total silence as far as the music itself is concerned. For more than thirty years, Arnold Schoenberg's compositions have been excluded from the Soviet repertoire, and the post-Stalin "Thaw" did not bring any change in this respect. In Soviet writings on music, the name of Schoenberg is barely mentioned. A five-volume set of a Soviet bibliography, *Literature on Music*, spanning the years 1917 to 1959, contains more than 10,000 entries; yet the name of Schoenberg appears only six times, of which three are merely in passing. This conspiracy of silence prevents a whole generation of Soviet musicians and listeners from knowing the real issues as far as twelve-tone music is concerned.

However, this was not always the case. In fact, prior to the First World War, Schoenberg enjoyed a certain vogue in Russian intellectual circles. In December 1912, he was invited to St. Petersburg to conduct his own orchestral suite *Pelléas and Mélisande*. Previously, his piano pieces Op. 11 and the Second String Quartet Op. 10 had been heard there. (Sergei Prokofiev remarks in his *Autobiography* that he had been the first in Russia to perform Schoenberg's piano music.) Schoenberg's personal appearance in Petersburg aroused considerable interest. The critic Venturus went so far as to compare the importance of Schoenberg's Russian visit to that of Richard Wagner in 1863. Articles on Schoenberg and his music, written by experts like

* This article is a somewhat expanded version of a talk given for B.B.C. (London) on Aug. 28, 1965. Reprinted by permission of the British Broadcasting Corporation.

Anton Webern and Richard Specht, were translated and published in Russian journals, as were some of Schoenberg's own essays. His *Harmonielehre*, just off the press in Vienna, was reviewed by Russian critics. Most revealing, perhaps, is an essay by Vyacheslav Karatygin written for the influential newspaper *Ryech*. Karatygin was a critic of modern orientation, an early champion of Scriabin, Stravinsky, and Prokofiev, and the guiding spirit of the group sponsoring the "Evenings of Contemporary Music." Karatygin noted that Schoenberg's music reached the Petersburg audiences in reverse chronological order: first the complex piano pieces Op. 11 which were greeted "with homeric laughter"; then his "marvelous" String Quartet Op. 10 which met with "less obstruction"; and finally the early *Pelléas and Mélisande* Op. 5, received with applause. Clearly, Karatygin was most deeply impressed by the Second String Quartet which he found "laconic, thoroughly original, wildly bold yet rigidly logical." He continued, "Knowing the Quartet, I could detect weaknesses in *Pelléas*—excessive length, lack of form (despite thematic unification), and occasional shortcomings in harmonic and modulatory logic. Even more objectionable is the orchestration: despite some original timbres the immense orchestra often sounds too thick and viscous, obscuring many interesting contrapuntal lines." Nevertheless, Karatygin was convinced of Schoenberg's "enormous talent" and praised him as "the most daring, most paradoxical, and perhaps the most significant of the German modernists." This evaluation, one must remember, was written in 1912.[1]

Shortly afterwards, Karatygin received a letter from Igor Stravinsky. Though living at Clarens, Switzerland (where he was at work on the *Sacre*), Stravinsky obviously kept in close touch with events at home. The letter, dated 26/13 December, 1912 (note the double dating of new and old style), reads as follows:

Dear Vyacheslav Gavrilovich!

I just finished reading your review about the Siloti concert at which Schoenberg conducted his *Pelléas*. I gathered from your lines that you really love and understand the essence of Schoenberg—that truly remarkable artist of our time. Therefore I believe that it might interest you to become acquainted with his latest work which reveals most intensively the unusual character of his creative genius. I am speaking about . . . *Pierrot Lunaire* Op. 21 which I recently heard in Berlin. There is a work which you "con-

[1] V. G. Karatygin, *Zhizn', deyatel'nost', statii i materialy* (Leningrad, 1927), pp. 222–24.

temporaries" ought to perform! Perhaps you met him already and he told you (as he told me) about the work?

In sincere devotion
Yours,
Igor Stravinsky[2]

This letter is noteworthy because it reveals Stravinsky's early sympathetic attitude toward Schoenberg which cooled in succeeding years. Two decades later, in his *Autobiography*, Stravinsky virtually retracted his earlier favorable opinion of *Pierrot Lunaire*.[3]

After the 1917 Revolution, there was increased Russian interest in Schoenberg and his ideas. Among his new disciples was the Russian composer Nikolai Roslavets who was quite successful during the 1920's, only to disappear in the 1930's. In 1923, Roslavets wrote a perceptive essay on *Pierrot Lunaire*[4] which included a knowledgeable discussion of Schoenberg's approach to melody, harmony, and rhythm. He sensed a dichotomy between the *im*pressionist text of Giraud and the *ex*pressionist musical setting of Schoenberg. The Pierrot of Schoenberg is actually not the "spectral 'lunaire' but a 'ferroconcrete' Pierrot, an offspring of the contemporary industrialized mammoth-city . . . in whose sighs we hear the clang of metal, the drone of propellers, the howl of automobile sirens. . . . It is indeed a strange amalgam of irreconcilable world outlooks. . . ." Roslavets predicted confidently that "Schoenberg's principles and methods of creativity will gradually conquer the thoughts of contemporary artistic youth; already now we can speak of a 'Schoenbergian School' as of a fact, which is of decisive importance for the immediate future of music."

In 1925, Russian interest in modern Western music was stimulated by the founding of the Leningrad Association for Contemporary Music. Its guiding spirit was the remarkable Boris Asafiev, also known under the pen name Igor Glebov, who was active as a composer, music historian, pedagogue, and author. Asafiev and his associates—mostly his young students—published a series of booklets dealing with modern music. One of them was devoted to Alban Berg's *Wozzeck*, to coincide with its first staging in Leningrad in 1927. The same year, Nikolai Malko conducted the first performance, in Russia, of Schoenberg's *Gurre-Lieder*—a work conceived in 1901 and orchestrated ten years later. (The reduced orchestration was used for the Leningrad performance.) In reviewing the event, the critic Valerian Bogdanov-Berezovsky (himself a composer and today one of Lenin-

[2] *Ibid.*, p. 232 (in Russian). The allusion to "contemporaries" refers to the "Evenings of Contemporary Music" in Petersburg.
[3] *Chroniques de ma vie* (Paris, 1935; reprint, New York, W. W. Norton, 1962), pp. 43–44.
[4] In *K Novym Beregam* No. 3 (June/August, 1923), pp. 28–33.

grad's leading musicians) recognized the work as a key to Schoen-berg's evolution and an "integral page of history"; yet, he said, "much of the music has lost its burning actuality and resembles a museum piece."[5]

Schoenberg continued to arouse much discussion among Soviet mu-sicians, though more often in print than through actual performances. A perceptive analysis of his piano works (up to, and including, the Suite Op. 25) was published by Mikhail Druskin in a modest-size book, *New Piano Music*,[6] which was given added importance by a preface written by Asafiev-Glebov. The twenty-three-year old Druskin was a student of Asafiev but had also worked with Artur Schnabel in Berlin where he acquired an insight rare among Soviet musicians of the day. The traditional minds of the Leningrad Conservatory must have been startled by some of Druskin's evaluations: he described Schoenberg's Opus 25 as a "sample of highest mastery, placing this Suite on a level with the best polyphonic achievements of J. S. Bach." At present, Dr. Druskin is professor of musicology at the Leningrad Conservatory and remembers his youthful book with a faint smile.

But there were also dissenting voices in Russia, and they grew stronger. In 1927, the composer Alexander Veprik visited Schoen-berg in Vienna and returned with negative impressions, "Today, Eu-rope realizes that atonality is a blind alley which leads nowhere. And what is more: Schoenberg himself is constitutionally alien to it." Vep-rik's essay is illustrated by two musical examples, one from *Pierrot Lunaire*, the other from Beethoven's Piano Sonata Op. 7; and he com-ments with sarcasm,

> Schoenberg, in contrast to the prototype of the post-war composer, honors Beethoven. And the true Schoenbergian, Erwin Stein, is determined to prove that both masters share certain principles of thematic development. This may be so, but Schoenberg's music does not gain hereby. He may develop with great mastery, but it does not reach the listener. Both examples have musical logic, with only one difference: in Beethoven it sounds, in Schoenberg it does not. One cannot deny external mechanistic logic in Schoenberg. But who can hear his thematic development? Who can hear his contrapuntal contrivances. . . ? All this, at best, pleases the eye and appeals to the intellect. But this music is not designed for actual listening. It is dead. It lives only a graphic life.[7]

When Veprik told Schoenberg that the atonal method made all com-

[5] In *Muzyka i Revolutzia*, No. 12 (December, 1927), p. 34.
[6] M. Druskin, *Novaya fortepiannaya muzuka* (Leningrad, 1928), pp. 88–90.
[7] In *Muzyka i Revolutzia*, No. 4 (April, 1928), pp. 18–21.

posers sound alike, he received a predictably irritated reply, "W[?]
do you mean—alike? Look at Alban Berg—that's one way; then listen
to Hanns Eisler—that's something quite different." (Incidentally, the
alleged "sameness" of twelve-tone music is a recurrent Soviet criticism.) The objections raised by Veprik were not only musical but
also ideological, "Schoenberg's theory of atonality, born in the labora-
tory, *broke the link between him and the mass audience.* His creative
work lost all social significance. He leans on emptiness. . . ." And
again, "One cannot break with the masses unpunished. . . . When this
happens, as in Schoenberg, the means of musical creativity degen-
erate."

Within a few years, in the early 1930's, the Association for Contemporary Music faded out of the Soviet musical scene while a new
cultural force, the "Proletarian Cult," gained strength: it stressed a
down-to-earth popular appeal. In 1933, the confused musical situation was clarified by the dissolution of *all* musical organizations, to
be replaced by a single Composers Union. This was considered progress by some, including Prokofiev, who had returned to Russia that
year; but the actual result was centralized political control of creative
work.

The year 1933 also brought Hitler's rise to power. Schoenberg,
branded by the Nazis as a "Kultur-Bolschewist," had to flee. As a
victim of fascist persecution, he was assured a measure of sympathy
in the Soviet Union. Thus we read, "Schoenberg, in his fight against
fascism, is aligned against Richard Strauss and the Catholic semi-
fascist Igor Stravinsky." This sentence is contained in a Russian
monograph on Schoenberg, published in 1934 under the imprint of
the Leningrad Philharmonic. The author was Ivan Sollertinsky, a
brilliant young music historian and close friend of Shostakovich.[8]
Sollertinsky's 55-page booklet is essentially non-controversial. He dis-
cusses twelve-tone technique in factual, general terms and gives a sympathetic survey of Schoenberg's works up to Opus 35, the Six Songs
for male chorus. Sollertinsky's attitude toward Schoenberg is not one
of unqualified admiration. He calls him a musical innovator of genius
"who created completely new means of musical expression and discovered hitherto unknown musical resources." But he also brands
Schoenberg as "the most striking representative of that ideological
crisis afflicting the petty-bourgeois intelligentsia of Europe." In fact,
the Soviet author speaks rather contemptuously of what he calls "German post-Versailles Expressionism." Aside from occasional socio-
political stabs, Sollertinsky expresses many perceptive views on

[8] Shostakovich dedicated his Trio Op. 67 to the memory of Sollertinsky who died
in 1944 at the age of forty-one.

Schoenberg, his theories and his music. Also praised are some of Schoenberg's disciples; in fact, Sollertinsky calls *Wozzeck*, despite its "atonal language," a music drama of genius, worthy to stand next to *Tristan*, *Carmen*, and—*Pique-Dame*. (To a Russian, the comparison with Tchaikovsky's opera is indeed high praise.)

Sollertinsky expressed the hope that Schoenberg, shaken by the political events of 1933, might find his way into the "camp of proletarian world revolution." At the time, Schoenberg seemed indeed interested in coming to the Soviet Union. As evidence of this interest, Sollertinsky mentioned a letter written by Schoenberg to Fritz Stiedry, the German-born conductor of the Leningrad Philharmonic. Since Schoenberg's published correspondence does not list such a letter, I asked Dr. Stiedry, now living in Switzerland, to verify this matter. In his recent reply to me, Dr. Stiedry confirmed that Schoenberg wrote to him from New York in 1934. Here are a few pertinent sentences from Schoenberg's letter to Stiedry in translation,

> . . . Hanns Eisler asked me through my son whether I might come to Russia, and I sent him an outline for the establishment of a musical institute, to be submitted to the proper Soviet authorities. May I ask you to further this project, should the opportunity arise. . . .

In his comment to me, Dr. Stiedry describes the whole project as a "crazy idea" of Eisler and adds, "At that time, Russia was under the totally reactionary whip of Stalin; under those conditions, friend Schoenberg would have been the least suitable musician imaginable . . . I strongly advised him against it, and I never heard anything further." The day after writing to Stiedry, Schoenberg departed for California where he was to establish his new home. This must have disappointed his Russian well-wishers.

Sollertinsky's monograph of 1934 contained the last sympathetic words written in Russian about Schoenberg and his school. Actually, it took considerable courage on the part of the author to speak with such warmth of a musician whose work was considered anti-social by a growing number of Soviet critics. In fact, the 1930's in Soviet Russia were a period of increasing hostility against *all* modernism, Western and Russian alike. After the Second World War, the campaign against so-called "Formalism" culminated in the notorious decree of 1948 which Alexander Werth once described as "Musical Uproar in Moscow."[9] It was far more than an uproar—it was the public castigation and humiliation of virtually all leading Soviet and Western com-

---

[9] Alexander Werth, *Musical Uproar in Moscow* (London, 1949).

posers of modern orientation. Singled out among foreign musicians were Stravinsky and Schoenberg.

Respected and well-informed music critics joined in this concerted campaign of vilification. Typical is an article in the monthly journal *Sovietskaya Muzyka*, official organ of the Composers Union, which appeared in August 1949. Entitled *Arnold Schoenberg, liquidator of music*, it had the illuminating subtitle "Against decadent atonal direction and its defensive disguise." The author was Joseph Ryzhkin, then—as now—a member of the Moscow Institute of Musicology. Mixing musical and ideological criticism, Ryzhkin asserted that, for forty years, atonality had exerted its disastrous influence on contemporary bourgeois music. Schoenberg's system, he said, actually leads to a "liquidation of music as an art, to be exchanged for senseless cacophony." Atonality has become "an organization, a sect" everywhere in Europe and America, except the Soviet Union. The center of the "sect" is in America, with Schoenberg—settled in California— acting as a "pedagogue-consultant" of many American composers. Ryzhkin appears fully conversant with the literature on dodecaphony and extends his acid criticism to the writings of Joseph Matthias Hauer, Herbert Eimert, Ernst Krenek, René Leibowitz, and Hanns Eisler. On this subject, he says, "Lately, articles and books have appeared in the West (written by Krenek, Leibowitz, and others) attempting to rekindle the fading interest in atonality. Leibowitz praises Schoenberg and his adherents with such abandon that he includes, among his geniuses, a mediocrity like Anton von Webern." Ryzhkin's evaluations reflect the party line when he declares that "atonality is actually a highly reactionary system though it tries to hide behind the false legend of its alleged progressiveness." This was the time when *Pravda* referred to the "reactionary composers Hindemith and Schoenberg," when Stravinsky was called "the apostle of reactionary forces in bourgeois music," when *Izvestia* described the American musical scene as *Dollar Cacophony*.[10] Observing that the so-called "creative" method of Schoenberg had influenced composers outside his immediate school—like Hindemith and Messiaen—the Soviet author declared, "Hence, we do not have an isolated case demanding clinical diagnosis, but a definite social occurrence, a kind of social impoverishment in need of an ideo-political, class-conscious analysis." Indeed, what could be more nefarious from the Soviet point of view than "the deep-seated disregard for the people, their lives, cultures, and aspirations which brought the atonalists to the negation of folk melodies and the idiom of folk music."

10 Boris Schwarz, "Stravinsky in Soviet Russian Criticism" in *Musical Quarterly* (July, 1962), p. 349.

Aside from his ideological tirades, Ryzhkin gives a well-organized, fairly detailed account of Schoenberg's evolution as a composer and theorist. His central musical argument against the twelve-tone system is the assertion that the abnegation of mode and tonality must lead to the destruction of the basic concepts of music. The acidity of Ryzhkin's critique reflects the ideological climate of the "purge" year 1948; yet, in essence, the views expressed by him still circulate widely in Soviet musical circles.

The most recent Soviet appraisal of Schoenberg and his school is contained in a book by Grigory Shneyerson, *Of Music, dead and alive*.[11] The first edition of 1960 devoted 35 pages to Schoenberg; the second edition of 1964 expanded that chapter to 50 pages. But the expansion consists merely of a more fully documented rejection of Schoenberg and his theories. Among Soviet critics, Shneyerson is one of the best informed and most internationally minded. His treatment of Schoenberg is one of hostile objectivity. He quotes extensively, not only from Schoenberg's own writings, but also from such well-disposed authors as Hans Redlich, Hanns Eisler, Roman Vlad, and Hans Stuckenschmidt. Yet, the quotations are selected in such a way as to stress those points which make the dodecaphonic system appear absurd in the eyes of the Soviet reader.

To illustrate the twelve-tone technique, Shneyerson uses Schoenberg's Wind Quintet Op. 26: he prints the tone row and four brief excerpts, demonstrating the use of the row. Other examples include fragments from the Piano Suite Op. 25, from Berg's *Lulu* and Webern's Opp. 17 and 26. To the Soviet reader, who has no opportunity whatsoever to hear or study the complete works, these excerpts must appear as cerebral aberrations—which is exactly the effect Shneyerson undoubtedly planned to produce. To be fair, Shneyerson quotes Schoenberg's repeated plea to judge his works on the basis of musical quality, not mathematical equation. Yet, in Soviet Russia this opportunity is not available since there are no performances. Shneyerson tends to belittle Schoenberg's opinion that the strict application of twelve-tone technique is extremely difficult. In refutation, he quotes Hanns Eisler, one of Schoenberg's early disciples, who said, "The style whose creation is the historic achievement of Schoenberg, the style which once was bold and new, can today be aped by any undersized graduate of a secondary music school." In summing up, Shneyerson says,

> Schoenberg's role in the history of music was extremely negative.
> He succeeded in confusing and destroying much in musical art, but

[11] G. Shneyerson, *O muzyke, zhivoi i mertvoi* (Moscow, 1960 and 1964).

he did not succeed in creating anything. . . . Dodecaphony as a system was already fully compromised in the early 1930's. The aura of "great innovator" surrounding Schoenberg's name has long since paled and withered. Obviously, life did not confirm the truth of his teaching. . . . Schoenberg contributed much to the decadent schools of composition diguised as "Avant-Garde." Such manifestations as dodecaphony, abstract painting, existentialist philosophy are natural and unavoidable results of bourgeois decadence and its reactionary ideology.[12]

Shneyerson reflects the opinions held by the leading Soviet composers of today. As proof that these negative views are not isolated, prominent Western composers—opponents of dodecaphony—are used as witnesses; among them are Honegger, Hindemith, and Bartok. Despite this reinforcement, one can sense that much of Soviet rejection is based on prejudged information disseminated mainly by musical journalists. Among young Soviet musicians, the thirst for information is great, yet they seem ill prepared to absorb it. Stravinsky, lecturing before a group of young Leningrad composers on the "seriation principle" in the fall of 1962, was confronted with questions like "Doesn't it constrain inspiration? Isn't it a new dogmatism?" The Russians fear the "leveling" effect of serialism, the loss of individuality, and—more importantly—the loss of a national musical idiom. There is a certain provincialism in that fear, and Prokofiev remarked as early as 1934, "The danger of becoming provincial is unfortunately a very real one for modern Soviet composers." This problem is multiplied today: having missed Western musical developments from the 1930's to 1960, Soviet composers are bewildered by the latest trends. Robert Craft, who traveled with Stravinsky to Russia in 1962, had this to say, "My own feeling is that to the custodians of this outward-growing society, Webern's music can only seem like the nervous tic of a moribund culture."[13]

Nevertheless, young Soviet musicians strain to make up for lost time. They start anew where a previous generation left off—with Alban Berg's *Wozzeck* which is studied avidly at the Leningrad Conservatory and elsewhere. The work is also the subject of a detailed analysis by one of Russia's foremost musicologists, Yuri Keldysh in the March 1965, issue of *Sovietskaya Muzyka* ("*Wozzeck* and Musical Expressionism"); and though Keldysh's final evaluation is essentially negative, it may well precipitate a new discussion of the entire topic. When I visited Leningrad late in 1962, I received an

[12] *Ibid.*, pp. 276–78.
[13] R. Craft, "Stravinsky's Return, a Russian Diary" in *Encounter* (London, June 1963), p. 46.

BORIS SCHWARZ

urgent request from the Conservatory to obtain George Perle's book *Serial Composition and Atonality* which had just been published. The books by Hans Jelinek and René Leibowitz circulate among young composers in Russia. A few of these twelve-tone "rebels" have achieved some fame (or better, notoriety), and they have been scolded publicly. Among them is Andrei Volkonsky, born in 1933 as a Russian *émigré*, who returned to Moscow as a student, only to be expelled from the Conservatory; and Arvo Pyart (born 1935), a gifted young Estonian, castigated for his allegedly atonal *Necrologue* (1960). There is a group of young Ukrainian composers who are experimenting in the twelve-tone idiom.[14] But in the face of official disapproval, all these musical experiments bear the aspect of an "underground" operation in stark contrast to the innovative zeal of the early revolutionary years. Thus in 1918, Lunacharsky—serving as Lenin's cultural commissar—said to young Prokofiev, "You are a revolutionary in music, we are revolutionaries in life: we ought to work together." The spirit of exploration was driven out of Soviet art in the Stalinist purge of the 1930's, but it is not necessarily lost forever. Polish composers have proven successfully that Communism and Serialism are not incompatible. Well-remembered is Hanns Eisler, the German composer, who was an adherent of both Marx and Schoenberg, much to the discomfort of some Soviet critics. Actually, it was a Russian composer, Alexander Scriabin, who contributed significantly to the dissolution of tonality in music. Were it not for Scriabin's premature death in 1915, Moscow might have joined Vienna as the citadel of non-tonal music. In fact, the affinity between Scriabin and Schoenberg was pointed out by Russian and Polish musicologists some decades ago.

The next few years will show whether young Soviet composers will be permitted freely to join their Western confreres in musical experimentation. A more flexible official attitude toward modernism in the arts has been evident in the past months. Leningrad has heard a new work by Volkonsky which in itself is significant, since this gifted young composer has been virtually excluded from the Soviet repertory because of his modernist leanings. The new composition, *The Laments of Shchaza*, scored for soprano, violin, viola, English horn, xylophone, vibraphone, and harpsichord, was written in 1962 and is said to have assimilated the influence of Webern as well as post-Webern trends. Another talented young composer, Boris Tishchenko (a post-graduate student of Shostakovich at the Leningrad

[14] Cf. Boris Schwarz, "Soviet Music since the Second World War" in *Musical Quarterly* (January, 1965), pp. 280–81, including an example of a twelve-tone piece by Valentin Silvestrov, a young Ukrainian composer.

Conservatory) had the temerity of closing his new ballet, *The Twelve* (based on Alexander Blok's revolutionary poem) with a twelve-tone chorale, but the ending was eliminated prior to the *première*. Even such musical conservatives as Kara Karayev and Rodion Shchedrin, known primarily for their assimilation of folk materials, are reported to have used some twelve-tone devices in their latest symphonies, first performed in the spring of 1965. Shchedrin, now thirty-three, declared only two years ago that "there is no cleavage between the generations [of Soviet musicians] . . . we have our Soviet socialist musical culture, powerful in the unity of ideals and strong ethical aims. . . ."

Yet, some cleavage seems to be developing lately, for the interest of the younger generation of Soviet composers in dodecaphony and "avant-gardism" is strongly opposed by the older leaders who are still in firm control. Once their excessive tutelage of the new generation is weakened, once the outdated concept of *Socialist Realism* is revised to fit the increasingly sophisticated needs of Soviet society, Soviet music will undoubtedly regain its contact with the mainstream of Western musical thought.

PROBLEMS OF PITCH ORGANIZATION
IN STRAVINSKY

ARTHUR BERGER

ANYONE WHO undertakes an investigation of the essential relationships of tones in the works of Stravinsky may find himself somewhat at a
disadvantage as a result of the fact that no significant body of theoretical
writing has emerged to deal with the nature of twentieth-century music
that is centric (i.e. organized in terms of tone center) but not tonally
functional.[1] There are, to be sure, a number of labels in circulation for
referring to this music: pantonality, pandiatonicism, antitonality,
modality, tonicality—even "atonality" has been stretched to embrace it.
But their function is largely identification, and where any one of them
presumes to represent a theory, this is more likely to be descriptive of surface detail than in the nature of an interpretation of internal relations
or structural significance. Moreover, instead of searching for the differ-
entia of the music they designate by ascertaining, for example, its own
unifying principles, the tendency has been to rely rather too heavily on
the established rules of formation.

A worthwhile objective is certainly an approach that would no longer
use tonality as a crutch, a new branch of theory, as it were, starting from
what this music itself is, rather than dwelling upon its deviation from
what music was previously. (Granted we might still be ultimately obliged
to come to terms with traditional schemata, since it is untenable to claim
for the music in question anything like the degree of cleavage with tonality
that characterized twelve-tone composition.) But until such a theory is
crystallized and implemented with a vocabulary of sufficient currency
to make it reliable as a means of communication, we cannot legitimately
be expected to more than simply attempt to gravitate in the general

---

[1]Tonality, according to the restricted sense in which it is construed here, is defined by those
functional relations postulated by the structure of the major scale. A consequence of the fulfillment of such functional relations is, directly or indirectly, the assertion of the priority of one
pitch class over the others within a given context—it being understood that context may be
interpreted either locally or with respect to the totality, so that a hierarchy is thus established,
determined in each case by what is taken as the context in terms of which priority is assessed.
It is important to bear in mind, however, that there are other means besides functional ones for
asserting pitch-class priority; from which it follows that pitch-class priority per se: 1) is not a
sufficient condition of that music which is tonal, and 2) is compatible with music that is not
tonally functional.

direction of the self-contained approach the new theory may someday provide. That the attempt might indeed be rewarding was one of my main thoughts as I undertook this discussion of Stravinsky's "pre-twelve-tone" works, prompted by a desire to assemble some observations that seemed to me interesting enough to share. In organizing the observations I found it convenient to group them into four sections: I) diatonic writing in which "tone center" is not functional "tonic";[2] II) a symmetrical scale used in such a way as to emphasize tritone relation; III) the same scale with minor-third emphasis; IV) interaction between diatonic elements of I and the symmetrical scale of II and III. The prognosis for self-contained treatment seemed encouraging to me in the ground covered in I and II, but III is a turning point—a concern with the traditional minor third itself, perhaps, being symptomatic. In IV the synthesis produces a curious alchemy that brings tonal functionality in its wake. Yet this conclusion does not, I trust, invalidate the initial intention; since it is better for tonal functionality to insinuate itself gradually, than for it to confine all discussion at the outset to the level of established theory.[3]

I

A suitable point of departure from which to approach one of the main problems of concern to us is the familiar *Danse Russe* (in the 1911 version),[4] where the "white notes"—which I take to conveniently represent the total content of any of the so-called "diatonic" scales—may be said to comprise the referential collection of pitch classes inferable from the main theme of the rondo and/or the codetta at No. 44. The referential order of intervals, on the other hand, varying independently of the referential collec-

[2] For purposes of non-tonal centric music it might be a good idea to have the term "tone center" refer to the more general class of which "tonics" (or tone centers in tonal contexts) could be regarded as a sub-class (see note 1).

[3] Any attempt at a statement of what I assume tonal functionality to be would, I fear, result in a disquisition—consigning the Stravinsky discussion to a postscript. This article could not have been written without the author's relying on the reader to supply the precariously evasive first principles and to take it on faith that thought has been given to the much needed revaluation of tonality that is now taking place. Indeed, as a gesture to this revaluation I have taken what may, perhaps, be the needless precaution of borrowing the latest terms (e.g. "simultaneity" where "chord" might have been perfectly adequate); but having done so, I feel I should say a few words, however informal, regarding them. In the first place, those who are in close touch with the rethinking responsible for the new nomenclature and who tend to forget its limited currency, are the ones whose obligation it is to define and justify it, which thus is not my intention here. To avoid the linguistic battle over what constitutes a "chord," I shall simply add to what I have already remarked about "simultaneity" that its attraction for me has something to do with its being a fair substitute for the German *Zusammenklang*. "Pitch class" (or "p.c.," in the folksy abbreviation used by a young contributor elsewhere in this issue) is useful to distinguish an observation about a pitch, say C, that may occur in any octave from an observation about a given C (such as middle C). Finally, notwithstanding the suggestion in note 2 regarding "tone center" vis-à-vis "tonic," for that future time when a new theory is evolved, I feel uneasy about present usage which equates them: hence the precautionary "priority," a more noncommittal term than "tone center." By virtue of its freedom from conventional

tion, is defined by the pitch class to which priority is assigned, and this, in turn, is decided on the basis of contextual evidence. In Ex. 1, G priority is indicated by the simultaneities in the strings on the first beats of the odd-numbered measures (where G is emphasized by doubling and its "low" registral position); and at its first return (No. 38) it is confirmed by a G tremolo. (The melodic line itself gives inadequate information for this priority.)[5] The referential ordering of intervals that may be inferred from G as 0 yields the following scale (in semitonal measurement): 0, 2, 4, 5, 7, 9, 10.

Ex. 1

---

associations it even lends itself to being applied below to a tone that is hierarchically at the head of a three-tone group in the "*Petrouchka* chord" without necessarily being a tone center as it is here understood. But normally "C priority" will mean "C is the tone center." It may be idle to add that the borrowing of these terms (as also the semitonal numbering, 0–11) is no more to be taken as evidence that the writer shares the total philosophy that gave rise to them than the use of the terminology of logic by some of my most esteemed colleagues is to be taken as a proof of the logical consistency of their arguments.

[4] Use of this version (except in one instance where the new orchestration is more practical for quotation) should avoid the objection that what are cited below as similarities between Stravinsky's early and recent practices are not altogether reliable simply because the new version of *Petrouchka* may embody some of his recent attitudes.

[5] The argument for G priority is supported by Stravinsky's own interpretation of this passage in the 1947 revision. Thus, among other things, the G is further emphasized by virtue of the fact that it is doubled by the basses not only, as in the old version, in its first appearance but in each subsequent appearance as well. Considerable "interference" qualifies G: e.g. an A pedal point (potentialized in the A priority of the subsidiary themes at Nos. 34 and 41) and a doubling of the tritone, to both of which I shall return later (see p. 22 below). In Exx. 1 and 2, the alternation of the triads B-D-F and C-E-G produces the whole step of the opening tremolo of the work (D-E or A-G)—a relationship that is made explicit when the opening section returns in its D-major metamorphosis at the beginning of the fourth tableau. Such are some of the large structural issues that are, of course, also relevant in different ways to other musical examples given here, insofar as complete data in terms of the totality of relations is to be sought. But especially since music is heard in time, local events may also, I believe, be considered as having independent validity, since they are more than a *tabula rasa* to be inscribed by total structure.

The codetta affirms the familiar referential ordering of the C major scale, for which the main evidence is the cadence, and especially the final simultaneity (Ex. 2b), which gradually materializes over a G pedal after No. 44 (x in Ex. 2a) and then persists to the end.

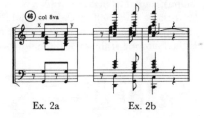

Ex. 2a   Ex. 2b

It may be wondered why we should be burdened with two referential categories: the collection and the ordering of intervals, since theme and codetta could both be referred to the C major scale, in terms of which the G-emphasis could be regarded simply as a prolonged functional "dominant seventh"; or the theme could be referred to one interval-ordered pitch-class collection, and the codetta to another. Now, the first alternative leads to the proverbial historical search for correspondences which we should like to avoid if possible; while the second alternative, although it allows the independence of a G priority among white notes—and is to this extent preferable—ignores common pitch-class content. To retain both categories, therefore, seems desirable.

Since the major scale and tonality are strongly inter-identified, however, it may be insisted that the functioning of the referential collection tonally when the referential ordering is that of the major scale, but not tonally when the same referential collection has the referential ordering of the other available white-note scales, engenders an interaction between tonal and non-tonal procedures—such interaction being implicit in the very existence of common pitch-class content. It would therefore seem to follow from this that what to some may appear to be unjustifiable tonal bias is not only legitimate but necessary for dealing rationally with this music. A self-contained theory, in order to refute this argument, would ultimately have to demonstrate that, though elements of the major scale provide the conditions for tonal functionality, Stravinsky does not significantly realize these conditions.

This is something I am not prepared to demonstrate now. However, it is not insignificant in the present regard that in *Agon* (a transitional work between the "neoclassic" and the "twelve-tone" periods), relations similar to those in *Petrouchka* appear four decades later, with C priority (i.e. as distinguished from a tonal functional "C major") still treated as just one referential ordering among all the others obtainable within the white-note collection. The *Pas-de-Quatre* from *Agon* and the *Danse Russe* differ mark-edly from one another on every conceivable level, so that apprehension of any similarity requires a high degree of abstraction. For example, the pitch class C is prominent from the outset of the former, while in the latter it is not. But if we discount the support this C gets in *Agon* from repetition and instrumentation, the B-C in the first simultaneity (Ex. 3a) may be said to have its counterpart in *Danse Russe* (*y* in Ex. 2a), though its appear-ance in the *Petrouchka* movement is, of course, delayed until almost the end. Furthermore, the measures with the triplet figure (Ex. 3b) carry in dis-tilled form the G implications of the *Danse Russe* theme, return in like rondo fashion (MM. 21 and 36, though the last time with a problematic B♭), and stand in analogous relation to the C-dominated simultaneity at the movement's end (Ex. 3c).

Ex. 3a   Ex. 3b

Ex. 3c

Having taken due cognizance of the parallelism, however, let us pause over this last simultaneity.

G gives C the acoustical support of the fifth—the assumption of the possibility of such acoustical support being indispensable to this entire discussion. At the same time, G's association with D, and even, to a certain extent, with F, forms a sub-complex of the simultaneity relating directly to the referential order that governed the measures with triplet figure. There are other ramifications, since F serves a double purpose, being also associated timbrally (in the harp) with C, in such a way as to allude to F's role on a secondary level of importance—as lowest tone both in the open-ing simultaneity and in the one in winds in Ex. 3b. As such, the F may be compared to the A in the final simultaneity of *Danse Russe,* except that this A is not only an allusion to earlier events in the movement, but also a simple continuation of an insistent element of the immediately preceding measures. The main point, however, is that the G supporting C in the final simultaneity of *Danse Russe* does not, unlike the G at the end of *Pas-de-Quatre,* directly relate back—by virtue of special contextual associations—to the G priority that accounts for so large a part of the *Petrouchka* movement as to make the absence of such a relationship quite perceptible.[6]

Another example of what I have in mind—less complex than the one from *Agon* because the movement has less complex relationships—is provided by *Dumbarton Oaks* Concerto, where the referential white-note collection is that of "Eb major." Extra doubling and the neighbor-note motion around G at the opening of the finale substantiate the triad G-Bb-D (Ex. 4a), defining a referential ordering of the scale: 0, 1, 3, 5, 7, 8, 10, whose normal abstract representation (always reading upwards), incidentally, indicates an ordering of intervals retrograde-inversionally related to the ordering of the major scale, similarly represented. The last eleven measures of the movement do not deviate from the pitch content of Eb major, but Eb priority has only begun to gradually infiltrate the original G priority since about No. 74, and even now, in the final simultaneities, retains from the G priority a G (as lowest voice), and a D (Ex. 4b).

Ex. 4a

Ex. 4b

[6] The abruptness of the ending may well be a theatrical allusion to the character of a peasant dance. Thus, something of the same nature occurs on another dimension when the long continued motion ceases at this same cadence without warning.

Despite its triadic elements, the ending, like that of *Pas-de-Quatre,* is far from a "resolution" in the harmony-book fashion, yet in an empirical sense, the basic structural issues are all resolved.

It may have occurred to some readers that this discussion could benefit from the paraphernalia of "modality," which would seem so very appropriate for the identification of the different interval-orderings within the white-note collection. But quite apart from the multifarious confusions with which this notion is laden, it does not really apply here. To claim that the finale of *Dumbarton Oaks* is "Phrygian" discloses nothing of the peculiar symbiotic relationship between scales with common referential collection but different interval orderings. It is quite frankly only on the most trivial level that "modality" can be helpful, i.e. by freeing us from dependence on the concept of "major" scale for identifying the referential collection. "D-mode," "E-mode," etc. rid modern modal nomenclature of extraneous historical implications; and by simple substitution of "scale" for "mode" (e.g. "D-scale") we, in turn, may derive a nomenclature that analogously circumvents the implications of "modality," both modern and archaic. According to such a convention, each letter-name can define a different ordering of the white-note collection (including C), the same letter-name being retained for transpositions, so that *Dumbarton Oaks* may be said to open in the E-scale on G and to close in the C-scale on E♭.

Before dispensing with "modality," it is tempting to make a special case for the *Hymne* of *Sérénade en la,* which has an opening section in the E-scale on A (with few deviations from the referential collection up to m. 19), closes with a transitory allusion to it (m. 77), and has about a third of the movement (mm. 52-76) dominated, despite "black" patches, by a transposition of the E-scale to the form referable directly (i.e. without transposition) to the white-note collection. The symbiotic relation between referential order and referential collection seems unimportant here, until attention is drawn to the inside pun of the opening measures, at which point the modal interpretation collapses. In these measures, the referential ordering of the C-scale (transposed to F), which played such important a part in *Danse Russe* and *Dumbarton Oaks,* covertly intrudes by way of the elements of the triad F-A-C which, in a narrow grammatical sense, account for most of the simultaneities through the third beat of m. 5. But any realization of their potency for the assertion of F priority is studiously avoided owing to their employment in such a way as to firmly assert A by virtue of various kinds of articulation: repetition, doubling, registration (A in outer voices and the more exposed inner ones), and accentuation (both quantitative and qualitative).

This by now classic example of the extent to which pitch-class priority may be stipulated by compositional procedures, serves as an appropriate transition from contexts referable to the white-note collection to contexts referable to a more complex collection. In the latter, all possible modes of articulation become more necessary than ever for the assertion of pitch-class priority—so much so, in fact, that the absence of such articulation, as it soon will be seen, may place the music in those interstitial realms between the centric and noncentric.

II

Without criteria for selection of certain pitches over others, the passage from *Les Noces* (Ex. 5) cannot be referred to the white-note collection, though an observer with strong tonal bias might claim that, except for what may be regarded as a "closely related" E, all the tones are accommodated by B♭ "harmonic minor"—and thus (so the argument would go) what results is simply another "diatonic" scale of the white-note class.

Ex. 5

Now I do not wish to tangle here with questions of the "hybrid" minor formations, except to stress that they do not fulfill the conditions of the white-note collection of being capable of having its elements arranged in an uninterrupted series, the first and last tritone-related and the adjacencies separated by the identical interval—the only such possible interval being, within the white-note collection, the fifth. But even if the interpretation of the "hybrid" minor scales was acceptable in its tonal functional sense, it would be hard to prove that the F♯ (G♭) is treated *functionally,* so that if it is to be said that there is any correlation at all with B♭ minor it would seem to be more statistical than anything else.

Should this, too, be considered insufficient grounds for rejecting the "B♭ minor" interpretation, there would still remain the more serious objection that may be levelled against the low hierarchical position assigned in this scheme to the E♭—namely as appoggiatura to D♭. Thus the dyad formed by the linear expression of E♭-D♭ associates with D-C of the preceding section (No. 27ff.), where D may be interpreted as the pitch class of priority, as well as with the E-D at the opening of the work, where the insistence on the soprano's E_5 leaves no doubt at all as to the priority of E. The position of E♭ is, then, hierarchically of a higher order than that of appoggiatura to D♭, though there is insufficient evidence to establish its priority as *the* tone center; therefore, when the mezzo-soprano line at No. 35 is heard in transpositions on C (No. 38) and on A (No. 39) these tones by analogy also have a certain potentiality for assertion of priority, each tone in its turn.[7] If an assessment is made of the relative weight of these transpositions, it is observed that A priority receives most substantiation: 1) from the A's on each quarter beat of the pianos' ostinato at Nos. 35-40; 2) from the significant reinforcement just before No. 39 by the octave doubling and by the new A_4 on the offbeats; 3) from the bass voice's entrance (6 measures after No. 36 and 3 measures after No. 37) with what starts on A as another transposition, but continues as a variant that will be prominent at No. 40.

These bits of evidence, while not particularly effective in asserting A in this section of *Noces,* are significant in the light of the A priority ultimately realized in the modified return of the material at Nos. 82-87:

Ex. 6

[7] In the two transpositions, the original undergoes the following slight modifications: in both of them, m. 6 is truncated and the (B♭) grace-note omitted; where the transposition on C has the contour A-C-E, identical interval order calls for A-C♯-E, which is restored when this transposition recurs at No. 85.

where the E tremolo acoustically supports A_3 of the pianos, and the A priority operative since No. 78 predisposes the ear toward the continued acceptance of this priority as asserted by the A's of long duration at No. 82.

But the question remains: why, given reasonable evidence to verify it, is A priority still in a certain doubt at Nos. 35-40? A search for the answer may lead one to contemplate the curious consistence that pervades forty-five measures at Nos. 35-40, and the same number of measures (of slightly longer duration because of some 3/4 meter) at Nos. 82-87, as a result of which everything, both linear successions and simultaneities, fits together like well-meshed gears, so that it is not surprising to discover, from a tabulation of the total pitch content, that a single referential collection of eight pitch classes accounts for it all—with a few exceptions so marginal as scarcely to require mention (some dozen tones, mainly ornamental, and most of them at Nos. 35-40). If it is granted that the pitch class A is the most likely element to determine the referential order within the collection, the scale drawn from the collection may be represented as follows:

	i	ii	iii	iv	v	vi	vii	viii	(i)
	a	B♭	c	D♭	e♭	E	f♯	G	(a)
pitch numbers:	0	1	3	4	6	7	9	10	(1)
intervals:		1	2	1	2	1	2	1	(2)

A formal approach to this scale (hereafter referred to as "octatonic") would calculate the structure and enumerate the properties at once.[8] Here the approach will be inductive, so that only such properties will be considered as are demonstrated by the musical examples discussed. Thus, the passage from *Noces* makes us aware of the high degree of similitude that the scale generates to the end that it yields identical interval content for the reproduction of the linear configuration at 0, 3, and 6 (hence the lower-case letters in the scale representation above). Substantial preservation of pitch content from one transposition to another is also available. The form on A, for example, requires no pitch classes not present at the original statement on E♭—provided the piano's A is counted. Naturally, what holds true for 0, 3, and 6 will hold true for 9, and indeed a transposition on this element is ultimately suggested between Nos. 83 and 84, where we are again reminded of the common pitch content, since it is

---

[8] Messiaen classifies this scale among "modes of limited transposition" in *Technique de mon langage musical* (Paris: Leduc, 1944, pp. 52f.). Its limitation to three transpositions becomes evident when the twelve pitch classes are arranged into the three available diminished-seventh chords: combination of any two yields the scale's total pitch content, and only three such combinations are, of course, possible. Also, between any two collections of scale content there will be one of these chords in common. (If the chords are designated X, Y, and Z, they yield XY, YZ, and XZ.) Taking his cue from Messiaen, Roman Vlad draws attention to Stravinsky's use of the scale (*Stravinsky*, London: Oxford University Press, 1960, pp. 7f.), without, however, exploring the special properties that will presently be seen to arise out of the ordering in which there is a semitone between first and second degrees.

produced as a result of the transposition at 0 crossing over to the one at 6.

Since each trichordal partition defines the interval order: 1, 2, it is easy to see what accounts for the symmetry. In combination, the four partitions produce a scale of whole and half steps. The fifth scale degree, at the interval of 6 semitones from A, is an axis around which the two halves of the octave are symmetrical; and at the interval of 3 or 9 there is another axis around which two quarters of the octave (halves of the tritone) are analogously symmetrical.

When we had only the simpler relations of the white-note collection to cope with (in Part I), the following condition prevailed: within any given white-note collection, for each pitch class there was only one possible referential interval ordering in which it could have priority. Within any given octatonic collection, by contrast, the first element of any of the partitions of the octave at 0, 3, 6, and 9 has the potentiality of being the pitch class of priority in an identical ordering referable to the same given octatonic collection, and this also holds true, analogously, for 1, 4, 7, and 10, with respect to a different ordering, of which more will be said later. That is to say, not only is each of the partitions a "transposition" of the other, in a sense, but the interval ordering of the total collection defined in relation to the first element of each partition is also identical; hence, each of the four possible orderings is also a different "transposition" of the octatonic scale. (Strictly speaking, this is really "rotation," since the collection has only three transpositions—see footnote 8.) Therefore, in the interval ordering of the scale as represented above, there are, loosely speaking, four potential "tone centers" of equal weight and independence.

In *Noces*, the two-part partition of the octave concerned us more and seemed more prevalent than the four-part partition. If the octave is assumed—as I have already assumed the fifth—then a hierarchy is thus established, contingent on the octave as a fundamental construct within the semitonal system. This attaches special importance to the fact that A-E♭ and its complement E♭-A are intervals each adding up to 6 semitones, while A-C, which is 3 semitones, has a complement of 9. For if the octave takes precedence the symmetrical position of 3 within the tritone is of less consequence than the relation of 3 to the octave, thus placing it on a different, or "lesser," hierarchical plane with regard to its potentiality for symmetry than the relation of 6 to the octave, but on a higher plane with regard to its potentiality for differentiation.

The, so to speak, equality (i.e. numerically) between the interval of a tritone and its complement is, if not the final verification, then at least highly symptomatic of the identity relation between these "two" intervals, or between their elements, or, specifically in *Noces,* between A and E♭. In addition, each tritone-related element has the potentiality, within the octatonic scale, to stand in an identical relation to any available interval ordering (this order and relation being parallel rather than symmetrical)

—i.e. to be an element of a transposition with identical interval ordering and/or identical interval content. Therefore, given any two tritone-related pitch classes within the octatonic scale, to establish the priority of one over the other within the scale's limits, this identity between the configurations of which they are respectively the members must be eliminated. One of the ways in which this can be brought about is demonstrated by the section of *Noces* between Nos. 82 and 87, where the high degree of similitude observed earlier at approximately No. 39, between the elements gravitating around A and those gravitating around E♭, is now scarcely present at all, as a result, on the one hand, of the continuing fifth (the E tremolo)—the E♭'s fifth being transitory—and on the other, of the sustained A's, all of which leaves no doubt as to the pitch class of priority, even though the transposition at 6 lingers on after No. 86 in very nearly its original form.

Since each scale degree of the octatonic scale is tritone-related, the noticeable presence of this interval is stipulated for any context referable to the collection of this scale; and any part of *Noces* where it is used will be more or less associated with the basic simultaneity at No. 1, where E is in the voice and B♭ is in the piano. (Thus, the mezzo-soprano's E♭ and the piano's A at No. 35 actually reverse the opening roles of the "black" and "white" notes.) Similarly, in *Petrouchka* it is clearly evident to the ear that the scale emerges directly out of the frequent expression of the tritone as a dyad (usually linear) in the first tableau: B♭-E at Nos. 7, 9, 17, 22; F-B at Nos. 8, 11, 23; both forms alternately between Nos. 24 and 27, and, the form of most immediate concern here, C-F♯ in the interlude between the first and second tableaux. (In the total structure, the limited associations of identical pitch-class content also lend significance to F-B in the main simultaneities of *Danse Russe* (Ex. 1 above) as a veriticalization of the linear dyads at Nos. 8, etc. According to this interpretation, G priority is a prolongation of the fourth degree of the basic D-scale of the first tableau, indeed, of the whole work; and the A pedal is an allusion to the supporting fifth of this D priority, an allusion clearly pointed up by the return of the tritonal dyads of No. 8 in the section of *Danse Russe* following No. 42.)[9]

To regard C-F♯ of the interlude as a foreshadowing of the "*Petrouchka* chord" is to admit some evidence for the standard interpretation of this configuration as a confluence of two sub-complexes "based" on these two pitch classes, rather than as a unitary sonic event. So Stravinsky considered it, and, to judge from one of his most recent published remarks, probably still does: "I had conceived of the music in two keys in the second tableau as Petrouchka's insult to the public. . . ."[10] However, since the entire configuration may now be subsumed under a single collection with a single referential order, i.e. the octatonic scale, the dubious concept of

[9] See note 5.   [10] *Expositions and Developments,* New York: Doubleday & Co., 1962, p. 156.

"polytonality" need no longer be invoked; nor does such an interpretation make it impossible to acknowledge a certain compound nature of the configuration, since this can be done entirely within the referential collection of the octatonic scale, by means of the partitions.

To evaluate the pitch-class priority, if any, of the "*Petrouchka* chord," it is well to determine beforehand toward what priority the ear may be disposed at its entrance, especially since the eight measures that precede this entrance deploy the octatonic scale from which the "chord" is drawn. The brief introduction to the second tableau involves, to begin with, the placing in the clearest relief a prolongation of G as the supporting fifth of the C which is carried over from the final simultaneity of the first tableau (Ex. 2b above) by a kind of liaison—the liaison, namely, of the C of the linear tritone in the interlude between tableaux. Example 7 shows how the piano both articulates the C-G and segregates, from the intervening stepwise semitonal activity (mm. 3-6), the following six elements of the octatonic scale: c, Db, eb, E, f♯, G. (Since all the essential features are preserved in the more concise 1947 orchestration, this version is quoted here. No. 93 of the new version corresponds to No. 48 of the original.)

Ex. 7

The simultaneity in the woodwinds in the third and fourth measures dissociates itself from the prolonged "neighbor-note" motion of the intervening elements by virtue of its duration, so that its content, all of it referable to the octatonic collection, may be applied to the higher level on which the scale is deployed—especially the A, which is not supplied by the piano. Whether the A♯ at No. 94 is similarly qualified to be applied to that level is very dubious, despite the octave doubling, accent, and exposed position at the beginning of a phrase. The understatement of this A♯ is far more striking—viz. the descent from G of m. 1, in Ex. 7, via flutes and violins, to G of m. 6, which deviates from stepwise semitonal motion only to avoid it, with the result that "in the place" of A♯ there is an extra B.

A♯ is a crucial element in more than one way; kept in reserve, essentially, for the first dyad of the "*Petrouchka* chord" (Ex. 8), it provides special conditions for a relationship which strongly counterpoises the tritone-related triads of the standard interpretation. Thus, if we assume that the horizontalized C triad of the first clarinet preserves the registration of the same pitch classes just as they occurred in the piano left hand at No. 93, the A♯, which can belong to an identically ordered triadic complex in relation to F♯, is precisely the element that avoids the identity by initiating a registral distribution for the F♯ triad (i.e. a first inversion) that is different from the registration of the C triad. Furthermore, the interval of 2 semitones formed by the simultaneity of this A♯ with C becomes a principal defining agency of the total configuration. (Notice how it is stressed by the registral extremities of the contour at *x* in Ex. 8.)[11]

Ex. 8

The other vertical dyads in Ex. 8, if less prominent than that just indicated, should also be weighed against the tritone-related triads, since these dyads, along with the A♯-C, describe the interval content of the conjunct trichordal partitions of the octatonic scale: 2, 3, 1, in that order.

When, however, during the vertical statement at No. 51 (to return to the 1911 version), there is a concurrent linearization from which the F♯ triad is filtered out, isolating the C triad (cornets and trumpets), the interpretation of the chord as two triadic sub-complexes is strengthened, as is also the priority of C. Then, in the continuation of the linear statement, when the sub-complexes intersect, the balance shifts to the unified

[11] A♯-C verticalizes the important unifying whole step, i.e. the opening D-E (see footnote 5). The interval's prominence as a linear dyad in *Noces* will also be recalled.

interpretation, substantiated by an arrangement of the elements (Ex. 9b) in what corresponds to "stepwise" representation of an incomplete octatonic scale "gapped" at two parallel positions (namely, where the interval of 3 occurs):

Ex. 9a   Ex. 9b

A♯ is first element in the above representation not because of priority, but on contextual grounds (the registration of the tremolo in piano and strings as in Ex. 9a); for in so symmetrical an arrangement even C priority, with all its backing (among other things, the support of the fifth) is not conclusive. Surely, an eventuality of this order must be what Stravinsky had in mind when he spoke of "polarity" in *Poétique Musicale,* and though he now cautions us that the book was one of those "written through other people,"[12] I take the liberty of quoting him on that concept:

> What preoccupies us, then, is less tonality, properly so called, than what might be described as the polarity of a sound, of an interval, or even of a sonic complex [*complexe sonore*].[13]

While the meaning is perfectly clear, it is tempting to speculate on whether Stravinsky's choice of "polarity," a word which cannot accurately be applied (as he applies it) to one thing without its opposite, either had implications that escaped the intermediary who transcribed his thoughts, or—which seems more likely—reflected an awareness, if only on a sub-verbal level where it was difficult to articulate, of the special properties of the tritone which make it possible for pitches at 0 and 6 (capable of graphic representation as "poles" in a circle of fifths, whether or not one accepts the assumption on which this circle is predicated), by virtue of similitude or equal and thus independent weight, to remain in equilibrium or—to the end that a tone center is asserted by neither—to stand in a certain opposition. This speculation might easily take flight in a direction which would establish, as a necessary condition of "polarity," the denial of priority to a single pitch class precisely for the purpose of not deflecting from the priority of a whole *complexe sonore*. And from here, it would be a simple step to the conclusion that short of twelve-tone and so-called "atonal" procedures, nothing provides this condition better than the

---

[12] *Op. cit.,* p. 153.

[13] *Poétique Musicale,* Cambridge, Mass., Harvard University Press, 1942, p. 26 (translation mine). Later statements of the pre-twelve-tone Stravinsky take a more positive attitude toward tonality. Only a decade ago, speaking of his Cantata, he declared, "tonality is my discipline" (New York *Herald Tribune,* December 21, 1952; sec. 4, p. 5).

octatonic scale. It is not the intention, however, to make exalted claims for this scale, but rather, to observe its behavior in such concrete manifestations as the *"Petrouchka* chord," to which, after this digression, we had better promptly return.

From the vantage point of the "gapped" scale, the C and F♯ can figure just as prominently as they do in the familiar interpretation, with the important distinction that they now function as basic elements not so much in terms of two triads, but primarily, in terms either of two trichords, each with the interval order of 2, 1 (the notes with stems down in Ex. 9b), or of two tetrachords, each with the order of 2, 1, 3 (the notes with stems up)—in the latter case, the result of a partitioning of the octave to produce two conjunct segments. And the reason C and F♯ rather than, say, A♯ and E, are hierarchically higher terms for defining the relationship, is that since C has a certain priority, F♯, which stands in an identical relation to its two adjacencies, will also have analogically a certain priority within its own trichord (though one priority may be more strongly asserted than the other)—which brings us back to the statement made above as to the scale's potentiality for more than one tone center.

The inexhaustible *"Petrouchka* chord," needless to say, is far from accounted for by this brief treatment, the ramifications of which the reader will have to infer for himself. Yet, before leaving it, two small points should be resolved. First, there is the A♯, whose important function would seem to render it worthy of consideration for priority. Such priority, however, would yield the interval order 2, 1, for the conjunct trichords of the complete octatonic scale, instead of 1, 2, which—for reasons that will later become more apparent—has been posited as the fundamental form for Stravinsky. If nowithstanding this, A♯ priority is still considered, it might be well to keep in mind that it makes for conditions distantly akin to those determined by the "B♭ minor" interpretation in *Noces*. But, as the reader must be aware, though evidence has been given for C priority of the chord, no firm commitment has been made here with regard to this or any other priority at all. Which brings us to the second point: namely, the "polytonality" of the chord. Though I realize the disadvantages of making such a statement without a disquisition on one's theory of tonality, a "polytonal" interpretation, insofar as it may have any validity at all, is even more problematic than the determination of single priority. For the "gapped" scale affords far too little information for the delineation of "keys" of any kind.

III

Let us make a fresh start, at a place in no way remote from this discussion up to here, but somewhat closer to the generally accepted analytical approaches. For it is untenable to pass from the tritone-related elements to those relations defined by the interval of 3 semitones without acknowledging Stravinsky's acceptance, until very recently, of the triad and its related chordal complexes, the permutations of which, often metamorphosing but never completely disguising the "basic" interval content (by such means as doubling, vertical spacing, inversion, etc.), have produced results admittedly very far indeed from the concept "triad" called to mind by the textbook representation. That this acknowledgement of preassumed interval complexes will not involve relinquishing the notion that certain compositional procedures arise directly out of the independent choice of intervals should soon become evident. Meanwhile, it will be necessary to resort to chordal nomenclature—though often purely denotationally.

To say that *Jeu de rapt* is a veritable primer of the ways in which the octatonic scale may be arranged into four major triads or seventh chords is not to deny its abundance of detail. In considering the six measures at Nos. 42-43 of *Sacre* (two representative measures of which are given in partial reduction in Ex. 10), I shall ignore most of this detail (articulation, etc.) and concentrate upon the chordal regimentation of the elements

Ex. 10

ushered in by the return of the first simultaneity (that at No. 37) as a kind of signal for the filtering out, at this point, of all pitch content not referable to the octatonic scale. In triadic terms, these are the discernible configurations: 1) major triads on C, E♭, F♯, and A (horizontal at, for example, x; vertical at x'—the latter being double-reed timbre rather than simultaneities as such); 2) dominant sevenths in first inversion (horizontal at y', but mostly vertical, y); 3) a brief vertical statement of the C triad at y^x (part of the simultaneity of No. 37); 4) a linear expression of the diminished-seventh chord (z).

Configuration z places directly in evidence a determining factor of similitude: it partitions the octave at different positions from those at which the four roots drawing the pitch-class content of their triads and dominant sevenths from it partition the octave; at the same time, z has an interval content identical with that of the only possible configuration (another diminished seventh) that can be formed by these chord roots; and the two semitone-related diminished sevenths (or any two diminished sevenths with no "common tones" at all) will, of course, always contain the total collection of an octatonic scale (see *Sacre*, Nos. 30 and 70, where these parallel diminished sevenths, horizontalized, are articulated to show their "whole-step" relation). The identity is stressed by the order in which the vertical configurations enter: y^x(C) and y on E♭ (the latter being the second element by virtue of duration), then y on F♯, and finally, y on A—piling up a simultaneity of three sub-complexes in m. 2 (note the weak articulation of G in the dominant on E♭). The "pyramided" entrances of y on E♭, F♯, and A are twice repeated; but the C triad (which took the form y^x at No. 42) does not recur in its original vertical form, though it is significant that among the linear triads (x) the one on C is timed to replace y^x (in Ex. 10, x^y is the beginning of one of these). Each tritone-related pair (either y on E♭ and A, or the combination of y^x with y on F♯) inevitably contains the same interval content as the "*Petrouchka* chord," but note in the combination of y^x with y on F♯ the similar interval order as well. (Pitch-class content, incidentally, is identical, too.)[14] It should also be noted that the tritone-related triads and/or dominant sevenths, such as are contained in the "*Petrouchka* chord," are not very different from those complexes that are related by the interval of 3 and/or 9. For by simply exchanging, in the "*Petrouchka* chord," the

[14] This is a mild form of a phenomenon that may be observed again and again in much more noticeable fashion in Stravinsky, as will become apparent from a comparison of the musical examples presented in the course of this discussion: namely, the association of given chordal relations with fixed pitch classes. In this sense, as in many others, Stravinsky is like the old masters who, as has often been remarked, for each key had their special way of writing. Thus Mozart, for example, had his "E-flat" manner or style, and this was different from his "C-major" style, etc.

F♯ for an E♭, we derive a configuration whose sub-complexes are the dominant sevenths on C and E♭—all of which is nothing but a function of the diminished seventh that is the common pitch-class source for the chord roots that define the other diminished seventh encompassed by the octatonic scale.

If, from Ex. 10, the interval content of any two transpositions with adjacent roots (i.e. related by the interval of 3 semitones) is extracted out of the four available ones, the tritone-related triads are no longer present, but it follows from what has been just said, that there will still remain a substantial degree of interval content in common with the "*Petrouchka* chord"; and if, moreover, the amount of timbral differentiation that was present in the passage from *Sacre* is reduced to a minimum in the articulation of these two triads as sub-complexes in a larger configuration, common interval content will then be supplemented by another common factor: the special timbral consistence of the famous "chord." From all this, a family resemblance should result—as may be observed in the configuration of brief duration in *Dumbarton Oaks*:

Ex. 11

where, when the elements are apprehended as a whole, the typical Stravinskyan "accordion"-effect, much retarded, but belonging to the same general class as the "*Petrouchka* chord," will be recognized by anyone who does not take the analogy too literally. With sufficient confidence, therefore, it may be said that what passes for one of the most peculiarly Stravinskyan "sounds," rises out of the octatonic scale.

Detailed analysis of this excerpt, to be sure, reveals the subtleties of differentiation to which the referential relationships lend themselves, and it becomes apparent that, in compensation for absence of marked timbral differentiation, the longer durations on the alternate beats dwell separately on each dominant seventh: first, the one on A♭, then the one on F. This phenomenon, of course, is simply a product of the different intersections of the stationary element (A♭-A-C) and the vertical dyads in the flute and clarinet lines; and in this process, according to conventional interpretation, A♭ and A each assume the opposite roles of "chord tone" and "non-chord tone"—roles that they reverse when· the intersection changes.

Whereas *Jeu de rapt* delineated two diminished sevenths—one formed by the dominant-seventh roots and the other formed by the common pitch-class content source of the dominant sevenths—only the second type is evident here, demarcated by the octave-doubled C in terms of which the elements of the diminished seventh are clearly apprehended as agents of the four-part partition. But the diminished seventh seems to me, in significance, to be secondary to the trichordal stationary element which is capable of providing a modest exemplification of a useful compositional procedure, the preserved consistencies of which it would be profitable for us to follow within contexts referable to the octatonic scale.

The nature of these manifestations becomes apparent from a correlation of the stationary trichord a♭-A-C with a trichord formed from elements of the combined dyads: E♭-f-G♭. In each trichord the common intervals (the semitone and 3 semitones) are in a different arrangement. Or if it is assumed that the somehow "disembodied" intervals constitute a "basic cell," then they may be said to have undergone "transformation." Now, since each conjunct partition of the octatonic scale contains the intervals of 1 and 3, the scale is singularly adapted to transformation involving these two intervals. Hence when the above-mentioned trichords are conjoined, other transformations will result: f-G♭-a♭; f-a♭-A; G♭-a♭-A.

At the same time, it would be injudicious to ignore the conventional interpretation of "non-chord tone" and "major-minor" when the interval of 3 or 4 is taken as a "fixed" quantity and the semitone as a "movable" one, so that the latter is—to pursue the metaphor of the "disembodied" intervals—like something capable of being "attached" at any of the four possible positions "inside" or "outside" either form of the third (which is sometimes said, as a result, to be "bracketed"). But if somewhere in the background the procedure of transformation exerts any effect at all as an operation in which essentially no single interval has any priority, chances are very good that the implications of such a procedure will insinuate themselves into a context that is either tonal or otherwise centric, with the result that the choice or assertion of the "fixed" interval may be insidiously placed in doubt; and it is thus that there arises in Stravinsky's music another occasion for the pun, different in detail from that of the *Sérénade*, but not altogether dissimilar in intent.

In this regard, the theme with variations from the *Octuor* (Ex. 12) is singularly apropos:

Ex. 12

for here, permutations of four pitches, to which the main linear aspect of the theme is entirely confined through the Bb of m. 7, horizontalize such transformations as those just discussed. The representation of the scale of *Noces* (p. 20) could serve here, too, and though it cannot be claimed that relations between one work and another are compositionally valid, a study of both contexts enables us to check one against the other to substantiate the A priority. The *Octuor,* to be sure, shares this priority only insofar as the position of A within the linear statement of the melody is concerned, since the simultaneities on the offbeats assert D. The A may thus be said to have "second-order" priority, for, as the dominant segment of D, it both supports and is subservient to D. At No. 39, the second-order is replaced by first-order priority, since the context also asserts A.

The pun this passage was chosen to illustrate involves both A and Bb. Thus, whereas A offers acoustical support to the D minor of the simultaneities, the collection to which the linear statement that gravitates around A is referable has no D at all! Furthermore, the pitch succession of the linear statement is to D minor something like what the passage in Ex. 5 from *Noces* is to Bb minor—namely, to a certain extent the affinity is purely statistical: as witness, the "irregular" progression of C. The very foundations of A-C# as the "fixed interval" are thereby shaken—hence, the irony of Bb, which carries with it implications of the statistical Bb minor that was rejected in *Noces* but that becomes more compelling here, owing to 1) the fact that the "foreign" E and irregular F# are not heard until m. 7; 2) the separate timbral plane of the melody (so that the ear may hear it as something unaffected by the D minor harmony), and 3) a degree of Bb-orientation among the simultaneities. From the viewpoint of a basic cell, Bb-C# could be the "fixed" element onto which C and A are variously "attached."

Into the larger context of the D minor, Bb introduces a doubt, and the doubt is an irresistible excuse for the pun which assumes the form of a susceptibility to the accidental suggestion only to make it immediately apparent that within the octatonic collection it is the A, rather, that has priority. What fleetingly takes place is like that familiar optical illusion, which makes us see checks of a linoleum, alternately with white in relief on black, and black in relief on white. To equate this with "keyshift," "polytonality," and such, is to miss the point, for it is rather, as may be seen below, merely a function of the affinity between the minor and the octatonic scales (Roman numerals denote scale degrees; the sixth degrees of both minor forms are included):

	i	ii	iii	iv	v	vi	vii	viii
	a	Bb	c	Db	eb	E	f#	G
Bb minor	VII	I	II	III	IV		VI	VI
D minor	V	VI	VII	VII		II		IV

Other ambiguities interpretable mainly in terms of basic cell and/or major-minor are observable in the relation between the melody and chordal accompaniment. For example, D-f-F♯, formed by the indirect relation of the simultaneities of mm. 1-2 with those of m. 3, results from the infiltration of the linear A-c-C♯, or its retrograde inversion, a-B♭-C♯, into the rest of the context.

From the frequency with which this interval complex (i.e., 1 and 3) occurs in the *Octuor* it is obvious that the most important determinants of both motivic and structural relationships in Stravinsky's "neoclassic" music were already crystallized in 1923—such determinants, for example, as those that were to invest *Orpheus* twenty-five years later with a special imprint, and in their most familiar form, dominate the *Symphony of Psalms.*

IV

"[T]wo minor thirds joined by a major third":[15] such is the way Stravinsky recently characterized the "double" version of the basic cell as manifested in *Psalms,* from which it is evident that both major-minor and the semitone-related dyads defined the relation in his mind. The arrangement of the four pitch elements is the same as in the *Octuor;* and here once again we encounter the pun, but on a higher structural level, where the "optical illusion" is exploited in such a way that, to pursue the image, both white checks and black checks are alternately validated, each for a substantial period of time. Equating "fixed" with "priority," in the first movement of the *Psalms,* the lower third of the pair may be said to be the "fixed" element (*x* in Ex. 13a); whereas in the C-minor fugue, the relationship is reversed (*y* in Ex. 13b). The motive on B, the supporting fifth (*y* in Ex. 13a) which has second-order priority, anticipates the relationship as it is found in the fugue subject.

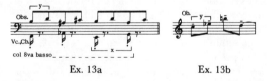

Ex. 13a   Ex. 13b

The four-element configuration receives mostly simple motivic treatment in the first movement. Versions of the basic cell like those in mm. 2-3 (e.g. at *x* in Ex. 14), articulated by the extremities of the contours and their directional changes, are rare here. Transformation is much more likely to be found in the last movement, but details of that movement are beyond the scope of the present discussion.

---

[15] PERSPECTIVES OF NEW MUSIC, Fall, 1962, p. 16.

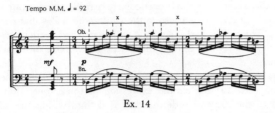

Ex. 14

The broad structural plan, unifying the main pivots of all three move-ments, also reveals the influence of the configuration, *qua* basic cell. Taking the main pitch classes of priority, without regard to temporal ordering, they could almost have outlined the motive if E-G-e♭ were followed by G♭. That the tritone-related C, instead, is the other term in this relation-ship, not only places the whole plan in the category of transformation but has provocative implications as to the significance of the octatonic scale for compositional structure. Among these implications, the presence of supporting fifth is a significant one to which I shall return, but right now let us contemplate the symmetry (absent from the parallel dyads of the motive) created by the two intersecting retrograde-inversionally related trichords:

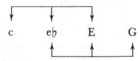

While the basic cell provides the means to circumvent triadic interpre-tation, it is very doubtful indeed that such interpretation, along with its tonal implications, can be ignored here, especially in view of the fugal statements. Even the first movement, which least calls for such an inter-pretation, since of all three it is the one where the octatonic scale plays the largest role, cannot readily escape it altogether, dominated as it is by an E-minor triad. True, the celebrated *"Psalms* chord" is like no E-minor triad that was ever known before, but if its uniqueness should be consid-ered by anyone to free it from tonal association, its implications do not; for it is implicated indirectly with the fate of C minor through that special registration that exposes the octave doublings of G in the quasi-mirror arrangement of intervals. Whenever the *"Psalms* chord" punctuates the movement, it not only asserts E priority but prefigures the alternate G priority which will eventually serve as dominant of C minor.

Thus, the *"Psalms* chord" is involved, either directly or indirectly, with all three of the principal structural issues of pitch-class priority with which the first movement is concerned. (E♭ priority does not become an issue until later.) As to these issues themselves in terms of the broad plan of the present discussion, they are particularly significant inasmuch as they return us by a circuitous route to the white-note scales that occupied us in Part I. The E-, G-, and C-scales, it will be recalled, were precisely those that Stravinsky favored among the orderings available in the white-note collection.

In dealing with these three priorities, let us take them in order by first observing (Ex. 15) the simple expression of those tones that may be referred to the interval ordering that E defines within the white-note collection:

Ex. 15

The white-note collection stated at No. 2 without deviation provides the basis for bringing the G- and C-scales into direct contact with the E-scale in what was described above as a symbiotic relation. Whereas formerly such a symbiotic relation was achieved with either the E- or G-scale vis-à-vis the C-scale, now for the first time we have all three scales at our disposal at once—which should provide optimum conditions for the diatonic exchange. That this result does not obtain, derives from the fact that both the number and character of the terms involved in the symbiotic relation have now been expanded to encompass the octatonic scale, which acts as a catalyst upon the others.

Examination of this symbiotic relation not only reveals more clearly the nature of different referential interval orderings and Stravinsky's reasons for bringing some rather than others into contact with the octatonic scale, but in addition—as another aspect of the same thing—it illuminates the structure defined by the order of intervals in the octatonic scale itself. Further, it even answers questions that may have been bothering the reader in regard to it—such as, in particular, why is the form with the semitone between first and second degrees fundamental?

To this end it will be useful to set up the octatonic scale as a norm against which to measure degrees and types of similitude and differentiation of each ordering, along the lines of what was done above to collate the minor and octatonic scales. Let us imagine the octatonic scale acting as a filter through which only the intersecting elements will pass. Now, as may be seen from comparison of Tables A and B, the results are very different, according to whether the intersecting white-note scales start on odd or even degrees of the octatonic scale.

TABLE A*

	i	ii	iii	iv	v	vi	vii	viii
	e	F	g	A♭	b♭	B	c♯	D
	0	1	3	4	6	7	9	10
C	I			III		V	VI	
D	I		III			V	VI	VII
E	I	II	III			V		VII
F	I			III	IV	V	VI	
G	I			III		V	VI	VII
A	I		III			V		VII
B	I	II	III		V			VII

TABLE B

	i	ii	iii	iv	v	vi	vii	viii
C		VII	I	II	IV			VI
D			I	II	III	IV		VI
E			I		III	IV	VI	
F		VII	I	II		IV		VI
G			I	II	IV			VI
A			I	II	III	IV	VI	
B			I		III	IV	V	VI

TABLE C

	i	ii	iii	iv	v	vi	vii	viii
C		III	IV	V		VIII		II
D		II	III	IV		VI		I
G		VI	VII	I		III		V
E (on G)			VII	I	II	III		V
"A" (on C)			IV	V	VI	VII		II

* (Large Roman numerals refer to white-note scale degrees.)

The results of rotation, inferable from comparison of Tables A and B, concern us mainly where they reveal a reversal of the entries under columns v and vi, so that while the lower tetrachords remain more intact in Table B, the perfect fifths above the pitch classes of priority are "filtered out"—a critical loss in terms of the assertion of nonfunctional tone center, assumed as fundamental to the organizing principle of the music being considered here. In this sense, the scales represented by the intersecting elements in Table B stand hierarchically lower than those in Table A in their relationship to the octatonic scale. Certain qualifications of this statement, however, are in order: (1) the B-scale, by its nature, cannot fulfill (because the diminished fifth is its normal fifth degree) what is here assumed to be Stravinsky's requirements; and since he treats it generally as the usual stepchild that it has long been taken to be, it may be eliminated altogether; (2) the C- and A-scales, with but four intersecting members in Table A, are at a disadvantage, not only numerically, but because their so-called "pentatonic" arrangement does not fulfill the conditions of the white-note collection with regard to the tritone and the series of fifths mentioned above (p. 18), so that, depending on what is assumed to be their "filtered-out" elements, the C-scale could equally be the F- or G-scale, and the A-scale could be the D or E; and even where this is rectified, in Table B, the absent third of the C-scale leaves room for the possibility of "minor," while the fourth degree of the A-scale is particularly "weighted" by the presence of its associated triad (i.e., Bb-Db-F).

Since the special value placed on the presence of the fifth in support of the first degree is due to the fact that we are dealing with a system based on pitch-class priority, it follows that every other means for defining this first degree is of primary importance. In this regard, it is immediately striking that the E-scale, under the conditions of intersection of Table A, is the only scale (i.e. satisfying the requirements of supporting fifth) that retains both elements that stand in relation of adjacencies to its first degree. On the other hand, it could be argued that the tetrachords remaining intact in Table B provide significant means for identity, precisely in the environment of any potential tone center. The tetrachord with interval order 2, 1, 2, it could be pointed out, is one that proliferates in manifold folktune-derived motives and melodic fragments throughout Stravinsky's "Russian" period, especially in the compound form that yields the D-scale (cf. *Petrouchka,* Nos. 5, 8, 20, 42, 103, etc., etc.). What could be more natural than a merger of two predilections—the other being his well-known one for the tritone—out of which would issue a new scale: D, e, F, g; G♯, a♯, B, c♯, two tritone-related tetrachords thus bringing the D-scale into the orbit of the octatonic scale? The answer to this question is fundamental: if such were the case the octatonic scale would suffer a severe loss of identity. Thus, in terms of the important first degree (or of each "accented" element of the disjunct dyads in the normal representation of the scale), the succession of consecutive scale degrees would yield nothing different from any referential ordering of intervals in the familiar white-note vocabulary until the fifth degree were reached—and even this, in terms of Classical practice, could be a so-called "tendency tone." It is the new "rhythm," in the ordering of intervals, that defines the uniqueness of the relations Stravinsky employed: namely, an ordering that gives up its secret, not at the fifth, but at the *fourth* degree, defining a tetrachord whose first and fourth elements are related by the interval of 4 semitones.

We may now, after this digression, return to *Psalms* and the "minor thirds joined by a major third, the root idea of the whole symphony"; and by the same token, the "root idea" of the octatonic scale, of which this work is an epitome, since in its motive and/or basic cell, as expressed at No. 7 (Ex. 13a), on both B and E, in terms of E priority, there is clear delineation of the scale's total interval content. The minor thirds define the conjunct symmetrical equal partitions of the octave; and the "major third" defines the tetrachord. And the motive, along with its transposition at the tritone (starting on B in the second and fourth oboes in diminution), yields the scale's total pitch content. The similitude between the octatonic scale and the E-scale, moreover, is such that any statement to the effect that the first movement is in the E-scale, is immediately subject to qualification, since it is almost equally in the octatonic scale.

That this movement is less tonally oriented than the others, is a function of this E priority, whether in the form referable to the white-note collection or not. An important symptom of this function is the absence of the "subdominant," A, from the intersection of the E-scale with the octatonic, subdominant having no structural function here. Stravinsky does, however, make a minimal concession to tonal treatment of E in m. 8, where A, the first deviation from the octatonic collection, brings F♯ in its wake, with the significant effect that nowhere else but here is the *"Psalms* chord" attacked without caesura—thus giving a sense of "E minor cadence," "justified" ostensibly by the liaison, or vice versa. (Compare F♯ followed by F♮ before No. 12, and also m. 10 of the *Concerto per due pianoforti soli.*)

Pursuing the image of the symbiotic relation, let us consider further the E, G, C (priorities) and the octatonic scale's effect on them. Both the E and G priorities will come into contact with C priority, but the relationship will not be established through common pitch-class content, such as we observed much earlier in *Danse Russe,* for example, since the C priority reached will be not that of C major, but that of C minor (of the fugal exposition). Moreover, since the pitch class C is not referable to the collection of the octatonic scale deployed here, that scale will be prevented from being placed in a direct relation with any C priority. (It is also quite significant that E♭, too, is absent from this octatonic collection.) If E priority has potentiality for relating to C minor, such potentiality is a product of the octatonic influence on G priority.

As intermediary, G priority assumes the various characteristics of all the others. For example, just before No. 2, in the piano, there is a linear statement of the E-scale on G (*x* in Ex. 16) in anticipation of the first "pure white" statement of the E-scale.

Ex. 16

A certain symmetry between E and G here flows out of those by now familiar properties of the octatonic scale, as a result of which G can define the octave partitioning on 3 in terms of E as 0, each one capable of relating to identical interval order and/or content. At the same time, it should be noticed that the present characteristics of G-priority may also be interpreted in relation to C minor, as a linear expression of the pitch content of the A-scale on C (what is called "natural" minor)—compare *E (on G)* and *A (on C)* in Table C.

The chameleon-like behavior imposed in the compositional process on the tones surrounding G whenever it comes into prominence, is adumbrated in the first three measures, where allusion is immediately made to the three main structural pitch classes. (I shall not discuss the usual claims as to the anticipations of Eb major.) I cannot even begin to defend this statement in available space, but I should like to draw attention to these conditions favoring G: (1) the "*Psalms* chord" predisposing us to it; (2) the change of contour where G follows Ab; (3) G-B in the "chord," returning —this time as a familiar element— after Bb-Ab.

If all this is so interpreted because of the later contextual amplification of the G-relation, it is nonetheless significant that the elements are here already present: e.g. the intersections of the E-scale on G and of the G-scale itself, respectively, with the octatonic scale—see Tables A and C. And the other set of elements that should be mentioned here is the similar intersection of the E-scale itself. (In each of these cases, there are the five intersecting scale degrees observable in the Tables.) While there are other intersections as well, these are the ones concerning us, because in this movement they will be the predominant issues. It will be noted that according to this interpretation, the "harmonic" minor of C results from the further intersection, on a "lower" level, between the E-scale on G and the G-scale.

Though a resemblance to the relationship that obtained among the three dominant sevenths in *Jeu de rapt* (on Eb, F♯, and A) may still be observed, it is obvious that there is less identical interval content here, with E as root of a minor triad, G as root of a dominant seventh in first inversion, and Bb as root of a dominant seventh in root position. The dominant seventh on E, in woodwinds (*y* in Ex. 16), could, of course, if used at the opening, have restored some of the parallelism. But the composer of *Psalms* avoids such parallelism, much more than the composer of *Sacre.* Thus, a comparison of what are, broadly speaking, the same relations, in four different works—two earlier examples (Ex. 17a and b) with two more recent ones (Ex. 17c and d)—reveals, in the last two, the establishment of the relationship in mm. 1-2 of *Psalms* as a kind of norm—the relative emphasis varying considerably from one work to the other. The different degrees of—to borrow Edward Cone's concept[16]—"stratification" (that is, the merging of "strata," their intersection, coexistence, separation, etc.) would make a fruitful study in which the comparison, not simply of one work to another, but rather—and far more significantly—of the various parts of the *Psalms* itself, would yield manifold relational fluctuations of such a kind that these degrees could be virtually represented on a graph.

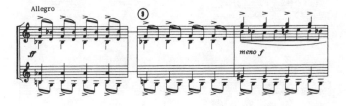

Ex. 17a, "Danse du diable," *Histoire du Soldat*

Ex. 17b, *Symphonies of Wind Instruments*

16 "Stravinsky: The Progress of a Method," below, pp. 155-64. Though, as it should be obvious by now, my "harmonic" analysis would be somewhat different from Cone's, I find that the "stratification" approach has possibilities for further development in, so to speak, a "stratification of strata." The various dimensions could be stratified—priority itself, for example—both in themselves and in relationship one to another. It is significant that Cone places Nos. 4-6 on a single stratum, which is appropriate in view of the perseverance of the octatonic scale. A stratification within this stratum or on another level could draw attention to the shift from a stratum for E priority to a stratum for G priority.

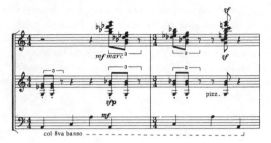

Ex. 17c, Symphony in Three Movements

Ex. 17d, *The Rake's Progress,* Act II, Sc. 3

Note that in the earlier examples (17a and b) the entrance of the E (F♭ in the *Symphonies*), which is the first element in *Psalms,* is delayed; while in Ex. 17d it is near at hand but still the last of the elements to be heard. Ex. 17c, the only one of the three in which the relations are transposed (the A corresponds to E of *Psalms*) is otherwise closest to *Psalms* in the temporal order in which the three chords are presented, and in their disposition.

The elements of mm. 1-2 of *Psalms* are encountered again in prolongation at Nos. 4-6, where the octatonic scale perseveres for eleven measures (Exx. 18a and b), which is longer than anywhere else in the work. (There is a notable deviation in the tenors at No. 5—the A, which again tries to upset the octatonic hegemony.)

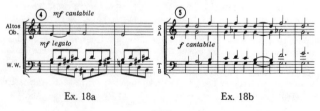

Ex. 18a   Ex. 18b

Assertion of E priority at No. 4 is followed by a shift to G priority at No. 5, articulated timbrally and by increased density and loudness, though within the ostinato context of pervasive eighth-notes suffused in double-reed sonority, the differentiation is not serious. The implications, by contrast, are very serious, indeed, since this is as close as the music will ever come to the outlining of tones of a dominant of C, such as that at the movement's end. If the fugato had started at No. 6 as the result of a ruthless cut, the approach to it, loosely speaking, would be similar to what it actually is.

Though the movement of F to D (sopranos at Nos. 5-6) does not favor tonal functional interpretation, the vertical B-D-F at No. 6 (Ex. 19) invests this section—retroactively, as it were—with dominant seventh association:

Ex. 19

In this reciprocal relation the simultaneity at No. 6 has the function of a continuation of whatever degree of dominant seventh is, indeed, associated with Nos. 5-6, establishing the conditions for one of Stravinsky's most striking ironies: here, ostensibly within easy reach, is the goal not only of the movement, but of the entire work. Yet, we shall not achieve it now, as long as the "incomplete" dominant seventh is not "resolved." Since, moreover, the "key" implied is that of the referential ordering defined by C within the white-note collection, it may be said, pursuing further this anthropomorphic description of tonal behavior, that the referential ordering defined by E within the white-note collection, "wants to"—insofar as its influence is indirectly exerted here—go to "C major." But C is not referable to the octatonic collection, which repeatedly in the course of the movement exerts its influence against the assertion of the pitch class C.

Confronted with broadly tonal issues such as these, the critical question is, again, where to draw the line between an intervallic, incipiently serial, "non-tonal" interpretation of this music and the tonal bias that obviously governed its conception. To be sure, since there is no "resolution," there is no yielding here to the imperatives of tonal functionality. Furthermore, it is significant that what tonal implications do present themselves are distinctly parenthetical—part of the irony being that the most important issue of the whole composition is tossed off in a little woodwind aside, well-nigh frivolous in this reverent atmosphere. It is also true that the context is typically "neoclassic,"—more precisely,—"neo-Baroque"; so that the transitory tonal investiture could conceivably be regarded as merely a form of parody, à la manière de . . . , of a kind not to be expected from the "Russian" works. But then all at once one may think of the F at No. 46 in *Sacre* which, despite the intervening measures, is similarly related to the octatonic collection at No. 42 as a pitch class not subsumed within the collection—the C-major triad operative since the beginning of *Jeu de rapt* having prepared all along for this goal.

If an adequate theory is to be developed to deal with such relationships as have just been discussed, what attitude should be adopted toward them? Are they actually tonal functional relations or are they "semblances,"[17] and if the latter, in what sense? Surely it is illuminating to approach Stravinsky's music from the angle of the octatonic scale and the basic cell. But Stravinsky, for all his genuine independence and original musical outlook, was born into a generation that had, in a manner of speaking, a "congenital" orientation toward those concepts of "traditional harmony" that are now being questioned.

Consequently, even though an attempt was made here to avoid tonal theory as a norm from which to depart, we found ourselves eventually obliged to confront it as a result of certain potentially tonal interpretations which arose out of what I believe to be the essential nature and significance of the music. The validity of these interpretations, their relation to tonal functionality or, conceivably, their relevance to a functionality of a new order—these are problems that ought to be seriously explored, preferably in a concerted effort. Our ultimate desideratum in doing so should be an approach from the vantage point of contemporary concepts. But it need not follow from this that because music is written today without reference to the postulates of tonality these should not be taken into account when they illuminate structural meaning in such works as those composed by Stravinsky before he undertook the discipline of twelve-tone composition. (That they should be applied to the music he wrote since undertaking that discipline, I am not, however, convinced.) Thus, any residuum or—if such is the case—"semblance" of tonality must be dealt with accordingly, both in the light of our total theoretical knowledge and in the light of interval relationships, whether of the basic cell, independent pitch-class formations, or the diatonic and symmetrical scales. I leave these considerations as a query in the hope that a new branch of theory may someday provide an answer.

---

[17] I choose this word instead of "resemblance" for the reason that somewhere in back of my mind I have the archaic sense, according to OED, of "an appearance or outward seeming *of* (something which is not actually there or of which the reality is different from its appearance)."

STRAVINSKY:
THE PROGRESS OF A METHOD

EDWARD T. CONE

I

FOR MANY years it was fashionable to accuse Stravinsky, like Picasso, of artistic inconstancy: of embracing a series of manners instead of achieving a personal style. Today it is becoming increasingly clear that Stravinsky, like Picasso, has been remarkably consistent in his stylistic development. Each apparently divergent phase has been the superficial manifestation of an interest that has eventually led to an enlargement and a new consolidation of the artist's technical resources.

This does not mean that all questions concerning Stravinsky's methods are now settled. Some of his most persistent characteristics are still puzzling, and as a result it is hard to explain why some of his greatest successes really work. But they do work, and this essay will try to throw some light on how they work by examining one of these characteristics: the apparent discontinuities that so often interrupt the musical flow.

From *Le Sacre du Printemps* onward, Stravinsky's textures have been subject to sudden breaks affecting almost every musical dimension: instrumental and registral, rhythmic and dynamic, harmonic and modal, linear and motivic. (Almost every one of these can be found, for example, in the first dozen measures of the *Symphonies of Wind Instruments*.) Such shifts would be noticeable in any context, but they are especially so because of other peculiarities of Stravinsky's style. A change of chord after a long-continued static harmony comes as a shock; so does a melodic leap interjected into a predominantly conjunct line; so too a new temporal context after a metrically persistent rhythm.

It could be argued that such points of interruption in scores like *Le Sacre* and *Les Noces* are meant to be analogous to corresponding actions on the stage, and hence that their origin is primarily extramusical and practical. Even so, none of the stage works exhibits so consistent and musically functional use of the device as the "abstract"

Symphonies—which would indicate that, whatever its origin, the method was musically important to him. That he has never relinquished it suggests that it is musically necessary.

On examination, the point of interruption proves to be only the most immediately obvious characteristic of a basic Stravinskyan technique comprising three phases, which I call stratification, interlock, and synthesis. By stratification I mean the separation in musical space of ideas—or better, of musical areas—juxtaposed in time; the interruption is the mark of this separation. The resultant layers of sound may be differentiated by glaring contrast, as at rehearsal Nos. 1 and 2 of the *Symphonies*, where changes of instrumentation, register, harmony, and rhythm, reinforce one another. The effect may be much more subtle, as at No. 6, where instrumentation overlaps and there is no change of register. (All references, in this as in other works, are to the revised scores because of their more general availability.) In almost every case, however, there is at least one element of connection between successive levels. In the first example cited the interval of the fourth, F-B♭, is the foundation common to the two areas despite their striking difference in sound.

Since the musical ideas thus presented are usually incomplete and often apparently fragmentary, stratification sets up a tension between successive time segments. When the action in one area is suspended, the listener looks forward to its eventual resumption and completion; meanwhile action in another has begun, which in turn will demand fulfillment after its own suspension. The delayed satisfaction of these expectations occasions the second phase of the technique: the interlock. To take the simplest possible case, consider two ideas presented in alternation: A-1, B-1, A-2, B-2, A-3, B-3. Now one musical line will run through A-1, A-2, A-3; another will correspondingly unite the appearances of B. Although heard in alternation, each line continues to exert its influence even when silent. As a result, the effect is analogous to that of polyphonic strands of melody: the successive time-segments are as it were counterpointed one against the other. The alternation of the first two contrasting areas of the *Symphonies* is an elementary example of this kind, but much more complicated alternations of three or more layers are common. (See Exx. 1–3.) (The device is not without precedent, as a glance at the successive partial statements of the ritornello in the first movement of the Fifth Brandenburg Concerto will show. In this connection Stravinsky's own predilection for the Baroque concerto style is illuminating.)

The most interesting phase of the process, the synthesis, is the one most likely to be overlooked. Some sort of unification is the necessary

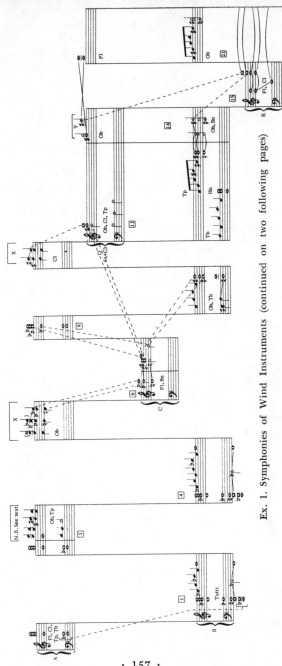

Ex. 1. Symphonies of Wind Instruments (continued on two following pages)

· 157 ·

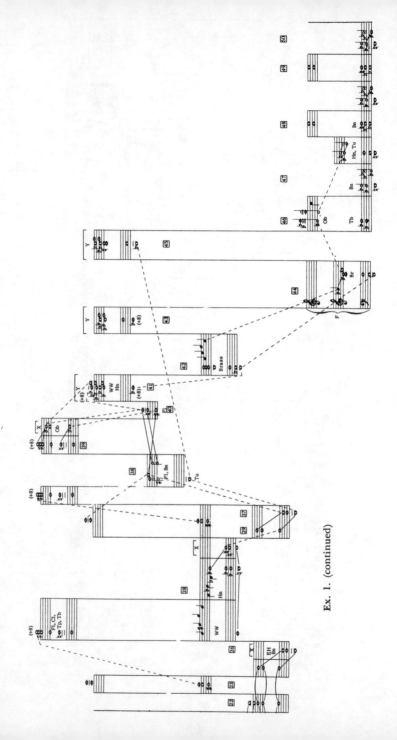

Ex. 1. (continued)

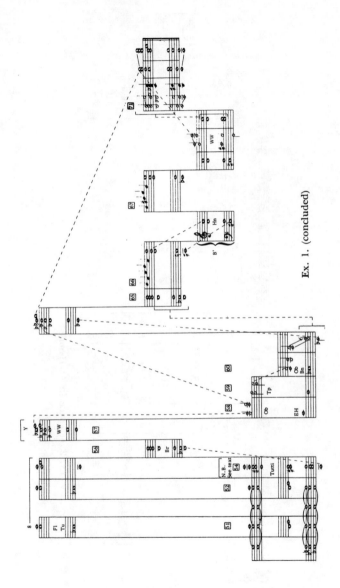

Ex. 1. (concluded)

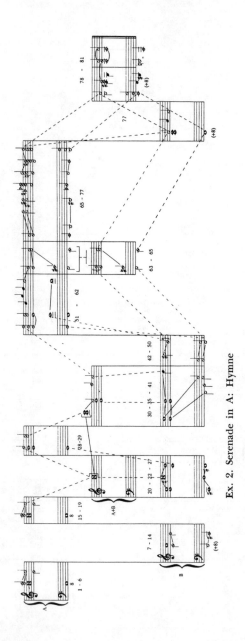

Ex. 2. Serenade in A: Hymne

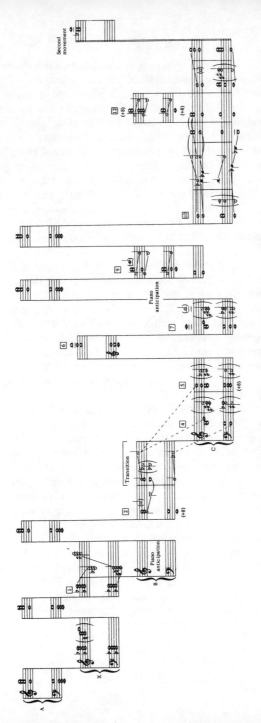

Ex. 3. Symphony of Psalms: First Movement

goal toward which the entire composition points, for without it there is no cogency in the association of the component areas. But it is seldom as explicit as the original stratification, and it almost invariably involves the reduction and transformation of one or more components, and often the assimilation by one of all the others. The diverse elements are brought into closer and closer relation with one another, all ideally being accounted for in the final resolution. But the process is by no means confined to the end of a movement; sometimes it is at work from the beginning. It can take many forms: rhythmic, contrapuntal, harmonic. A small-scale example referring to a limited section begins at No. 46 of the *Symphonies*. The material, first presented on levels separated by register and instrumentation, moves gradually into a *tutti* in which all strata are simultaneously stated.

A description of the technique would be incomplete without mention of two devices the composer uses for mitigating the starkness of the opposition between strata. One is the use of a bridge, such as the two measures just before No. 6 of the *Symphonies*. This motive, linking the preceding statement at No. 3 with the new area of No. 6, effects the gentler stratification previously noted. It is not a transition in the conventional sense, but an area with a life of its own, as its future development shows. Although acting as a bridge in the immediate context, it reaches forward to its next appearance in the interlocking pattern.

The other means at Stravinsky's disposal is what I call divergence: the division of an original single layer into two or more. When the chorale, so long suspended through the course of the *Symphonies*, succeeds in achieving its full expanse, it engenders a divergence (initiated by the horns after No. 66, carried on later at No. 68 by the oboes). A more subtle example is the one introduced by the oboes at No. 3. Here it sounds like a continuation of the first motive, but it proves to be the source of the entire large area beginning at No. 46.

All the examples so far have been taken from the *Symphonies*, the most thoroughgoing of Stravinsky's works in the employment of the technique. Its entire form depends thereon, as I hope the following analysis will make clear. During the years that followed its composition, however, Stravinsky refined his method, as I shall try to show in analyses of the first movements of the Serenade in A and the *Symphony of Psalms*. Finally, a few references to more recent works will attest its continuing importance.

II

The sketch of the *Symphonies of Wind Instruments* is not meant to serve as a complete linear and harmonic analysis but is rather intended to make clear to the eye the way in which the strata are separated, interlocked, and eventually unified. The thematic material represented by the capital letters is easily identifiable through the corresponding rehearsal numbers in the score; my own notation presents the minimum necessary for following the important lines of connection. These should be read first of all straight across—from the first appearance of A to the second, thence to the third, and so on. If this is done, the continuity of each layer should become immediately clear. When the voice-leading is unusual, or when it has been abbreviated in the sketch, paths are made by unbroken lines, as in the bass of the first appearance of B. Broken lines are used to show connections and transitions between areas, divergences, and elements of unification. The fourth underlying both A and B, for example, is indicated at the outset as a common factor. The transition from A to C at No. 6 is similarly shown, as well as the double connection from C to the following statements of A and B.

One thing the sketch does not show is the contribution of the meter to the differentiation of strata. Taking $\quarternote = 72$ as the common measure, we find the following relationship:

B:	$\quarternote$	$= 72$			
A:	$\eighthnotebeam$	$= 72$			
C, D, E:	$\tripletbeam$	$= 72$	(actually notated:	$\eighthnotepair$	$= 108$)
F:	$\fourbeam$	$= 72$	(actually notated:	$\eighthnotepair$	$= 144$)

These relationships also contribute to unification. In the first important step toward synthesis, at No. 11, the area referred to as D brings A and C together at a common tonal level against contrapuntal interjections by B. A is assimilated into the faster tempo of C as well, a movement at first resisted but eventually joined by a B transformed for the occasion. Out of this synthesis appears E as a long divergence that shows its close connection by retaining the same tempo. E in turn suffers frequent contrapuntal interjections by D, and after several more serious interruptions it returns to its parent, never to reappear.

The latter half of the piece is largely concerned with the development of the new area F. It has already been suggested that F contains several levels that are unified in the climactic *tutti* at No. 54. The result is an unmistakable emphasis on the fifth A-E as a neighbor to the G-D of the beginning and end. At the same time, another line initiated by the original G-D fifth has descended through F♯-C♯ (No. 9) to E-B (No. 15, and especially after No. 26), and its gradual return to the original level is completed in the final synthesis.

It is thus the role of the late flowering of area B to resolve both of these motions, a role beautifully fulfilled by the last chord. The linear aspects of this synthesis are indicated in the sketch, but even more impressive is the masterly way in which the harmonic progression toward the tonic C is handled. Foreshadowed by the premonitory chords at Nos. 42 and 56, delayed by the long development of section F, clearly approached at No. 65, momentarily circumvented by the divergence within section B, it arrives with inevitability and finality. And although its root is C, the chord is broad enough to contain within itself the triads of G major from the opening and E minor from the long central passage.

This connection of G to E is important for another reason: it demonstrates the influence of the opening motive on the entire course of the piece. Area A is concerned with the contrast of two fifths (or a fifth and a fourth) at the distance of a minor third: G-D and B♭-F. The expression of the same relationship horizontally in the upper voices gives rise to the basic opposition between areas A and B. The progression from G to E and back, again expressed in terms of their fifths, reflects the minor third in the opposite direction. The third thus operates within a single area, by contrast between areas, and through the movement of the whole.

Two recurring transitional passages should be noted: the ones marked X and Y. The former is first used between areas A and C; but later it occurs cadentially attached to A, B, and E—a significant unifying element. Y always functions as a preparation for a longer section: it is used to herald E, F, and the final B.

The most interesting detail of all, however, is the little passage at No. 3. Interpolated as a conclusion to A, it looks forward, both metrically and motivically, to the future F. At the same time it summarizes the two important movements of fifths mentioned above: the neighboring motion from G-D to A-E and back, and the descent from G-D through F♯-C♯ to E-B. And the English horn, its lowest voice, forecasts clearly the tonality of C toward which the entire composition is to move.

III

The first movement of the Serenade in A is both a simpler and a subtler example of the same techniques—simpler because it is based on only one predominant stratification, and subtler because the two areas develop the same material and are consequently always in close touch with each other. The initial statement of the two strata sets up the immediate contrast: A is *forte*, relatively high in tessitura, and based on a Phrygian mode. B is *piano*, lower in tessitura, and more chromatic, moving from the Phrygian to the major. The "Hymne" records the progress of the gradual assimilation of these levels to each other. The first step on the way, the sudden harmonic shift in m. 22, exemplifies Stravinsky's more flexible approach to his own method, for this passage functions as both a divergence and a unification. From the point of view of B, it is a divergence toward the more diatonic realm of A, a divergence that returns to its origin only at m. 42. But in a larger context this area represents a convergence of A and B, the first of a series leading to the synthesis of the final measures. The sketch tries to make clear both relationships.

Stratum A makes an important step toward unification at m. 52, where for the first time its *forte* interruption is continued *piano*, a dynamic level heretofore associated exclusively with B. In mm. 63-65, a divergence occurs that, like the one noted previously, is at the same time a step toward synthesis. Here A enters the lower tessitura and outspoken chromaticism of B, and even when it returns to its own melodic level in m. 68, the harmony is still colored by the association.

The synthesis of the last few measures is within the range of B, it is true, but it specifically resolves both levels as the sketch indicates. The concluding open octave sounds appropriately neutral.

The opposition set up in the first few measures thus not only explains the immediate interruptions so characteristic of this movement, but also underlies the divergences within the larger sections. As in the *Symphonies*, an initial detail controls the course of the form. It can hardly be an accident that if one adds all the sections labeled A and those labeled B, the results are equal in length almost to the eighth note.

IV

The refinement already noted in the Serenade is carried still further in the first movement of the *Symphony of Psalms*. Here the areas I have designated as B and C represent successive expansions of, and divergences from, the original area A, which is the pure E minor chord. (Pure but not simple: its unique orchestration and doubling already suggest the important role of G as a future dominant.) B, always easily distinguishable by the predominance of the piano, permits diatonic motion within the static E minor; but C, the vehicle of the vocal lines, contains in its instrumental parts chromatic neighbors that are continually pushing the voices toward C minor or E♭ major. Why?

The answer takes us beyond the confines of this movement. The last appearance of C ends squarely on the dominant of C minor, the key of the second movement. E♭, on which this movement in turn ends, is also prominent in the finale, which resolves its constant struggle between that key and C major in favor of the latter. This completes the circle, so to speak, by its close relation to the opening chord. The following diagram, linking by means of a double line those chords in which the root of one is the third of the other, indicates the progression of the whole symphony:

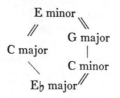

This progression is forecast in the stratum labeled X, which unlike the others does not relate directly to the opening chord. It begins by alternating the dominants of C and E♭ and moves now toward the one key, now toward the other. It is also an important element of unification. Its sixteenth-note motion constantly underlies B; its harmonies are constantly suggested in C, the accompaniment of which is appropriately based on an augmentation of X. But the true resolution of X comes only with the statement of the fugue-subject of the second movement.

Here, then, is the same technique, but used in a highly complex way. B, although divergent from A in rhythm, develops its harmony; although in instrumental and harmonic contrast to X, it utilizes its rhythm. (At one point—during the transition to the first appearance of C—B even embraces the harmony of X.) C, in turn easily distinguished from its neighbors by its orchestration, nevertheless includes and synthesizes the harmony of them all; and the climax at No. 12 combines C with B, and by implication with A. Interesting overlaps occur, as when the piano twice anticipates the entrance of B (once before No. 2 and again before No. 9), or when voices—the property of C—reinforce B's tonic pedal (No. 9). Stratification in one dimension thus proceeds simultaneously with unification in another, and the process embraces not this movement alone but the symphony as a whole.

V

It was suggested at the outset that Stravinsky has never relinquished the method of composition outlined here. A cursory glance at almost any typical piece written before his present twelve-tone period will bear that out. An analysis of the first movement of the *Symphony in Three Movements*, for example, becomes much easier if the principle of stratification is applied. The introduction not only furnishes the basic material of successive divergences forming the important areas of the movement, but also returns at the end to complete its own line and to synthesize the whole. The chief strata of the body of the movement, those beginning at No. 7 and at No. 38, are presented in interlocking pattern; and much that goes on internally within each can be explained by sub-stratifications—such as the contrasting *concertante* areas that comprise the central section.

What is more surprising is to find the same principles at work in the twelve-tone pieces. There is no clearer example of the interlock, for instance, than the recurrent Hebrew letters in contrast to the Latin texts of the "Querimonia" and "Solacium" sections of *Threni*. Each stratum here forms a line unified by melody, harmonic progression, instrumentation, and choice of voices. A more primitive example of the same kind is to be found in the recurring orchestral refrains throughout the *Canticum sacrum*.

It could be argued that these are special cases analogous to stage works, and that only their textual and liturgical demands have elicited a technique characteristic of Stravinsky's earlier period. Yet I believe that a closely related method underlies *Movements*. Here, in a style characterized by wide-ranging, pointillistic melodies, a complete harmonic exploitation of the chromatic scale, and a flexible rhythm free from obvious ostinato patterns, instrumental differentiation becomes the chief source of stratification. This practice is especially obvious in the third and fourth of the *Movements*. In the former, one level is initiated by the piano, one by the oboe and English horn, and one by the harp and trumpets. Only the piano remains unchanged throughout. In the second level, the English horn is replaced first by the clarinet, then by the flutes. In the third, the trumpets are joined by the bass clarinet and are eventually replaced by a clarinet tremolo.

EDWARD T. CONE

This element serves as a unifying pedal in a final synthesis of all three layers.

The fourth movement presents one level always opened by flutes and sustained by chords in string harmonics. Each statement of this area is answered by one of the piano, but each phrase of the piano is in turn introduced and interrupted by an orchestral interjection. The interrupting area is always the same: solo cellos or basses. The introductory area constantly changes: from cello harmonics (m. 98) to clarinets (m. 111) to trombones and bass clarinet (m. 125).

These two movements are the most thoroughgoing in their use of the orchestra in this way, but all the sections are influenced by the same approach. It is symbolized by the peculiar layout of the full score—a notational scheme that in fact suggested the one I have used in my own analyses. What is more, the entire work shows evidence of a single plan of orchestral stratification, working its way through all the movements. This can be seen in characteristic idioms of certain instruments: the trumpets, whether playing intervals or lines, constantly emphasize the fifth; until the last movement the trombones are heard only as a group; the clarinet tremolo is carried over from the third to the fifth movement. The succession of the interludes emphasizes first the individual sound of each group in turn—woodwinds, strings, and brass—and then the unification of the three. Prepared as it is by the exceptionally clear differentiation of instrumental areas of No. IV, this interlude comes as a climactic synthesis—the only *tutti* in the entire work. It is typical of Stravinsky's current phase that this is followed by a movement of relative attenuation, decomposing the orchestra once more into stratified layers. It is symptomatic that even the harp tone is here divided as it were in two—into a harp and a celesta component (mm. 183ff.).

Many listeners have noted that *Movements*, for all its references to post-Webern serialism, still sounds unmistakably like Stravinsky. The foregoing account of an enduring feature of his style may suggest one reason why.[1]

---

[1] Since writing the foregoing, my attention has been called to Nicolas Nabokoff's "Christmas with Stravinsky" in Edwin Corle's *Stravinsky* (Duell, Sloan and Pearce, New York, 1949, pp. 123-68), in which Stravinsky describes his composition of the fugue in *Orpheus* in terms remarkably close to my own: " 'Here, you see, I cut off the fugue with a pair of scissors. . . . I introduced this short harp phrase, like two bars of an accompaniment. Then the horns go on with their fugue as if nothing had happened. I repeat it at regular intervals, here and here again. . . . You can eliminate these harp-solo interruptions, paste the parts of the fugue together and it will be one whole piece.' " (p. 146) I could not ask for a more authoritative confirmation of my theory.

REMARKS ON THE RECENT
STRAVINSKY[1]

MILTON BABBITT

NEVER BEFORE the year of Igor Stravinsky's eightieth birthday had I been privileged to speak publicly or to write about the music of Stravinsky. That I was then invited to do so, and that I accepted this invitation happily and proudly might have been construed by some simply as evidence that invitations to birthday celebrations are tendered in a spirit of generosity and forgiveness, but must certainly have been interpreted by some less credulous others as a further evidence of a sinister realignment of allegiances, which has attended and reflected certain aspects of Stravinsky's compositional activity during the past decade. My only concern, then as now, with this journalistic view from below of the world of musical composition, is that it carries with it the imputation that had I or certain of my colleagues been asked to speak on the occasion of Stravinsky's seventieth birthday, we would have lacked both the will and the authority. As for will, and may the *Symphony of Psalms* be my witness, I can but assert that had I been asked then or now to discuss the then latest works, or of the works preceding them, or—indeed—of any work or collection of works later than the Piano Sonata of 1904, a composition which I must confess to knowing not at all, I would have done so with the same sense of involvement, the same sense of wonder, and the same need of study and preparation, as I approach the now latest works. And if my present presumption of authority derives merely from such a phrase of Stravinsky, in discussing his own music, as "the combinatorial properties of this particular series," and the indubitable serial and twelve-tone attributes of this latest music, then allow me to suggest that my particular dispositions may be (and I like to think are) necessary conditions; they are scarcely sufficient bases for authority. At least as necessary, if not yet sufficient, is that kind of reflective, contemplated, and total knowledge of the individual compositions themselves, which I cannot profess as yet to possess of *The Flood,* or the *Sermon, Narrative and Prayer,* or even the *Movements,* and which so many of us possess, and have had to possess for so many years, of the Concerto for Two Pianos, or the Octet, or *The Rite of Spring.* The convenient notion that prior to 1952 all contemporary compo-

[1] From a lecture given under the auspices of the Santa Fe Opera as part of its Festival in honor of Igor Stravinsky's 80th birthday.

sition was susceptible of assignment to one of three disjunct areas of activity —one associated with the music of and the ideas embodied in the music of Schoenberg, another similarly associated with Stravinsky, and a third associated simply with neither—and that composers, or, at least, younger composers, swore professional loyalty to one and unyielding opposition in the form of at least complete uninterest in the other two, is not merely preposterous but factually inaccurate. However absorbed some of us who were very young composers in the late 1930's were by the possibilities and the already considerable compositional achievements of twelve-tone composition, we were little less involved in studying, learning from, and experiencing such a work as the Concerto for Two Pianos; nor in so doing did we suspect ourselves of disloyalty, or loyalty, or of attempting to court public or even professional approval of our catholicity. For those then latest works of Stravinsky, which now are momentos of a comfortable and irretrievable past to many, were then—to at least as many—unfortunate and deliberate refusals on Stravinsky's part to write another *Petroushka*, or, at least, *Rite of Spring*. But we marveled at the subtleties, at the genuinely innovatory in conception and realization, whereas the slogans "back to Bach" and "neo-classicism," invoked as encomiums and pejoratives, were presumed to characterize and settle the issue completely and finally and to eliminate the occasion for a specific investigation and responsible assertion. It is as symptomatic a commentary on the climate of musical discourse as it is a considerable irony that Schenker's analysis of only sixteen measures of the Piano Concerto, for all that it bristles with normative irrelevancies, provided the most revealing insight into the procedures of Stravinsky's composition. His work suggested further modes of analysis while, not incidentally, demonstrating that the path was not backward but forward to an extension of certain means of prolongation and continuation which provided a basis for increasing the span of certain traditionally non-stable, thus non-extensible, conformations. If the rhythmic texture superficially suggested Bach, the dynamics of pitch progression were suggestive only of a future in sound and in design, and in the means of motivating such a rhythmic texture from different causes and with very different effects.

So we studied such works, as composers are wont to do, selfishly in our own interests; our loyalties were primarily to ourselves, to our own music, and to music. And we, as twelve-tone composers, or as non-twelve-tone composers, but more particularly as twelve-tone composers, were not ones to deny ourselves the discoveries and lessons of a composer who, in his music and in his writings—I think here particularly of the *Poetics of Music*—was so involved with and aware of the nature and resources of musical temporality, rhythm in every sense of the concept, on all levels, in a multitude of extensions. No composer's work has reflected more of an awareness that "music moves only in time," a consciousness of the capacity of music to provide specified control of time passage, and that a musical composition may be regarded in some significant sense as a time series. And it was Stravinsky who also had characterized so aptly an essential aspect of his conception of his musical structure with the expression "composing with intervals." I shall have something to say later of the fundamental relation of the temporal and the intervallic to the very foundations of twelve-tone thought. But first, consider a little of what Stravinsky offered us then. The accentually delineated variable durational rhythms, the fundamentally associative contextual function of intervallic structures in *The Rite of Spring* contributed significantly to its extraordinary character and influence, which were not and can never be minimized. But we had not experienced its revolutionary impact directly; this experience belonged to the previous generation. To us it was exciting; but nonetheless it was assimilated history. How much more tantalizingly problematical seemed the less assertively new, the latently more intricate, the—if you wish—less literal means of the later works. One need but recall that apparently simplest of passages, the single line opening of the second movement of the *Symphony of Psalms*, with its rhythmic polyphony defined by the durations between absolute and relative upper and lower extrema, by contour durations, and by the distribution of pitch repetitions of equal and unequal durational value; and the interrelation of such rhythmic characteristics—for example, in the *Symphony in C*—with timbral rhythm, registral rhythm and, above all, the rhythm of phrasing—phrasing not so much in the musico-grammatical sense, as in the sense of instrumental phrasing and articulation, which provided each individual line with still another level of durational relationships. The repeated complexes of the earlier works, often taking the form of periodic ostinati, now were replaced in function by the single note or interval, separated temporally from its repetitions or similitudes by variable durations which counterpointed the linear rhythms delineated by immediate succession.

"Composing with intervals" was, first of all, the reflection of a desire to reexamine the very foundations of this irreducible relation between two pitches and of two of the essential properties of perceptual constancy in music: octave equivalence and interval invariance under transposition. And with this reconsideration came the possibility, realized by Stravinsky in this music, of employing far more constrained criteria of similarity by insisting upon the identificational necessity of every intervallic entity contained in a simultaneously or temporally unfolded complex. Two such complexes functioned as identities independent only of time point; beyond that there was the availability of a multitude of differentiations, founded on the assumption that any degree of difference, the minimal difference, can be employed as a musically significant difference. Recall the celebrated recurrent chord of the first movement of the *Symphony of Psalms;* it is ever structurally the same: the same absolute intervals in the same spatial distribution with the same instrumental assignments. It is not merely what would be termed conventionally a root position, E-minor triad, but is so uniquely a specific representation of such a triad that it is possible for Stravinsky, throughout the entire movement, until the final sound, to use no root-position triads other than E-minor triads; and this apparently highly circumscribed class of structures is transformed into a whole structural and functional hierarchy, so that there is motion between, contrast within, and articulation obtained, by different members of this conventionally identical family. The final sound of the movement is a G-major root position triad, defining—by structural parallelism—a motion of a minor third from E to G. And just recall a few of the ramifications of this interval in the work: the C to E♭ motion of the second movement, the conjunction of these two minor thirds in the C-minor-major structure of the third movement, the linear role of minor thirds a semitone apart throughout the whole first movement (from the moment of the chorus' first entrance) and in the fugue subject of the second movement, which consists entirely of successive tetrachords constructed of minor thirds a semitone apart. The very instrumental sound which is termed "Stravinskyian" cannot arise from techniques separable from the particular compositional conception or inferrable from purely instrumental properties; it derives from this concern with each interval in its spatial placement, the relation not just of each note to its adjacent note, or between extrema, but the relation of every note to every other note within and between timbral groups, and with the structural role of orchestration. The same E-minor chord of the *Symphony of Psalms* is not, in instrumental spacing or pitch assignment, closely similar to any other simultaneity in Stravinsky's music; its relation is to the structure of the movement in which it occurs. For its uniqueness resides in its distribution of G's, emphasized by the number of its occurrences and its exposed octave representation within the chord; thus does the first chord adumbrate the destination of the movement, G.

Finally, there was that conjunction of Stravinsky's concerns for recurrence, pitch rhythm, and intervallic distribution, in the domain of the speed of circulation of pitches and pitch classes, an issue of central importance for twelve-tone composition, where such speed of circulation is significant not only for the total progression but for the assignment of pitches instrumentally and registrally, and for the assignment of immediate repetitions. Again, one need not look beyond the fugue subject of the *Symphony of Psalms,* where the first four pitches are stated four times in succession, but with any possible effect of ostinato moderated by the fact that each of the occurrences occupies a different total duration and possesses a different internal rhythmic structure.

But I have been presuming to speak outside my intended period, which begins with the Cantata of 1952, and includes those works which can be described as serial or twelve-tone (two terms which I have used already without explanation). Presumably, explanation of these two terms is no longer necessary, a state of affairs that can be inferred from their frequent occurrence, without explanation, in the popular press. With that unerring inaccuracy engendered by mass circulation and invulnerability to instruction or correction, an anonymous expert wrote, in the pages of one of the most widely circulated weekly newsmagazines, the following: "Stravinsky . . . began writing dodecaphonic music himself, even embracing serialism in *Canticum Sacrum, Agon,* and *Threni.*" This, if true, would be news any week. For it is not merely untrue, but necessarily meaningless. It is transformed into a meaningful and approximately factual statement by the interchange of the words "serialism" and "dodecaphony." The writer was unaware, manifestly, that all "dodecaphonic," that is, twelve-tone, works are necessarily serial, but that one daren't assert the consequent, that is, serial works are by no means necessarily twelve-tone, and the three compositions mentioned are indubitably twelve-tone in those movements where they are most aptly described as serial at all. So, though explanation may be superfluous, clarification in the spirit of correction may not be entirely gratuitous, if for no other reason than that the circulation of the weekly newsmagazine in question probably exceeds the combined circulation of *Journal of Music Theory* and PERSPECTIVES. Briefly, then, a serial relation is one which induces on a collection of objects a strict, simple ordering; that is, an order relation which is irreflexive, nonsymmetric, transitive, and connected over the collection. The term "serial" designates nothing with regard to the number of elements in the collection, to the relations among these elements, or the operations—if any—applicable to the elements or the relations among them. A musical work, then, can be described as serial with regard to, say, pitch, if the pitch content is completely and most simply characterized as fulfilling such an ordering with regard to temporal and/or spatial precedence. In truth, any work can be so characterized, if—as might be required in the most extreme case—the whole work is regarded as a single serialized collection. But, in music, the term has come to designate a work in which the pitch content is describable as deriving from operations on a relatively small, temporally serialized pitch collection or interval succession. A twelve-tone set is a serially ordered collection of the familiar twelve pitch classes, but the fact that each class occurs exactly once in the collection and that the systematic transformations of this set are the similarly familiar ones of transposition, inversion, retrogression, and their combinations, are over and beyond the conditions of mere serialism. These principles of formation and transformation constitute a statement of the twelve-tone system, and thus, a work can be characterized as an instance of this system if each pitch element is identifiable as a representative of a pitch class belonging to a set form arrived at by these systematically defined operations. The purpose here is neither to discuss further or "vindicate" the presuppositions or implications of this system; but there are those, and Igor Stravinsky appears to be one of them, who recoil at the word "system," presumably because of its common-language connotations of a prescription or legislation of immediate procedure. But the word "system" in the expression "twelve-tone system," as in customary rational discourse, simply designates a specification of the elements, the relations among the elements, and the operations upon these relations, exemplified by a work or collection of works. In this sense, every composition is an instance of a system or systems, just as every language utterance is an instance of a language system. The twelve-tone system may be regarded as defined by the maximum number of characteristics shared by those works designated as twelve-tone, or a work may be characterized as twelve-tone if a complete explanation of its pitch content is embodied in a series of statements which are equivalent to, or entailed by, the principles of formation and transformation of the system.

Serialism, not yet by any means twelve-tone, made its first appearance in Stravinsky's music under a sonic surface, under auspices of timbre and texture that scarcely flaunted its presence. Most decidedly, serialism is not a determinant of what is customarily termed "style" or "idiom," however ill-defined these terms may be, but the Cantata seemed so continuous an extension of *The Rake's Progress* in its verbal characteristics that it was difficult not to hear Tom as the tenor, and Anne and Baba as the soprano. For, however great the verbal differences between the anonymous lyrics and the Auden-Kallman libretto, there were those singular techniques of Stravinsky's in employing uniquely musical means of securing verbal accent—imposed dynamics, relative metrical orientations, pitch placements, and instrumental supports—as substitutes for the quantitative, durational component of accent in spoken English, since duration, though conventionally characteristic, is non-phonemic and is therefore not a significant component of recognition and identification. But the Ricercar II, the tenor solo, is totally serial in the vocal part excepting the short ritornelli and a three-measure passage in which the serial progression is transferred from the voice to the second oboe. And Stravinsky, as if he wished to prevent the discovery of the fact of this serialism from obscuring the fact of the work, discovers the property for the reader of the score. The tenor part is initially labeled "cantus cancrizans," in reference to the grouping of serial units in retrograde related pairs, and the serial unit and each of its derivates is bracketed, so that every serially derived note of the vocal part appears under at least one bracket. The serial unit here consists of eleven ordered pitch elements, but only six different pitch elements. Since there are, then, non-immediate repetitions of pitch elements within the unit, the serial characterization, in terms of the relation of temporal precedence among pitches, requires that each occurrence of a pitch element which occurs multiply be differentiated ordinally; more concisely, if it is agreed to represent a pitch element of a serial unit by an ordered pair signifying the element's order number and pitch number, then the collection of such ordered pairs associated with the twelve-tone set necessarily defines a biunique, one-to-one function, while that of a serial order with repetitions cannot. This latter collection defines a function, but not a biunique one, and the inverse, therefore, is not a single-valued function.

If these two characteristics of the serial unit of the Cantata, total pitch content of less than all twelve pitch classes and non-consecutive repetition, differentiate it essentially from a twelve-tone set, the operations upon the serial unit correspond to those of the twelve-tone system. Their effect, however, is profoundly different. For whereas these operations in the twelve-tone system necessarily result in permutations of the elements of the set, in a non twelve-tone serial unit, they do not. Indeed, if the serial unit is not inversionally symmetrical, as it is not in the Cantata, the effect of inversion can never be to permute, but rather to adjoin pitches which are not present in the original unit. So, whereas an inversion of a twelve-tone set can be so identified only by virtue of order, in the case of such a serial structure as that of the Cantata, it can be identified by pitch content alone. Here, then, is combinational rather than permutational serialism, since each form of the serial unit represents a selection from the twelve pitch classes rather than a particular ordering of these classes. A significant criterion of similarity, of hierarchization, among such serial forms, then, is the number of pitch classes shared between and among set forms; and this, in turn, depends entirely upon the exact intervallic content of the serial unit constructed by the composer as a contextual norm.

In the Ricercar, although the six-note unit is so chosen that there is no inversional form which contains a duplication of the content of the original unit, there is one that contains five notes in common, with the result that there is maximum pitch intersection between these forms. The statements of the four forms of the unit, constituting the first section of the tenor solo, contain only seven different, chromatically contiguous notes. Since the order of forms is: prime, retrograde, then inversion, retrograde inversion, the first two forms employ only six pitches, and the following two—which as a compound unit are the retrograde inversion of the first two regarded as such a unit—similarly employ only six pitches, differing by one only from those associated with the first two forms. These combined constraints of pitch content and pitch order reflect a continuation of the Stravinskyian concern with the time rate of change of pitch replacement, as does the very structure of the serial unit, the placement of whose repeated pitches results in the avoidance of the repetition of a temporal distance between such pitches, be that distance measured in terms of the duration resulting from the assignment of rhythmic values, or merely in terms of the number of intervening pitches. The assignment of repetitions within the unit so that the notes so emphasized are retained under that inversion which creates the maximal pitch intersection, may be taken as a vestigial, if highly refined, manifestation of ostinato technique, but—in all accuracy—it is more closely related to the concern for pitch replacement and retention; not any one of the eleven sections contains more than ten different pitches, with the note F♯ reserved for a single occurrence at the end of the tenth section, while the highest note in each of the other nine sections is always the same, F. The maximal representation through inversion also preserves extrema, which emphasize the similarity rather than the difference between different unit forms. The explicit rhythmic structure of the unit never is repeated, but immediate repetitions of pitch elements are introduced as representations of a single occurrence. The pitch elements of the serial unit are specific, registral pitches rather than registral representatives of pitch classes, as is customarily, though not necessarily, true in twelve-tone composition; this leads not only to explicit pitch repetition within and between unit forms, but in the preservation of absolute or relative contour structure from form to form. In the language that today is frequently employed to describe characteristics of 14th- and 15th-century music, the Ricercar is not isorhythmic but isomelic, if we permit the prefix "iso" to signify identity of interval succession to within complementation. And it should not be forgotten that when the Cantata first appeared, it was the name of the 15th- and 16th-century composer Isaac which was invoked, and not that of the editor of the volume of Isaac's works, which Stravinsky suggested should find a place in every household; the editor, of course, was Anton Webern.

Perhaps it is obvious already that what is at least as interesting as how Stravinsky's music changed with his adoption of serial methods is how it remained the same. If even within the strictly serially determined structure of the tenor line Stravinskyian predispositions are strikingly evidenced, in the relationships among the voice and instrumental lines they are even more so. These lines are more often explicitly related to each other than to the vocal part, with the choice of the resultant simultaneities and the succession of simultaneities never determined by the principle of vertical representation of the horizontal serial structure; rather, an intervallic succession is created which fluctuates between a reflection of the intervallic structure of the line and a complementing of it—in the sense of providing intervallic and pitch adjacencies spatially which are not available linearly in the vocal part. Reflection often takes the form of providing unison or octave support of an element of the vocal line, thus superimposing still another stratum of rhythmic structure upon the line.

When one first confronted the score of the Septet, it was the final movement which demanded one's attention from the point of view of Stravinsky's serial concerns. Here, rather than directing one to the serial unit through the bracket notation, Stravinsky indicated what he labeled the "row" associated with each instrumental line. But whereas the term "row" always had signified, as a synonym of "set" or "series," an ordered collection of twelve pitch classes, thus removing one from the era of Isaac to a much more recent era, Stravinsky used the term to signify the unordered pitch class collection from which the serial unit is constructed, as in the Cantata, by ordering with non-successive repetition; the serial unit of the Gigue consists of sixteen pitch-time events representing eight different pitch classes. The compositionally most significant aspect of this collection is that the transposition interval which secures the maximal pitch intersection between transpositionally related forms is the perfect fifth (or fourth), quite different from the situation of the Cantata, where the minor second (or major seventh) fulfills this function; here is characteristic and important evidence of the structural significance of the contextually determinative serial unit, for the unfolding of successive serial forms in the *Cantata* occurs linearly, while in the Gigue the unfolding occurs from part to part, as imitation, or, more accurately, as fugal exposition. The interval of imitation, then, is the perfect fourth or fifth, corresponding to the contextually determined hierarchization of the serial unit. But, of course, this is the traditional interval of fugal answer, be it in Bach or in the Stravinsky of the *Symphony of Psalms,* where it provides not necessarily maximum content identification between forms of the subject, but serves as a representation of that functional area whose associated scale does possess maximum pitch intersection with the associated scale of the original subject. This motivation of traditional procedures by nontraditionally determined criteria is deeply Stravinskyian, in both the technical domain and the historical domain, wherein he presents himself for comparison with his great predecessors and announces his colleagueship with them, be they Baude Cordier, Isaac, the Schuetz of the God of two voices, Bach, or Schoenberg.

Since the serial unit of the Gigue functions essentially as a subject for imitation, it recurs in the same contour or inverted contour form. In the preceding movement, the Passacaglia, the same serialization of the same pitch collection is presented isorhythmically as is traditional in the passacaglia, but, nontraditionally in that each presentation of this theme involves different representatives of the indicated pitch class, thus producing an alteration on each occurrence of the contour rhythm of the subject, the registral lines, and the rhythms of exact pitch repetition.

It was the textural, instrumental character of the first, unaccompanied statement of the Passacaglia theme that suggested to some a relation to Webern; this linear partitioning of the sixteen-note theme into seven linear segments distributed among three instruments, however, is more a characteristically Stravinskyian compositionally presented analysis of those rhythmic and intervallic properties of the theme which are to be exploited in the course of the movement.

Neither the Cantata nor the Septet includes a movement that is completely serial in pitch content, while both contain movements which are not significantly serial at all. Neither statement can be applied to Stravinsky's next work, the *Three Songs from William Shakespeare*. The first of these songs can now be regarded as a definitive step toward eventual twelve-tone composition: the serial unit, of just four notes, manifestly is not twelve-tone, but there is no pitch or pitch class repetition within the unit. The first statement of the unit is followed by an inversion at a transpositional level selected so that a hexachord is formed, and, incidentally, phrase articulated, by the first four notes of the serial unit and the first two notes of the inversion, which contains no pitch repetition, and chromatically fills the fourth, G-C. Its structure can be further described as deriving from the first three notes of the unit by applying the operation of retrogression; this application of such an operation to, above all, a three note segment, is characteristically Webernian. And while the flute is stating this hexachord, the other two instruments are presenting an ordered, diatonic pentachord filling—directly and in retrograde—the fifth, C-G. It is with the explicit statement of these, the only two pitches in common between the hexachord and the pentachord, that the instrumental introduction ends. The vocal line consists completely of successive statements of forms of the tetrachordal serial unit; to be sure, at one point two pitches are interchanged within an inverted form, but it must be assumed that here serialism provides a means of word-painting by providing a criterion of deviation from an established norm, for this inverted form sets that part of the text which contains the phrase: "do offend thine eare."

Unlike the Cantata, with which it palpably invites comparison, the accompanying instrumental parts here are components of a single accompanying line, which itself is derived completely from the tetrachordal unit; until the closing measures when the diatonic pentachord returns, there are no instrumental simultaneities other than pitch class doublings. The song, then, is a two-part composition, one part vocal, one part performed on a monophonic instrument with varying timbral characteristics.

The *In Memoriam Dylan Thomas* is even more completely and unifiedly serial in pitch structure. The serial unit of five notes, with no pitch class repetitions, is a chromatic spanning of the major third, and, therefore, each interval which occurs in the complex of ten intervals contained in this pentachord occurs with unique multiplicity. Further, the structure of the pentachord is such that there is, for the first time in Stravinsky's serial works, an inversional form which is a pitch permutation of the original unit. In this work, then, there is a permutationally related complex of four set forms embedded combinationally in the total chromatic. At the same time, the ordering within the pentachord is such that only two absolute values of intervals are available between successive pitches: descending and ascending minor seconds and minor thirds, whereas in the first of the Shakespeare songs no two linear intervals in the serial unit were of the same value. In the *In Memoriam*, with the vocal as well as the instrumental lines compounded from forms of the single serial unit, often with enjambment, the contrapuntal relations among these lines provide the remaining intervals and support recurrences of pitches in the vocal part with different complexes of associated pitches. The first accompanied pitch of the vocal part is a D♭, and successive recurrences of this D♭ are associated with every one of the other eleven available pitch classes; but, in extreme contrast, the first note of the vocal part, B♭, is never—in the whole movement—stated vertically and simultaneously with any note other than a B♭. This procedure is in no sense serialism, but it is a highly original method of endowing each pitch element with an individual harmonic environment in the course of a movement.

From the Cantata to *In Memoriam* is but a two-year span, in which the serial unit has been reduced in pitch content, pitch duplication has been eliminated, and the serial unit has been made to supply every pitch element of the work. The next composition, the *Canticum Sacrum*, is, in large part, a twelve-tone composition.

There is little point, in the name of discretion, in attempting to minimize the results of the appearance of an incontrovertibly twelve-tone work from Stravinsky; it engendered reactions and extramusical speculations which largely and conveniently displaced musical considerations with pseudopsychological and tactical ones. That Igor Stravinsky should now be creating works which were instances of a musical system originally associated with the name of Arnold Schoenberg appeared to destroy a fundamental preconception of how the activity of contemporary music had long since been compartmentalized and assigned, and how the issues had been patly and permanently drawn. Composers, presumably, are competitors, and never colleagues; their primary activity is that of consolidating their holdings while attempting to depreciate the value of the holdings of other composers. I can find no evidence of a similar response when, say, Albert Einstein—who already had created the theory of special relativity—turned his mind to matters in the field of quantum theory, and, incidentally, made such fundamental contributions as the theory of the specific heats of solids, for all that quantum theory was associated widely and previously with the name of his older colleague, Max Planck.

Similarly, there is little point in denying that there were attendant and peripheral satisfactions and gratifications experienced by some of us when Stravinsky asserted: "Those younger colleagues who already regard 'serial' as an indecent word, in their claim to have exausted all that is meant by it and to have gone far beyond are, I think, greatly in error." For this was Stravinsky's verbal verification of the musical act of awareness of those extraordinarily ramified, those deep resources of the twelve-tone system, which we also believed to have been yet but slightly explored and slightly understood, least of all—necessarily–by those who claimed to have exhausted them, and who have never, in word or in work, demonstrated either an understanding of the formal system or the qualities of those works which have employed it. None of us wondered what the twelve-tone system would do to Stravinsky, but we were and are profoundly interested in what Stravinsky has done, is doing, and will do with and within the twelve-tone system. The answer as to what particular properties Stravinsky discovered in the system which he regarded as most significant can be answered only by a complete explanatory description of the works. But I will run the risk of being accused of resorting to the easy infallibility of postdiction by stating that a composer who has throughout all of his creative life been consumed by the temporal, and—therefore—order, in music, by the constructive possibilities and significances of the interval, might well be strongly attracted to the first widely employed musical system which incorporates temporality into the very foundation of its structure and intervallic invariance into the fundamental formulation of its operations. The twelve-tone set is a serial ordering with regard to the relation of qualitative temporal precedence, and each pitch class of the set is associated with the unique ordinal time point. As a result, such an operation as that most familiar one of transposition must alter, depending on the structure of the specific set and the particular interval of transposition, the temporal relation among the elements of the set; the number of elements so effected can range from a minimum of two to a maximum of all twelve, while the intervallic succession necessarily is preserved. Perhaps the very name "twelve-tone system" has had the unfortunate result of appearing to emphasize the role of individual tones rather than the intervallic relationship between tones in the system. But the systematic operations derive their primary applicability, that is, their major perceptible consequence, not from their effecting permutations of the elements of the set but from their selecting those particular permutations from the totality of permutations, by virtue of those properties of the original intervallic succession which remain invariant under these operations. The fundamental conjunction of the temporal and the intervallic can be inferred from the mention of but one simple property: if the temporal distribution of the elements of any number of inversionally related set forms is interchanged in a passage, the pitch succession necessarily is altered, but the interval succession necessarily remains unchanged. Perhaps it is not superfluous to add that the very operation of inversion may be viewed as an operation which preserves the pitch content of dyads, while reversing the order of the pitches when the dyad is expressed linearly, and that the retrograde inversion operation merely reverses the order of the intervals of the set, and that under all of the operations of the system, the pattern of interval recurrence possessed by a given set remains unchanged.

These are familiar and rudimentary notions which depend upon only the most uncontrovertible and essential facts of musical perception: the capacity to recognize pitch identity and nonidentity, intervallic value under transposition in a semitonal system, and are properties which are assured by the nature of the system and with which the system endows any work which is an instance of it.

It is only anecdotally coincidental that the first twelve-tone movement written by Stravinsky involves a tenor solo, as does the first serial movement. But it does offer an easy means of comparison. In the twelve-tone movement, the second of the *Canticum Sacrum*, all of the parts, not merely the tenor solo, are twelve-tone determined, and the very first measure offers the first instance of vertical serialism in Stravinsky, the four-part chords being simultaneous statements of the elements of the successive tetrachords of the set, to be next presented in a purely linear performance by the tenor. Throughout this and the following two movements, the set form, as was the serial unit, is treated basically as a linear construct. The harmonic and contrapuntal relations between such lines determine coincidences of pitch classes, and these repetitions counterbalance the necessarily maximal pitch differentiations of the individual lines. In other words, the total progression of pitch structure, unlike the characteristic case of Schoenberg's music, is not in aggregates but in groups of a smaller number of elements whose extent is delineated by pitch repetition, and the durations of such groups thus are defined as rhythmic constituents. Short-range linear pitch repetitions were secured in works such as the Cantata and Septet by including such repetitions in the serial unit itself, in the Shakespeare Songs and *In Memoriam* by employing such short serial units that repetition be secured through the appropriate choice of juxtaposed forms. In the lines of the *Canticum*, set segments, often two-note segments, are repeated as compositional assumptions. Such repetitions often are associated with adjacencies which maintain between different set forms, while the emphasis imparted to the segment by such repetition is for the purpose of increasing memoratively the temporal range of inter-event influence of the segment.

The most fruitful initial approach to a twelve-tone composition is through an examination of the structure of its set, for this structure determines not only the nature of the local events, but those particular invariants which will obtain under the systematic transformations only as a result of the structure of the particular set. The pitch intervallic structure of a given set is a contextual determinant of the particular work, but the principle of construction of a set is a point of identity among all works of the system. For all of Stravinsky's complexity in distributing the elements of the set in his latest works, the set itself always is presented explicitly initially as the compositional assumption of the work, even in such otherwise intricate and novel works as *Movements, Sermon, Narrative and Prayer,* and *The Flood.*

The set of the second movement of the *Canticum* is described most reasonably as dividing into two hexachords, inversionally equivalent with regard to content. This internal division is presented explicitly by the first repeated dyadic segment, which occurs at the beginning of the second hexachord. Such set structure is employed by Schoenberg to provide a means for combining inversionally related set forms to create aggregates and retrograde inversionally related set forms to create secondary sets. Stravinsky, characteristically, is more inclined to emphasize the possibility of this property in effecting pitch identity between hexachords; the last set statements of the vocal part in this movement consist of an inversion at that pitch level which results in the first hexachord of the following prime form permuting the elements of the second hexachord of the inversion, and therefore the second hexachord of the prime is a permutation of the elements of the first hexachord of the inversion. Such set structure may be described as securing combinational structure within the permutational structure since a pitch subset—here a hexachord— is fixed in content under a subset of the operations of the system. The attraction of such set structure for Stravinsky probably should not be regarded as a last rarefied link to the world of the ostinato, through this complexly disguised repetitional subset within the larger unit, but rather as a profound connection to the world of intervallic composition, for it is the extraordinary property of any hexachord that its total intervallic structure is duplicated only by its complementary hexachord, thus equating in these terms the two disjunct halves of any twelve-tone set, and furnishing a unique basis of intervallic identity between two otherwise apparently highly dissimilar pitch complexes. Parenthetically, it is of considerable interest to compare this, the second movement of the *Canticum* with two works which employ sets of the same hexachord content structure: the Opus 34 of Schoenberg, and the *Sermon, Narrative and Prayer*. [This is left as an exercise for the listener.]

The third and fourth movements of the *Canticum* employ a set closely related to, but hexachordally significantly different from that of the second movement. The set is constructed of disjunct hexachords which are identical under transposition as well as inversion. Therefore, each hexachord of a set form can be content identified with either hexachord of another set form; such identification is explicitly presented compositionally at the end of the third movement in the trumpet duet, where corresponding hexachords of inversionally related forms are so related in total content: the final hexachord in the first trumpet consists of G♭, F, A♭, E, G, A, and in the second trumpet: G, A♭, F, A, G♭, E. This pitch identification between hexachords can be termed, more than metaphorically, a cadential resolution, for it is the final stage in a succession of juxtapositions of hexachords, beginning with a pair which is disjunct in pitch content and proceeding through set pairs with varying degrees of pitch identification.

Stravinsky recently has asserted that serialism in general interests him more than the twelve-tone system as such. This generalized interest in an order-defined norm with successive transformations often takes the form of literal imitations. In his transcription of his *Les cinqs doigts* as *Eight Miniatures for Orchestra*, the texture is enriched primarily by canonic elaboration, and his interruption of the composition of the *Canticum Sacrum* to transcribe that cornerstone of canonic writing, Bach's *Chorale Variations,* can thus be understood in the light of his conception of the canon as a traditional manifestation of serialism. Thus, by increasing the number of canonically related parts without, in general, increasing the number of different notes, by instrumental extraction and assignment, he therefore increases the serial content of the variations. And this conception of the nature of canon invests *Agon*, which—since it was begun earlier, to be returned to and completed after the *Canticum*—contains movements which are twelve-tone and those which are not significantly serial at all, as a means of relating such otherwise disparate materials. The structure of the twelve-tone movements is the simplest of all of Stravinsky's works. This is not to minimize their virtuosity, or their extension of the procedures already alluded to, or their extraordinary interrelation of serial methods with such eternally Stravinskyian procedures as the employment of instrumental doubling as a rhythmic determinant in the Four Duos, the design function of the variety of representations of the measure, or the extraordinary ensemble effected through timbrally relatively unrelated sound sources.

But it is with *Threni*, his first completely twelve-tone work, and his most extended one, that Stravinsky establishes what has become, for the *Movements*, the *Sermon*, and *The Flood*, his completely personal use of the materials of the twelve-tone system. Rather than working with a single form of a set, he more often employs a collection of set forms or segments of set forms as a unit and as a source of his pitch materials. Constituent set forms still provide the ordering criteria for the elements they contain, but the ordering of segments drawn from this collection, and the very number of such segments, constitute a rhythmic procedure, a pitch weighting procedure, and a method for the construction of linear elements, which seldom are themselves set forms. These explicit linear elements, be they presented as timbral lines or as lines temporally unfolded by a variety of timbres, may be said to, since they easily may be heard to, trace a path through this collection of sets. The path moves among set forms according to various patterns of regularity, selected to secure rhythm of pitch repetition, of pitch configuration repetition, and specified intervallic succession, and to secure emphases upon pitches through multiplicity of occurrence within a given time period, and to secure new thematic elements which serve to mediate among different such collections of set forms. This procedure may be regarded as the partitioning of a set form by the insertion of other set forms, which are thus mutually partitioned. Hexachords, much the most frequently employed of such set segments, come to be regarded virtually as independent units, subject—as a result—to order alteration with regard to one another, while internally the ordering of the elements is subject to order number transposition, the strict analogue of transposition in the pitch sense.

In *Threni*, the precise mode of application of this technique centers on a primary attribute of the structure of the set, an embedded hexachord which is, in content, equivalent to itself under inversion and, in order, equivalent to itself under retrograde inversion (Ex. 1a).

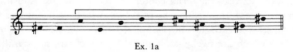

Ex. 1a

This latter characteristic makes it possible for this hexachord to be employed as a common region to, a pivotal region between, different set forms, so that a set may be traversed to the final element of this hexachord, and then continued to the conclusion of the retrograde inversion of the set form; since any retrograde inversional form duplicates the interval succession in reverse order, this technique results in intervallic repetition in shorter time spans than can be provided by the set itself. Stravinsky's concern with the importance of this hexachord is signified explicitly by the opening of the *Querimonia*, where—by order trans-position— this hexachord now becomes the opening hexachord of the set and the opening hexachord in the vocal part at the beginning of the move-ment (Ex. 1b).

Ex. 1b

This technique surely is the object of one of the allusions of Stravinsky's statement that he "composes vertically, including rhythmic combi-nations." Vertically denotes not only his permanent preoccupation with the contextual signification of precise spatial distributions, but also the vertical relation of set forms which are vertical only in their composition-ally uninterpreted state, and not in their explicit compositional presen-tation. And, as for the vertical interpretation of rhythm, Stravinsky merely is asserting his concern not only for the construction of the linear rhythmic component or the relation among such components, but for the resultant rhythm, its continuity and interrelationships. The measure has become increasingly for him not simply a grouping of durational units delineated by dynamic accent or contour identity, but a structural unit to be characterized by its accentual partitioning. The repeated measure virtually has disappeared, but an important role is played by measures which are rhythmically identical in their resultant form but which differ in the instrumentally delineated components which create this resultant rhythm. These components function rather analogously to segments of set forms, whose temporal relations can be altered with-out affecting the stipulated order within a segment. Such metrical reorien-tations of the individual components result, in general, in a different rhythmic representation of the measure.

Surely it was the use of collections of set segments as unit totalities that prompted the following statement by Stravinsky: "The *Movements* are the most advanced music from the point of view of construction of any-thing I have composed. No theorist could determine the spelling of the note order in, for example, the flute solo near the beginning, or the derivation of the three F's announcing the last movement simply by knowing the original order. Every aspect of the composition was guided by serial forms." I am obliged to believe that Stravinsky's derogatory use of the word "theorist" reflects a reaction to the many evasively unsatis-factory glosses of his own music, thereby inducing an acceptance of the common-language use of the word "theory" as an activity of undisci-plined conjecture which collapses upon confrontation by the facts of practice. But the serious occupation of empirical theory construction in any field is the providing of the most complete and meticulous rational reconstruction of the products of practice, the reconstruction founded upon the smallest possible number of simple and incontrovertible experiential premises. Certainly, Stravinsky could not have been implying that the relations and associations which endow these particular places in the *Movements* with their compositional coherence are undetectable in terms of the premises of the system and of the work; for if they are, they are irrelevant, if they are not, it is the theorist's task to detect them and explain them.

Stravinsky's description of *Movements* seems to me to be a modestly accurate one. Never before have his linear, and—above all—his ensemble rhythms been so intricate. Only the measure still remains inviolate as a rhythmical unit; for example, in the second movement, in only three of the twenty-eight measures is the first beat of the measure not explicitly presented, being omitted once in a duple measure, once in a triple measure, and once in a quadruple measure. Never before ·have registral, timbral, and—resultingly—dynamic elements been so manifestly ordered and organized. The orchestra is treated in what can be termed accurately a combinational manner, and it is merely to document quantitatively the most unavoidable immediate impressions of the instrumental variety of the work that I point out that nowhere in the work is the total orchestra heard, each movement employs a different total collection of instruments, the total string section is heard just once and then for less than a measure, one and only one instrumental combination in the first movement returns among the twenty-some combinations of the movement; so, too, this referential role in the second movement is played by a combination which is heard nowhere else in the composition; the rare instrumental repetitions from movement to movement are associated with pitch repetitions (for example, the two trumpets in the first and third movements). This compositional variety is mediated by a highly redundant set structure a second-order all-combinatorial set, each set form is hexachordally equivalent to or totally disjunct from fifteen other set forms, so that one-third of all the available set forms belong to a collection of sets which are hexachordally aggregate forming, that is, hexachordally identical. Further, there are order repetitions within the set to the extent of one ordered trichord appearing three times. It is this high degree of internal set organization which plays not only a fundamental role in unifying the highly differentiated rhythmic, timbral, and registral constituents, but which may be said to preside as a proxy for the ostinato, the dissolution of which is now complete; neither the periodic property of such repetition nor the conjunction of components repeated now remains. Indeed, there is little left of what can be called total recurrence; recurrences within different dimensions occur at different time points, so that coordinated repetition is replaced by a polyphony of repetition.

If the absence of correlated repetition creates initial difficulties in perceiving the work, or a movement, as a whole, the further application of "vertical composition" to hexachordal collections similarly induces difficulties in the comprehension of immediate pitch continuity and relationship, in the determination of "the spelling of the note order." Here—as, later, in *The Flood*—the collections are those which Stravinsky terms "alpha," "beta," "gamma," and "delta" collections. Each such collection is composed of six hexachords, derived by successive order transposition (rotation) and pitch transposition (by the transposition number equal to the mod. 12 complement of the pitch-class number of the element which, as a result of the rotation, occupies the initial order position in the so-derived hexachord) of the elements of—respectively— the first hexachord of the set, its inversion, the final hexachord of the set, and its inversion. The vertical presentation of such a collection often takes the form of the simultaneous statement of elements of the same order position in the six derived hexachords. But each such vertically arrived at "hexachord" will possess the number of pitch class duplications equal to the number of order-number interval pitch-class interval couples (or their complements, mod. 6 and 12 respectively) repeated in the original hexachord. For example, in the first hexachord of the set of *Movements* there are the three such couples $(1, 1)$, $(1, 1)$, and $(5, 11)$, and—therefore —in the "alpha" collection (Ex. 2)

Ex. 2

there are three occurrences of the same pitch class associated with order numbers 1, and—necessarily—with the complementary order number 5. The pitch-class numbers so repeated in association with complementary order numbers must be, themselves, complementary. Such duplications are not, in general, delineated compositionally by Stravinsky either registrally or instrumentally, or by such less explicit means as, say, dynamic or rhythmic emphasis associated with the single representation of the inceptually duplicated pitch class.

Since Stravinsky also has remarked on the reduction of the number of "tonal allusions" in *Movements* as compared with his earlier twelve-tone works, perhaps a word need be said on the subject. I would prefer that this "word" be merely that the formal systems—of which the tonal system and the twelve-tone system are, respectively, instances—are, under no conceivable principle of correspondence, equivalent; they are so different in structure as to render the possibility of a work being an extended instance of both unthinkable, and by so saying, there is no invocation of the fallacy of proceeding from the analytically valid to the empirically true, but only the fundamental rule of reason of proceeding from the analytically contradictory to the empirically false. Stravinsky must be assumed to have been referring merely to the appearance in a twelve-tone work of events which were quantitatively the most frequent events in works normally adjudged "tonal," because they were independent rather than highly constrained events whose role was that of providing a means of progression from independent point to independent point, and whose mode of arrival and departure was strictly circumscribed. But the mere individual presence of such events cannot be a sufficient condition for tonality or even for a significant "tonal allusion," for if it were, it would be a vacuous sufficiency, since it would admit virtually no counter instances, no invalidations, and would classify as tonal bodies of works which have never been so regarded, and which are not most completely and satisfactorily described in terms of concepts formulated in terms of tonal primitives. Schoenberg, too, once spoke of avoiding those events which are statistically most characteristic of tonal composition, but only— I assume—to avoid misleading cues, to avoid the invocation of connotations external to the work in question; but that is the crux of the issue, the externality and the actual irrelevancy. Concretely, the C♯ triad which ends Stravinsky's *Anthem* and constitutes a return to the opening of the work derives its structural function not from the fact of its triadic nature but merely from its being a terminal repetition of the initial measures, and this function would obtain to any structure so repeated; the function resides in the similarity relation, not in inherent structure.

Of course, the tonal and twelve-tone systems share one property: the physical materials, the elements, the same equal-tempered division of the frequency continuum, while their rules of formation and transformation are fundamentally different. But because of this one component of identification, it is conceivable that a musical work could be constructed comparable with Dean Swift's bilingual doggerel which makes sense when read aloud in both English and Latin, since it employs only those phonemes which are common to the two languages. But it makes different sense in the two languages, and only rudimentary sense in both. If *The Flood* is truly simpler than the *Movements,* surely it is not by virtue of any such sonic characteristics but perhaps because of its apparent literalness both in rhythmic and pitch structure. But, in yet another sense, it reflects Stravinsky's involvement with twelve-tone composition even more deeply and complexly than his preceding works. If there is a more profound simplicity, it is not in the sonic surface, not in the identification of set form and instrumental or vocal line, not in the coordinated repetitions of such as the voices of God, but in the set structure itself. The set is constructed as a succession of inversionally symmetrical tetrachords, so that there are four-note units which maintain their content under all transformations, and also eight-note units the pitch-class content of the first two disjunct tetrachords can be order-interchanged (Ex. 3).

Ex. 3

In sum, this set structure produces repetitions of short segments with regard to pitch, but not with regard to order. The tetrachordal aspect of the set's structure is presented explicitly at such a point in the score as that accompanying those words: "Welcome, wife, into this boat", a two-measure passage, framed by rests, changes of tempi, and orchestration, where the elements of the final tetrachord of the set are presented successively, and then as a simultaneity duplicating the registral dispositions of the elements in the succession, thus contextually establishing an identification of the linear and the simultaneous. But a level of complexity is imposed upon this tetrachordal structure by Stravinsky's utilization of hexachords as in the previous works, as independent elements which are compounded into new compositional units.

As so often has happened before, the latest Stravinsky work proves to be the newest Stravinsky work, and demands our study and attention long before we can claim to have probed the discoveries of his preceding works. How old he makes us feel, this remarkable composer, this extraordinary man who is 80. I can but selfishly hope that when he is 90 I will be regarded as an appropriate choice to speak on his then-latest works, and not merely on his works of the 1950's and early 1960's. In any event, in the meantime, I shall be doing my best to keep up.

NOTES ON STRAVINSKY'S *ABRAHAM AND ISAAC*

CLAUDIO SPIES

Thirteen years after the appearance, in 1950, of Schoenberg's Hebrew setting of Psalm 130, *De Profundis,* Op. 50B, Stravinsky has composed his latest Biblical work, on the text in Genesis 22: 1–19, in its original language. It can be assumed that both these works are destined to occupy a special niche in the pantheon of mid-twentieth-century music, not only by reason of their evident beauty, but because facts of our time's history led their composers, independently, to express an awareness of, and admiration for, a country born in our day and attached to our consciousness. Stravinsky has dedicated *Abraham and Isaac* "to the people of the State of Israel," and Schoenberg, in a letter dated May 29, 1951, wrote concerning the *De Profundis,* "... I plan to make this, together with two other pieces, a donation to Israel ..."[1]

Originally, the idea of a Hebrew setting was not Stravinsky's, but was suggested by Nicholas Nabokov. As the project began to take shape, the assistance of Sir Isaiah Berlin was much in evidence, and it was through his knowledge of three languages crucial to the undertaking that Stravinsky was able to begin composing the piece. Sir Isaiah read the Hebrew text to Stravinsky, in order to acquaint him with the sound of a language whose inflections were, until then, completely unfamiliar to his ear. The next step was to transliterate this text into phonetic Russian, so as to allow the composer to have the most direct grasp of accents, stresses, and pronunciation.[2] (Obviously, Hebrew is closer, phonetically, to Russian; the sound *kh,* for example, does not exist in the English language.) There followed the word-for-word rendering of the Hebrew text into English—that is, not a mere translation, but an exact reflection of the word-order and syntax in these Hebrew sentences. Finally, Sir Isaiah provided a transliteration into phonetic English, and this is what Stravinsky actually used for his setting.

It is of particular interest, in this connection, to observe that the composer's score contains the English phonetic transliteration in capital letters, while, immediately below this sung text, there appears the English word-for-word translation. This "English text" is, however, clearly not to be sung. Stravinsky placed it in his score both as a result of his own necessary procedure in composing this work—taking into account, simultaneously, the words of a language unknown to him and their

[1] See introductory remarks to the *De Profundis* in Chemjo Vinaver, *Anthology of Jewish Music,* 1955.

[2] See Igor Stravinsky and Robert Craft, *Dialogues and a Diary,* 1963, p. 178.

literal reflection into English words—and in expectation of the need for performers and public alike to be aware of each momentary meaning during the recital of this text. The unique circumstance of his setting a language unknown to him must also have modified to a considerable degree, if not explicitly, Stravinsky's often-stated notions about a text's *syllabic* primacy. These Hebrew words were perforce more than "good syllables", and their meaning therefore penetrated his musical setting to a greater extent than might ordinarily have been expected in a text whose language was familiar to him. In the published score, the Hebrew text occupies the principal position, its capitalized phonetic transliteration is immediately underneath, and the English translation, in small print, is placed above the corresponding vocal notation.

By way of an introduction, basic measurements and pertinent data may be given as follows: *Abraham and Isaac* is a cantata for baritone and a chamber orchestra consisting of fifteen wind instruments (two flutes and alto flute, oboe and English horn, clarinet and bass clarinet, two bassoons; horn, two trumpets, tenor and bass trombones, tuba) and strings numbering 6-6-4-3-2; thirty-six players in all.[3] Performance time is approximately twelve minutes. The work is in one large "movement," divided, according to differences of tempo, into six sections. The score was completed on March 3, 1963.

Any new work of Stravinsky moves its student to make comparisons between its distinctive traits and those of its immediate chronological predecessors. Whether, in the result, contrasts outweigh similarities, or vice versa, is not however germane. What is more essential is that certain threads always run from work to work and that, at the same time, no new piece has failed, in recent years, to contain at least an element of the previously untried, or a new solution to a consciously proposed, and accepted, problem.

The story of Abraham and Isaac is a narrative whose unfolding conveys, inevitably, a formal design that could be subsumed, roughly, as follows: instructions toward a particular action, preparations for this action, the action itself and the story's climactic moment, consequence of the action, and moral conclusion. The story is told in the Bible by means of dialogue between the protagonists, in addition to straight narration. In terms of a musical setting, it was necessary, therefore, to make a choice, in the first instance, as to the medium through which the text was to be presented, as well as regarding the length of its exposition. Stravinsky's

---

[3] Except for the "symphonic" forces used in *The Flood*, Stravinsky's preference in his recent works has been for chamber orchestras, including different combinations of wind instruments. The composition of these wind sections has revealed a new practice: Stravinsky no longer takes the pairing of equal ranges for granted. Rather, he calls for some couples of complementary range (i.e., in *Movements* and in *Abraham and Isaac*: oboe and English horn, clarinet and bass clarinet; in *A Sermon, A Narrative and A Prayer*: flute and alto flute, clarinet and bass clarinet) mixed with the conventional groupings (*Movements*: 2 flutes, 2 trumpets, 3 trombones; *A Sermon, A Narrative and A Prayer*: 2 oboes, 2 bassoons, 4 horns, 3 trumpets, 3 trombones and tuba; *Abraham and Isaac*: 2 flutes and alto flute, 2 bassoons, 2 trumpets, 2 trombones and tuba) and employing, besides, occasional single instruments (*Movements*: bassoon; *Abraham and Isaac*: horn).

The absence of percussion, and of harp or piano, in *Abraham and Isaac* adds to the numerous examples of Stravinsky's greater interest in selective instrumental exclusion than in orchestral all-inclusiveness; there are no horns in *Movements*, no bassoons in *Threni*, no contrabasses in *Monumentum*.

decision to assign to one singer both the narrative function and the rendering of "spoken parts" distinguishes *Abraham and Isaac,* in one sense, from the *Narrative.*[4] There the speaker and alto share the narration, while the tenor assumes the *role* of Stephen, and the alto temporarily—for one sentence—becomes "the twelve" (see mm. 82-89). Alto and tenor jointly tell of the stoning, and the interaction of "speaking" and narrating becomes especially poignant when the protagonist's final words, in mf, are followed, after only an 8th rest, by the same tenor voice singing, in p, the conclusion of the tale (mm. 203-206). In other words, the disappearance of a barrier between a sung narration and dramatically personified singing roles has been completely effected in *Abraham and Isaac,* the vocal participants having been reduced to the least possible number.[5] The consequence of this choice could, in other hands—and in anticipation of the baritone's sufficient stamina—have led to a very long piece of music.[6] A duration of no more than twelve minutes endows *Abraham and Isaac* with an extraordinary intensity, banishing any possible "relaxation" induced by meditative arias or other lengthy hortatory devices. The juncture, for instance, after the angel has cried to Abraham and has kept him from sacrificing Isaac, is composed so that the changes in "speaking parts" are underlined by dynamics (Ex. 1).

Ex. 1 (mm. 167–173)

The text is delivered with very little repetition of words or phrases; whenever something is stated twice, an intentional stress is given to important words (e.g., "thine only one"; "the place"; "the lamb"; "Isaac"). But repeated words do not

---

[4] *The Stoning of St. Stephen,* part II of *A Sermon, A Narrative and A Prayer.*

[5] Nevertheless, this is not to be confused with the *Sacred History* (*Ricercar II* from the Cantata of 1952), whose long tenor recitation is, consistently, in the first person singular.

[6] Oratorio lengths can, however, be produced today only by Catalonian cellists or British elegiasts.

necessarily connote musical repetition of any simplistic sort. In one such case (Ex. 2) an instrumental repetition does not coincide with the text that is repeated, and the baritone's repeated (but transposed) melodic pattern is not sung to the reiterated words.

Ex. 2 (mm. 23–32)

The single word which is emphasized more than any other in the whole piece has no accompanying instrumental sounds (Ex. 3).

With occasional melismatic exceptions, the greater part of the vocal line is set syllabically, and Stravinsky's customary rhythmic incisiveness is as much in evidence in setting Hebrew as it has been in his use of the various other languages of his texts. In *Abraham and Isaac* there is no evidence of the composer's desire to employ an ancient language for purposes of lapidary stylization; nor is there, in fact, anything to invoke comparisons, regarding matters of "style," "manner," "convention,"

Ex. 3 (mm. 232–239)

Ex. 3 (cont.)

or specific formal practices,[7] with any of Stravinsky's vocal works older than the *Narrative*. Furthermore, with the experience in mind of new, compressed values of

---

[7] I.e., the avoidance of musical refrains. Genesis 22 does not offer any poetic incentive to the invention of such unifying devices, save for the beautiful word *VAYOMER* (*and he said*). In this sense, the formal scheme of *Abraham and Isaac* stands in total contrast to the *Sacred History* (n. 5), whose network of refrains stems from more than the poetry itself.

CLAUDIO SPIES

musical timing in *The Flood,* it is not surprising to find the same precision and thrift in the use of that dimension for *Abraham and Isaac.*[8]

Formal considerations—meaning large as well as small elements of form—in this cantata can be derived with superb clarity from the text itself.[9] The succession of textual events is unambiguously conveyed in distinctly outlined musical episodes, and is supported, furthermore, by musical devices which provide "frame-works" and other varieties of structural emphasis. Through the musical setting the nineteen verses of text become ten units, in the following manner:

1. verses 1-2; mm. 1-50; tempo $\quad$ = 132
2. verse 3; mm. 51-72
3. verses 4-5; mm. 73-104; tempo $\quad$ = 120 (from m. 91 on)
4. verses 6-8; mm. 105-135; tempo $\quad$ = 92-96
5. verses 8-10; mm. 136-162
6. verses 11-12; mm. 163-181; tempo $\quad$ = 76
7. verse 13; mm. 182-196; tempo $\quad$ = 72
8. verse 14; mm. 197-206
9. verses 15-18; mm. 207-239
10. verse 19; mm. 240-254; tempo $\quad$ = 60

(In the above table, all places without text are incorporated into their adjacent previous units; i.e., units begin with the appearance of their respective texts.) Each of these ten segments may, in addition, exhibit a number of subsidiary structural factors, depending upon the necessities of the specific text.

The work opens with twelve measures of primarily linear music—one line only, distributed among violas and six wind instruments (except m. 7, to be discussed presently), at the end of which the baritone makes his first entrance. From here to m. 45, the orchestra plays only single lines (one at a time) given to wind instruments, with occasional, typical overlapping and unison doubling. The only "chordal" music is assigned to the strings, for two measures (16-17), at the moment that the words *V'HA-ELOHIM NISAH (and God did try)* occur. The strings articulate two-pitch tremolandi, détaché, sul ponticello, mf, during the last syllable of *ELOHIM.* Earlier, the violas had played a two-pitch tremolando with precisely the same articulation, bow-placement and dynamic (m. 7).[10] In the second segment there is a canon at the point in the text at which the two boys and Isaac become involved in the action (mm. 56-68), and this is followed by chords for the violins

---

[8] *The Flood* was conceived in theatrical (representational) terms for a medium which has yet to prove itself capable of dealing with this work's imaginative demands. If timing, in *The Flood,* was gauged to possibilities inherent in television, it is also equally persuasive (dramatically and musically) without that, or any other, means of representation. By the same token, the timing in *Abraham and Isaac* is pure theater, even if the composition has not the remotest connection with a scenario.

[9] This observation could, evidently, be made of most compositions based (in one way or another) on a text. However, the derivation of "form" from a text is often no more than a transmutation of words into a particular kind of musical delivery; a *manner* rather than a formal procedure (for instance, a recitative).

[10] This particular sonority, new in Stravinsky's usage, strikes the ear immediately. It only occurs, significantly enough, in the aforementioned two places.

and violas, sul ponticello, tremolando (each, however, on a single pitch and not détaché), p, to the words *ASHER OMAR LO HA-ELOHIM* (*whereof spoke to him God*).[11] Although, for the remainder of the text, the recurrences of the word *ELOHIM* do not bring about any further tremolando associations, these chords for strings return a hundred measures later and support a textual-formal fact. When first stated, the chords are identified with Abraham's preliminary obedience to God's instructions. Their return coincides with the angel's timely countermand and, with wonderful appositeness, they are heard in the retrograde of their prior succession.[12]

During the central portion of the story (section 5), when Abraham and Isaac are alone and the sacrifice is being prepared, the orchestra performs four brief, instrumentally homogeneous duets: bassoons, oboe and English horn, violins 1 and 2, trumpets. The design established by these four is pointedly interrupted by a subsequent duet, in a slower tempo, at the beginning of the next section (mm. 163-166). The preventing angel cried to Abraham "out of the heavens"; Abraham is below: the duet, a canon by inversion and diminution, is for flute and tuba.

Section 7 contains the episode of the ram caught in a thicket. It is introduced by four string chords and a characteristically articulated wind cadence (Ex. 4a). Twelve bars later (Ex. 4b), at the close of this segment, the postlude is a nonliteral retrograde.[13]

If the ten constituent segments of *Abraham and Isaac* are defined by such formal devices as consistency of texture, canon, "framing," structural retrograde, change of tempo, in addition to purely momentary textual supports, then it becomes apparent that the orchestra carries the main burden of articulating the form. (More will be said further on regarding canonic and other procedures in which the vocal and instrumental parts collaborate.) It is the orchestra, furthermore, which emphasizes separation between segments, by means of several independent interludes, as well as by a strikingly consistent placement of silences of 2/8 duration (see mm. 46, 50 —framing the first interlude; also 135, although longer; 146; 196-197). The interludes may be brief—providing a pause for the singer, principally—or they may gather about them a certain dramatic weight. Measures 89-104, between the third and fourth segments, for example, contain a "Cadenza quasi rubato" for flute, accompanied by strings, leading into a longer orchestral passage in a new tempo and in a consistent texture of low-pitch dyads articulated in a steady rhythmic pattern. (That this music may connote heavyhearted walking, or that dyads may imply two protagonists does not, under the circumstances, seem a far-fetched assumption.) The final page of the score comprises the concluding segment, which begins with five measures for viola, cello, and bass soli before the baritone

---

[11] Shimmering tremolando chords for upper strings may bring to mind mm. 182-246 from *The Flood,* but their ancestry in a "supernatural" context goes back to *Orpheus* (Nos. 36-40), *Babel* (Nos. 11-13), and *Apollo* (*Apothéose*).

[12] Mm. 173-177.

[13] The music cited in Ex. 4 serves as a structural frame for this section of *Abraham and Isaac,* just as the chords in retrograde (n. 12) have a bearing, dramatically, on the over-all structure. Either instance of "modified retrograde" is as unmistakably perceptible as the larger, *hin und zurück,* literal and self-sufficient retrograde in *The Flood* (mm. 399-455).

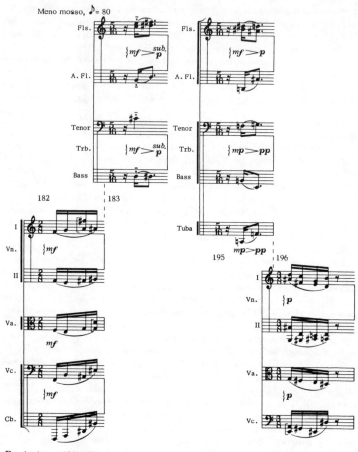

Ex. 4a (mm. 182–183)

Ex. 4b (mm. 195–196)

sings the last verse of the text. These few measures convey perfectly the peculiarly undramatic ending of the story; in fact, that the story should end "with nothing" is, perhaps, sufficient impetus for Stravinsky to have composed this very touching and beautiful page.

The orchestra, as the accompanying element, provides, on the whole, a general means for underlining the text through spare, well-placed musical punctuations. Of the numerous instances where, on the other hand, it adds a dramatic highlight to a single word or phrase, or to a particular action described in the text, let the following be cited: a) mm. 207-216 (beginning of section 9): before the angel speaks— for the second time—there is only a single line shared by horn and tuba (with no overlapping or doubling); immediately after the announcement of the angel's impending words (*VAYOMER: and he said*), these instruments each play their independent pitches together to identify the angel's speech (see Ex. 13); b) (see Ex. 5): the pizzicato quintolet occurs only here, just as the repeated notes in the clarinet are unique, and the rhythmic-dynamic inflection in m. 220 is to be found nowhere else in *Abraham and Isaac;*

Ex. 5 (mm. 220–222)

Ex. 5 (cont.)

and in Ex. 6, the dynamics, articulations and changes from pizz. to arco heighten the effect of Abraham's fearsome hocketing.

The preceding mention of ways in which the music in this composition enhances the dramatic tenor of the text may invite the employment of a variety of shibbo-leths: "word-painting," "programmatic," "Baroque," "musical symbolism," etc. None of that terminology, however, escapes the risk of possible semantic vagueness;[14] nor does it avoid the onus of a probable association with certain vulgarisms of prurient "illustration."[15] Call it, therefore, what one may (or gingerly eschew . . .), the fact remains that Stravinsky's latest work gives more evidence of

[14] Especially "Baroque," which means *savoir-faire* with respect to certain rhythms, tempos, and articulations, rather than luxuriances of speculation in the vagaries of *savoir-histoire.*

[15] The ram caught in a thicket (mm. 186-187) might, to satisfy a Richard Strauss, have bleated!

Ex. 6 (mm. 82–88)

Ex. 6 (cont.)

such musical usage than any of its predecessors,[16] and gains thereby an intensity and an immediacy of quite unprecedented eloquence.

Abraham and Isaac is built with a set whose characteristic properties can be shown in the following way. [The notation in this and the subsequent charts is in treble clef].

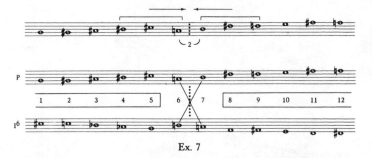

Ex. 7

(The third trichord is the retrograde of the second trichord at T^2; the prime inverts, at T^6, into its own hexachordally displaced retrograde, with the exception of notes 6 and 7, which invert into themselves by crossing the hexachordal bar; the set is non-combinatorial. The subjoined table of the four untransposed set forms includes all forty available hexachordal rotations.

[16] This is obviously not intended to imply that such practices are any the less present in the *Narrative, The Flood, Orpheus* or, for that matter, the *Symphony of Psalms* (for a description of whose symbolisms see *Dialogues and a Diary,* pp. 77–78).

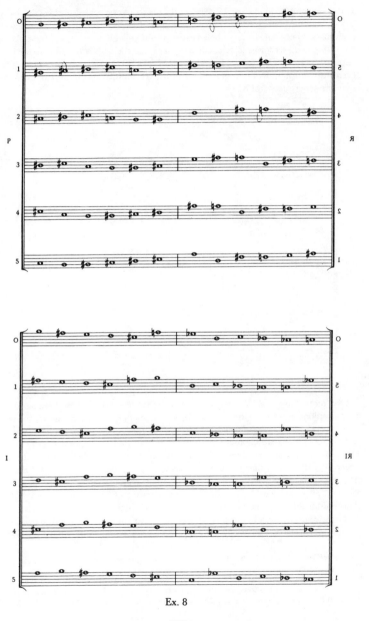

Ex. 8

For the sake of accuracy, the IR form of the set should be added to this table (see below, Ex. 9). Although IR, in this case, means, plainly, RI⁸, it is preferable to make a distinction between these symbols for the cogent enough reason that Stravinsky's "untransposed" set forms have consistently included the *inverted retrograde* in preference to the *retrograde inversion*. In *Abraham and Isaac* IR forms, their rotations, and even their untransposed retrograde forms (i.e., I⁸) are used much more frequently than the generic forms of RI.[17]

Ex. 9

One more table (Ex. 10) is needed in order to demonstrate how hexachordal transpositions geared around a "common tone" may be combined with rotations.

All these insistently hexachordal charts are intended, of course, to show the main criteria for the derivation of set orderings in this composition. It is noteworthy that the delimitation of hexachords within a twelve-tone set is always 1-6; 7-12—never 4-9; 10-3—and that the available symmetry between the second and third trichords is therefore given no direct expression. Stravinsky's interest lies, rather, in the multiplicity of possible succession among members of hexachords. He restricts that multiplicity however, by adhering to only one system of rotation (he does not rotate dyads or trichords in this predominantly "linear" music) which will guarantee a maximum of clarity for basic (and even perhaps "contextual") interval successions.

---

[17]RIᵃ occurs only once (mm. 51-52; see Ex. 12), and the only consistently used form of RIᵇ is its first rotation, RI₁ᵇ.

(The letters a and b designate, respectively, the first and second hexachord of a set form; numerals 1 to 5, placed below these letters, signify rotations (see Ex. 8); transpositions are indicated by placing transposition numbers next to hexachordal denominations.)

Ex. 10

The "scale formations" (notably in P^a-R^b and their inversions) are, in this sense, particularly meaningful: none of the five rotations obliterates the consecution of major, or major and minor, seconds between at least three successive hexachordal components.

The proof of the self-sufficiency of hexachordal ordering in *Abraham and Isaac* (in contrast to the presumably "fixed" succession within twelve-tone sets) resides in the fact that the complete *ordered* set is stated only once in the entire piece (Ex. 11), at the beginning:

Ex. 11 (mm. 1–5)

Hexachordal complementation occurs frequently enough, but the resultant "sets" display, consistently, unstable ordering due either to juxtapositions of P and R (or I and IR) hexachords, or because of independent hexachordal rotation, or a mixture of both.[18] Whenever complementary hexachords are stated consecutively, they pertain to either one or the other of the performing forces; baritone and orchestra seldom share in the enunciation (no matter what the order) of a complete "set." It is more usual for such complementation to be confined to whichever "force" has stated the hexachord to be complemented. This independence, regarding serial orders, of the performing elements is a remarkable feature of the cantata. Excepting, for the moment, canonic passages, one of the very few cases of an interdependence between baritone and orchestra in the formulation of a hexachord, occurs at the beginning of the second segment (Ex. 12).

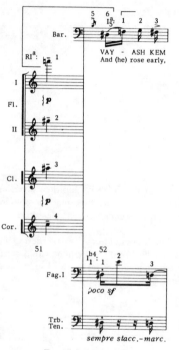

Ex. 12 (mm. 51–52)

Several of the segments begin, in the vocal part, with complementary hexachords. But complementation is not the sole criterion for hexachordal associations or successions, and there are several places in the score where no such association appears to be intended. Stravinsky may, as in previous works, link one hexachord to

---

[18] P[a], P[b], R[a], R[b], and their inversions can be found often enough *in order*—or in a rotation clearly derived from such order—to be readily identifiable as the basic set forms. Besides, the obviously intentional statement of P at the outset of the composition bespeaks Stravinsky's aversion to obscurantism for its own, or any other, sake.

another by means of an identity between the last note of one and the first note of the next, or, as in Ex. 13, through simultaneous rotation and transposition (see Ex. 10).

Ex. 13 (mm. 217–219)[19]

[19] For similar chains of rotating-transposing hexachords, see *A Sermon, A Narrative and A Prayer,* mm. 150-159; *The Flood,* mm. 127-130 and 277-282.

Ex. 13

In the absence of any material whose recurrence is sufficiently constant and frequent as to justify the inference of "refrains," certain striking repetitions should, nevertheless, be pointed out. On three separate occasions, the word *ELOHIM* (or *V'HA-ELOHIM*) is sung with interval successions that are readily committed to memory; at each of these appearances, however, the orchestra plays textures and pitches that are not "recapitulated," although there is an obvious relation between the first two (see pp. 110–11).

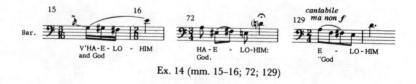

Ex. 14 (mm. 15–16; 72; 129)

A more self-contained example of vocal repetitions coupled, this time, with repeated instrumental punctuation, can be seen in Ex. 15, during whose fragment of dialogue the word *VAYOMER* supplies the incentive for a design (cf. n. 7):

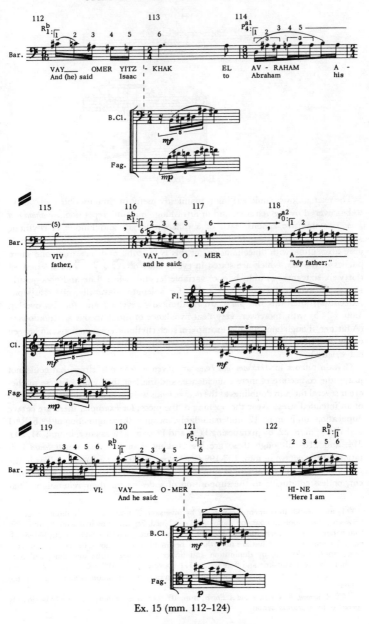

Ex. 15 (mm. 112–124)

CLAUDIO SPIES

Ex. 15 (cont.)

The exercise of canonic writing is manifestly useful in circumscribing an "area" to be covered by a given text, and in furnishing "built-in" repetition. *Abraham and Isaac* contains five canons, each of a different length and kind.[20] A rhythmic artifice in the first of these is of special interest, as it indicates Stravinsky's continuing absorption with "mechanisms" of this type: tuba and bass trombone share pitches of the *dux,* which are stated in even values of ♪♪♪ for a length of thirty-six sixteenths (within bars of variable length), while flute and oboe jointly answer in even values of ♪♪♪ (for a length, naturally, of twenty-four sixteenths); after this the parts are rhythmically reversed and the *duci* overlap (mm. 62-65) with, moreover, very neat avoidance of simultaneous articulations.[21] (A further, though non-canonic, example of such rhythmic constructions can be seen in the duet between bassoons (m. 136ff.) in which "sevens" alternate with "fives," if not strictly.)

Certain pitches in *Abraham and Isaac* are given a degree of stress that could not justify the conjecture of mere coincidence, and the fact that some of these pitches occur several times in doublings at the octave lends weight, clearly, to the assumption of an intended stress. Near the opening of the piece, for example, there are octave duplications on F: in m. 12, understandably, owing to the conjunction of P^b:6, R^a:1 and IR^a:1; in m. 22, by juxtaposing I$^5_3$:6 and P^b:6; as well as later, in mm. 41, 205, 214, and 218—although these are less striking than the very much *heard* imitations at the octave in mm. 198-199 (see below, n. 20, under 5)—as well as in the canon at m. 73. There are other pitches whose octave duplications are less consistent, or less conducive to the supposition of a design for their reiteration. That

---

[20] 1) mm. 56-68: instrumental canon *a 2* by inversion; 2) mm. 73-79: rhythmic canon *a 2* between the baritone and bassoon – solo violin combined, beginning by inversion; 3) mm. 129-135: canon *a 2* by augmentation between baritone and trumpet over a rhythmically independent tuba line, whose pitches are nevertheless pertinent to the canonic design; 4) mm. 163-166: canon *duplex a 3,* by diminution and inversion between tuba and flute, and only rhythmic between baritone and flute (see p. 111 above); 5) mm. 197-203; canon *a 2* between baritone and tuba, at the octave, and with the horn in rhythmic canon, beginning also at the octave.

[21] Cf. *A Sermon, A Narrative and A Prayer,* mm. 106-112: a less extensive, equally fascinating species of mensuration canon.

octave duplications should take place fairly frequently in this music is not, however, simply a foregone conclusion.

Among the other means employed for stressing definite pitches, there is one which successions of hexachords may reveal unmistakably enough, but which may nonetheless remain in some doubt for the ear. Exx. 10 and 13 have demonstrated the linking of hexachords through transposition-rotation. The same operation can be effected with two "common tones," in alternation. The notes C♯ and D♯ act as "seams" of this kind in mm. 136-145 in the baritone part, in addition to the conspicuous C♯ in the second bassoon (m. 142), followed directly by D♯ in the first. Both aforementioned pitches are, however, given a much more obvious emphasis during the concluding 14 measures—in effect, a coda. The baritone enters on C♯ and four of his six hexachords begin on that note—one of the remaining two begins on D♯—besides which three of his four C♯'s are in a fixed pitch-location (middle C♯), representing the highest sung notes of this segment. Furthermore, the notes C♯ and D♯ are the first to be heard at the beginning of the segment, and the location of *this* C♯ (viola) remains, until the end, the highest pitch. Each middle C♯ in the baritone is answered by the viola with a C♯ either above or below it, at a distance never greater than four 8ths. The final D♯-C♯ in the bass clarinet is repeated and the composition ends with this instrumental dyad, plus the baritone's A.

If a cadence by any other name would sound as sweet, that antiquated appellation may still be attached to four specific places in the score: m. 81 (with a fifth: F-C),[22] m. 145 (octave B), m. 194 (chordal), and mm. 205-206 (four-fold, octave-triplicated C♯'s). The latter's emphasis serves as a bridge to the repeated underlining of vocal C♯'s from this point on.[23] (It also reminds the ear of the G♯'s in mm. 475-479 of *The Flood*.)

The concluding factor of stress (and indeed, of over-all unity, perhaps) to be mentioned here is an intervallic one. The interval (or simultaneity) of the perfect fifth sounds so frequently in *Abraham and Isaac* that a list of the measures in which it occurs would make tedious reading. It would also be quite pointless to include such a catalogue, since fifths abound, in like fashion, in comparatively as many measures of any of Stravinsky's works written since 1954. This does not mean, of course, that fifths perform a sufficiently exclusive, tangible "function" (or that they arise from any remarkably peculiar set properties) so as to encourage interpretations of tonal emphasis or promote inferences of traditional harmonic practice (albeit through twelve-tone glasses, darkly). It is much more likely that the reason for an abundance of fifths in *Abraham and Isaac* is, directly, a predominant thin texture, in which this interval takes on, after all, a very precise musical meaning—a very accurately measurable amount of musical distance—for the ear. If the fifth has, in the practice of many centuries, implied stability more strongly than any other interval, then that fact is mentally recorded, if not necessarily verbalized, and Stravinsky's use of fifths in his serial works may best be explained in that straightforward context.

[22] Cf. other stresses on F mentioned above, p. 124.

[23] E.g., in mm. 207-208, 214, 223 (with octave duplication), 239 (cadence: see Ex. 3), 240ff., as described above. (See also Ex. 15 for doubled C♯'s, B's and reiterated A's; cf., in a broader context, the first *tableau* of *Les Noces* and the *Sacred History*, for stress on E.)

The features of *Abraham and Isaac* that have been discussed thus far (as well as those that have not)[24] reveal, essentially, an uninterrupted pursuance of those compositional practices exhibited by the vocal works written since *Movements.* There is, at the same time, a greater sharpening, a greater concentration in *Abraham and Isaac;* there is more consistent hexachordal variety and independence, and there is a further intensification in providing for a kinship between words and music. If this is the brilliant latest link in a chain of religious works going back further than half a century, then one's musical appetite is surely whetted at the thought that the *Variations* may be the heir to *Movements.* Lastly, it is a continuing absorbing fact that Stravinsky's changing twelve-tone technique is based—as was, of course, Schoenberg's—upon the accumulated practice derived from a long career rather than on any rigidity of theoretical postulation. This may go beyond most other considerations in explaining Stravinsky's "inclusive," if by no means thereby less rigorous, twelve-tone discipline.

ADDENDA

At the time of writing this article, my remarks explaining hexachordal transposition-rotation were somewhat tentative and certainly incomplete. The nomenclature proposed in Ex. 10 to identify the five transposition-rotations in P^x seems to me now as needlessly cumbersome as combing one's hair with one's feet. But I had not then inferred that Stravinsky's charts might extend this graphic transposition-rotation scheme to include all hexachords in the four basic set-forms (i.e., P^a, P^b; R^a, R^b; I^a, I^b; IR^a, IR^b collections), nor that the shared pitch-classes with which each of the hexachordal collections begin might have found their compositional application in certain octave-doublings, e.g., the C♯'s in mm. 205–206; the F's in m. 182, and that such exclusively vertical readings among these hexachord-collections might by the same token have yielded clues to the correct naming of several otherwise serially unclassifiable successions of six, five, or four-factor simultaneities in *Abraham and Isaac.* It was not until I saw Stravinsky's charts for the Variations, at the time of their first performance, that I realized that this manner of organizing his serial apparatus had become habitual.

The whole matter of verticals—for whose concise description, see Milton Babbitt's *Remarks on the Recent Stravinsky,* pp. 183–184—having been omitted, it will now be enough to summarize their usage in *Abraham and Isaac* as follows: only those in P^b, IR^a, IR^b, and R^b occur; of the eight separate instances of vertical-successions, only two include the single pitch-class vertical (see above), and several successions entail omission or displacement of other vertical-factors; mm. 220-222 provide the only instance of verticals articulated in collaboration with the baritone's part, and of non-simultaneous iteration in one vertical array.

In a few instances, the examples differ slightly from the corresponding measures of the subsequently published score. Measure 219 has been relieved of its momentary *meno mosso* (see Ex. 13), and time signatures have been rewritten so as to accom-

---

[24] E.g., the characteristically spaced, beautifully balanced chords in mm. 229-239 (see, in part, in Ex. 3); or the avoidance of any excessive audible "patterning" of the kind to be found in Stravinsky's music prior to the last ten years.

ADDENDA

modate conducting requirements: m. 16 must be beaten as $\frac{4}{16}$ (see Ex. 14); mm. 113 and 115 are in eighths, rather than quarters (see Ex. 15).

Moreover, the following additional, specific corrections must be noted:

Ex. 1: m. 169:   baritone: the C♯ is accented

       m. 172:   the text reads: YAD-KHA EL HA-NA'-AR

Ex. 2: mm. 29f.:   the text reads: ET BIN-KHA ET Y(e)-KHID-KHA, ET Y(e)-KHID-KHA

Ex. 4a: tempo: eighth-note = 72

       m. 183:   slurs and *dim.* indications are deleted (i.e., flutes, alto flute and bass trombone tongue the dotted eighth, *sub. p*)

Ex. 4b: m. 195:   the same deletions as in m. 183

Ex. 5: m. 220:   woodwinds: the *f* sixteenth includes a *tenuto* sign

       m. 221:   baritone: for the first sixteenth, read two thirty-second D's, the second unaccented; the text reads: A-VA-REKKE-KHA; the grace-note should read E, not D

                    violoncello: the first quintolet-sixteenth should read F♯, not F

       m. 222:   the text reads: -BEH' ET ZAR'-A-KHA

Ex. 6: m. 87:   strings: *mf*; the slurred-to sixteenth includes a *staccato* dot in all parts

                    the text reads: V(e)-NISH-TĄ-KHA-VEH

Ex. 11: m. 1:   dynamic: *mf marc.*

Ex. 12: m. 52:   baritone: the first two sixteenths are unslurred; the last two are slurred, with the accent on the G, not the F♯, accommodating the final syllable of the word VA-YASH-KEYM

Ex. 13: m. 212:   baritone: the second eighth should read C, not B; the two sixteenths are slurred

       mm. 216f.:   the text reads: HA-DA-VAR HA-ZEH V(e) LO KHA-SAKH-TA ET BIN-KHA ET YE-KHI-DE-KHA.

       m. 219:   the time signature is $\frac{9}{16}$ ($\frac{3}{8} + \frac{3}{16}$); delete eighth-note = sixteenth-note

                    baritone: the first three notes are eighths, not sixteenths

                    tuba: the first D♯ is an eighth, not a sixteenth; it should have a line with a dot ($\div$) over it; the two rests preceding it are eighths, not sixteenths

Ex. 15: m. 115:   bassoon: the grace-note D♯ is slurred to the D; the grace-note C♯ to the C

       m. 116:   baritone: there is a slur from the grace-note C♯

       mm. 122f.:   the text reads: HI-NE-NI B(e)NI VA-YO-MER

NOTES ON
STRAVINSKY'S VARIATIONS

CLAUDIO SPIES

HIS FIRST PURELY, and exclusively, orchestral composition since *Agon* (1957), Stravinsky's new Variations were written between July 1963 and October 1964 and were first performed on April 17, 1965 by the Chicago Symphony Orchestra conducted by Robert Craft. The score calls for woodwinds by twos (plus alto flute, English horn, bass clarinet); 4 horns, 3 trumpets, 3 trombones; no percussion; piano, harp; strings in four (i.e., *not* five) groups of equal weight: 12 violins, 10 violas, 8 cellos, 6 contrabasses. The Variations take a little more than five minutes to play, but one would hesitate to explain away this duration merely by calling the piece "short." It is, in fact, the chronometrical dimension of this music that is astounding in the first place, for this is no "small" composition either in regard to its content or with respect to the premises which it sets out to fulfil during its brief unfolding. The score gives evidence on its 25 pages of Stravinsky's conscious awareness of a new scale of timing, a new apportionment of time among various elements of the total design, as well as a new balancing and pacing in the constituent parts of interior, smaller structures. This is not to say that a concern with concentrated aspects of timing in the Variations is a reflection of the similar aims revealed in *Abraham and Isaac* and *The Flood:* in those works a narrative text and dramatic action or stress were primary factors in the musical design, and timing was contingent upon them; in the Variations all timing devolves upon musical factors alone, while all concomitant structural concerns are, obviously, only instrumental/orchestral. (In this connection, it may be reasonable, by now, to place a dividing line signifying "old" and "new" timing in Stravinsky's music of the past decade between *Threni* and *Movements*—or between, on the one hand, *Threni* and *A Sermon, A Narrative and A Prayer* and, on the other, *Agon* and *Movements.*)

Of Variations there are twelve, separated from one another, in most instances, by a measured pause, a fermata or a change of tempo (nearly always defined by a common unit). There is, however, no "Theme" on whose melodic, rhythmic or phraseological characteristics these variations are constructed. Neither can any specific compositional practices of the kind conventionally subsumed under the heading "Variation technique" be found here, nor any trace of the grand "Finale" with which many sets of variations were once endowed. Instead, a sectional design is postulated on varieties of change and contrast, rather than on actual transformation—diversity in phrase-structure, for example—on subtle or abrupt textural shifts, on rhythmic "variables," tempo-relations, as well as on a beautifully calibrated system of refrains and a perfect recapitulation. The following table will indicate the Variations' general formal outline:

I ♩ = 80	mm.	1-6:	*f* chords; *p* chords:	fls.; brass; hp., pno; strings
		6-22:	monodic presentation:	↓ ↓ ↓ ↓
II ♩ = ♪(= 80)		23-33:	12-part polyphony:	12 solo violins
III ♪ = ♪		33-39:	phrase (in one unit):	fls., bns., ob.
IV ♪ = ♪		40-46:	phrase (segmented):	↓ ↓ , then fls.
V ♪ = 80		47-58:	12-part polyphony:	10 solo vlas., 2 solo cb:
VI ♪ = ♩ (= 80)		59-72:	2 contrasting phrases:	fls., b-cl., bns. bn.; trps., trmb., str.
VII ♪ = ♪		73-85:	phrase (ant. + cons.):	obs.; hns.; hp., pno.; str. & trmbs.
VIII stesso ♪ (6/16; 9/16; ♩. = beat)		86-94:	phrase (ant. + cons.):	E.H., cl., b-cl., bn.; hn.; str.
IX stesso ♪		95-100:	phrase (ant. + cons.):	trmbs.; fls.-bns.; hns., trmbs.; low str.
X stesso ♩		101-117:	rhythmic *fugato:*	str.; bn.; pno.
XI ♩ = ♪ (= 80)		118-129:	12-part polyphony:	all woodwinds; hn.
XII ♪ = ♩ (= 80)		130-134:	*f* chords; *p* chords "varied"	fls., cls.; hn.; pno.; str.
		134-141:	*f* chords; *p* chords recapitulated	↓ ↓ ↓ hp. ↓

Sections II, V, and XI constitute the structural refrain mentioned above, and the music in these polyphonic measures provides the single most arresting feature of the Variations. This counterpoint *a 12,* presented at first in a completely homogeneous medium, is never imitative, nor are the 12 lines related to one another rhythmically. Each line achieves its individual internal rhythmic coherence, each part is melodically self-sufficient and each has its own particular articulation. There is hardly any rhythmic or articulative coincidence in these measures between any given two parts, yet the sound is clear because the steady, continuous iteration of eighth-notes (see VI. 12 in mm. 23-33) gives this music its pulsating rhythmic context. And the contrapuntal feat is the more extraordinary inasmuch as Sections V and XI are "returns" of this music *only* with respect to its rhythmic constitution. Not only is the instrumental context changed, the pitch range expanded (mainly downward), but the melodic lines are, in all 12 parts, dissimilar —if also, in some instances, inversionally related (as will be shown below)—in each of the three appearances of this polyphony. (A metric scheme, however, is common to all three: $\frac{4}{8}\frac{3}{8}\frac{5}{8} + \frac{4}{8}\frac{3}{8}\frac{5}{8} + \frac{4}{8}\frac{3}{8}\frac{5}{8} + \frac{4}{8}\frac{3}{8}$, plus $\frac{5}{8}$ rest in Section V, and $\frac{3}{8}$ rest in Section XI.) Similarly, the recapitulation of the opening 6 measures at the very end of the composition is perceptible as such on rhythmic grounds principally. No melodic-harmonic return here, nor even a restatement in terms of orchestral color; what supplies the foundation for this broad arch is a conjunction of rhythm, articulation and dynamics.

Stravinsky's unwillingness to allow for *any* extensive melodic restatement in the Variations bespeaks, of course, a particular recent solution to the generic problem of any kind of "recapitulation" or even "counterstatement." If, then, melodic phrases or statements are never repeated outright, the resultant "tightness" of construction is, perhaps, the most direct reason for the work's brevity and concentration. Yet, aside from the preceding truism, the terseness of the Variations' rhetoric is simply an expression of what Stravinsky himself has called "our new poetry"—a reaction against orotund utterance, in the most immediate sense, but also—far more interestingly—the direct outcome of his having forged, after the age of 75, his new musical syntax by means of serial procedures.

Wherever melodic fragments *are* reiterated, they function as phrase-openers (Exs. 1 and 3) or as punctuation within a phrase (Ex. 2).[1] Section VI begins as follows:

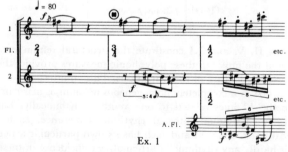

Ex. 1

[1] See also *Movements,* V, mm. 155-56.

The phrase "temporizes" later on, on an A♯ pedal (and will lead into a contrasting phrase):

Ex. 2

The *fugato* in Section X states a subject three times; its rhythmic structure is examined below:

Ex. 3

Such repeated fragments undeniably call attention to themselves and thereby justify their crucial locations. At the same time they may bring to mind certain of their relatives in other works—the third measure of the subject in Ex. 3, for instance, recalls mm. 498-99 in *Agon,* and there has, in fact, been no other *fugato* in Stravinsky's music since the one in that ballet (mm. 539-52).

Stravinsky's first idea for the Variations came in the form of a little melody.

CLAUDIO SPIES

Ex. 4

It is the first notation in the composer's sketch-book for the Variations. It is also a statement of the Prime, and, bereft of its rhythm, it becomes the basis for the composer's serial charts. Now, this little melody—a charming, spontaneous invention with a bit of "Russia" in its rhythm and, particularly, in its first five pitches—is never stated as such in the composition itself. Only its constituent intervals and pitch successions provided the impetus for further exploration. Stravinsky's charts (given here only for the two hexachords of P) read:

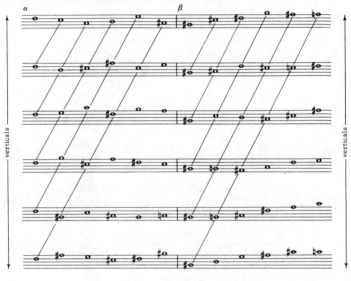

Ex. 5

It can be seen that hexachordal transposition-rotation occurs here in the same way as was shown in the charts elucidating this procedure for *Abraham and Isaac* (see pp. 198–201, examples 7–10), but the Variations include rotation among all 12 members of a set (without taking the hexachordal bar into account) rather more prominently. Thus, for instance, the monodic presentation in Section I states five different twelve-tone collections in a succession of transpositions governed by transposition-rotation in the first hexachord of P, before the untransposed P is actually revealed. (In all six collections the pitch D therefore assumes the function of either linking, beginning or ending a twelve-tone collection.)

mm.			
6-7:	P^4		(7-⌐ 6)
			⌐ D
7-9:	P^{10}		⌊ (5-4)
			D
10-12:	P^3		(4-3)
			D
13-14:		R^5	(11-10)
			D
15-17: {		R^2	(12-11)
18-19: {	P^2		(3-⌐ 2)
			⌐ D
20-22:	P		⌊(1-12)

A more complex mechanism of rotation by 12, operating again—but not always—with "common tone" links between set transpositions, determines the melodic content of the three instances of 12-part polyphony. Pitches F and D (= P: 12 and 1) are consistently prominent in all three appearances of this design, and most of the sets in the first two appearances are related by inversion.

		F		F		F		F	Rhythm
VI.	1:	R^{11} (2-1)		R^{10} (3-2)		P^2 (10-9)		P^9 (8-7)	1
	2:	⌐—D—⌐			D				
		RI^{10} (12-11)		I^9 (4-3)		RI^8 (8-7)			2
	3:	⌐—D—⌐			D				
		RI (1-12)		I^7 (3-2)		RI^2 (9-8)			3
	4:	D			⌐—D—⌐				
		I^{10} (2-1)		RI^9 (10-9)		I^8 (6-5)			4
	5:		⌐—F—⌐			F			
		I^6 (1-12)		RI^4 (4-3) → C♯ ← I^4 (10-9)					5
	6:	F			⌐—F—⌐				
		RI^8 (3-2) → F♯ ← I^8 (11-10)		RI^9 (6-5)					6
	7:	F			⌐—F—⌐				
		RI^6 (1-12) → G♯ ← I^6 (1-12)		RI^7 (2-1)					7
	8:		⌐—F—⌐			⌐—F—⌐			
		I^9 (8-7)		RI^2 (5-4) → D♯ ← I^2 (9-8)		I^7 (11-10)			8

9: R^9 (6-5) [F above] P^4 (9-8) $\rightarrow$ F $\leftarrow R^4$ (5-4) — 9

10: P (1-12) [D above] $\rightarrow$ F $\leftarrow$ I^9 (1-12) P^{11} (12-11) [F above] — 10

11: R^2 (4-3) [F above] $\dot{P}^{10}$ (11-10) [F above] — 11

12: I (1-12) [D above] ⌐—B—⌐ RI^7 (11-10) ⌐—D—⌐ I^2 (5-4) — 12

(mm. 23-33)

				Rhythm

Vla. 1: P^2 (2-1) [D above] R^3 (10-9) ⌐—D—⌐ P^4 (6-5) — 4

2: R^2 (12-11) ⌐—D—⌐ P^3 (4-3) R^6 (12-11) [D above] — 2

3: R (1-12) [F above] ⌐—D—⌐ P^5 (3-2) [F] R^{10} (9-8) — 3

4: P (1-12) [D above] ⌐—F—⌐ R^5 (11-10) ⌐—D—⌐ P^{10} (5-4) — 12

5: P (1-12) [D above] ⌐—F—⌐ R^2 (4-3) $\rightarrow$ A $\leftarrow P^2$ (10-9) — 5

6: R^{10} (3-2) [F above] $\rightarrow$ E $\leftarrow P^{10}$ (11-10) ⌐—F—⌐ R^9 (6-5) — 6

7: R^9 (6-5) [F above] $\rightarrow$ A# $\leftarrow P^9$ (8-7) $\rightarrow$ F $\leftarrow R^9$ (6-5) — 7

8: P^4 (9-8) $\rightarrow$ F $\leftarrow R^4$ (4-3) R^2 (5-4) [F above] P^{11} (12-11) [F above] — 8

9: RI^4 (4-3) [F above] I^2 (9-8) $\rightarrow$ F $\leftarrow RI^2$ (5-4) — 9

10: I^6 (1-12) $\rightarrow$ F $\leftarrow RI^6$ (1-12) I^7 (12-11) [F above] — 10

Cb. 1: RI^7 (2-1) [F above] RI^8 (3-2) [F above] I^4 (10-9) [F above] I^9 (8-7) [F above] — 1

2: RI^4 (4-3) [F above] I^8 (11-10) [F above] — 11

(mm. 47-57)

									Rhythm
Fl.	1:	I^6 (1-12) :‖	⌐—F—⌐ RI² (5-4)		RI⁶ (1-12) F				1
	2:	I^4 (10-9)	⌐—F—⌐ RI⁹ (6-5)						11
	alto:	I^6 (1-12)	⌐—F—⌐ RI² (5-4)		I^4 (10-9) F				10
Ob.	1:	F RI^6 (1-12)	I^7 (12-11) → F ← RI⁷ (2-1)						9
	2:	RI^8 (8-7)	⌐—D—⌐ I⁹ (4-3) → E ← RI⁹ (10-9) D			RI¹⁰ (12-11) D			8
E.H.	:	RI^2 (9-8)	⌐—D—⌐ I (1-12)		I^7 (3-2) D				5
Cl.	1:	RI (1-12)	⌐—D—⌐ I² (5-4) → G ← RI² (9-8) D						7
	2:	RI^9 (10-9)	⌐—D—⌐ I (1-12) → B ← RI (1-12)						6
B-cl.	:	D P (1-12)	⌐—F—⌐ R⁹ (6-5)		P⁴ (9-8) F				3
Hn.	1:	P^2 (10-9)	⌐—F—⌐ P¹⁰ (10-9)		R⁴ (5-4) F				4
Bn.	1:	F R^{11} (2-1) → E ← P¹¹ (12-11) F			P (1-12) F				2
	2:	P^9 (8-7)	⌐—F—⌐ R² (4-3)		P¹¹ (12-11) F				12

(mm. 118-128)

Stravinsky uses the "verticals" shown in Ex. 5 as generators of chords. In fact, the "verticals" explain the prevalence of some octave-doublings in chord-formations, as well as the predominance of six-factor chords[2] and the otherwise puzzling, tantalizing manifestation of "major-minor" triads (in P^α).

All six vertical arrays of P^β in retrograde furnish the Variations with its ending, and provide the clue to the eloquent single G♯.

[2] Verticals, similarly derived, account for chord-formations—also of six factors—in *Abraham and Isaac:* mm. 69-72, for instance, and mm. 229-39.

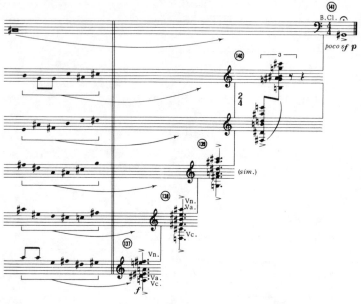

Ex. 6

The central portion of the piece is made up of a succession of six units, each of which has been described above with the general term *phrase*. To be sure, the substructure outlined by these six units is interrupted by the first return of the 12-part polyphony, but that only abets the composer's intention of sustaining an all-purposive asymmetrical bias: two refrains encircling the central eight Sections, the third of which is itself a refrain, while the last—the *fugato*—is the longest undivided unit in the entire composition. Now, granted that *phrase* is a barely apt or sufficient description for the extremely concise, delicate structures achieved in Sections III–IV, VI–IX, there is nevertheless such a subtle gauging of factors in the construction of each, as well as so gradual an over-all progression toward greater balance among antecedents and consequents, as to justify using this classical term. Individual phrases contain, independently, their specific structural components, with only infrequent functional cross references—the segment-opening bassoon at m. 44 and the bass clarinet at m. 62, for example—and with internal equilibria contingent upon varieties of rhythm, articulation, dynamics, segmentation, scoring, duration and other factors, but never upon direct melodic reflection nor *complete* symmetry of any sort. The first three units in this scheme act as precursors to the last three, whose increasingly balanced interaction of contrasting elements between and within antecedent and consequent clauses represents the final stage in this evolutionary précis. The most pertinent features in the first three units can be summarized in the following manner:

Section III: mirror-like rhythmic construction around an axis in m. 37 (Bn. G♯); contrast between triplet sixteenths and sixteenths, stressed additionally by their being exchanged between flutes and bassoons (mm. 35 & 39).

Section IV: three segments separated from one another by eighth-rests; tempo contrast (only in m. 40) in the first segment; approximately equal length of the first two segments; greater length in the last segment, but with a closer tie to the second (mm. 42-43 & 45-46).

(Since these Sections share rhythmic, dynamic, instrumental, and articulative traits, and are not juxtaposed in any too obvious way, they are played without interruption—the oboe entrance at m. 39 "anticipating," as did the flute in m. 33.)

Section VI: two antithetical phrases: the first (mm. 59-66) divided by m. 62 into contrasting, but related, segments of approximately equal length;

the second (mm. 67-71) more clearly made up of contrasting antecedents (mm. 66-67 & 70-71) and related, similar consequents (second eighth of m. 69 & m. 71).

For the last three units there can be a more schematic representation:

Section VII:

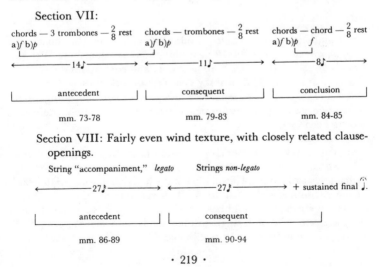

Section VIII: Fairly even wind texture, with closely related clause-openings.

Section IX:

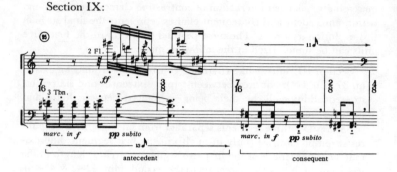

antecedent

consequent

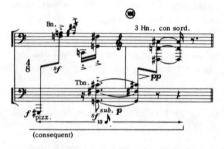

(consequent)

Ex. 7

The trombones' repeated notes in this place are, in the Variations, perhaps as unexpected as the 12-part polyphony is astonishing. The extreme contrast between such homophonic and contrapuntal writing is probably at the root of Stravinsky's choice, but these pulsating repeated chords are obviously also reminders of many accompaniment figures in his more distantly previous music—their most immediate predecessors having been used in *Agon*.

A word about the last Section—the only one from which a trace of more conventionally customary variation procedures can be inferred. The whole Section serves the purpose of recapitulating a rhythmic, articulative and dynamic distillation of the homophonic materials heard at the beginning of the Variations. This recapitulation occurs in two stages, of which the second bears the stronger likeness. The following diagram compares both stages to their model and shows, again, Stravinsky's asymmetrical, non-literal intent:

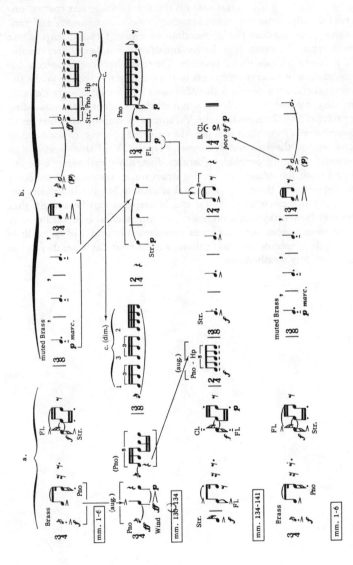

Ex. 8

In conclusion, Stravinsky may be said to have accomplished a double task in composing his Variations: on the one hand he has carried onward, logically, those elements of rhythmic-melodic continuity and consecution that signified the tremendous inventive forward leap of the *Movements;* at the same time, he has included a number of "remnants" of a previous compositional practice. There is, therefore, a perceptible consolidation of different elements into a constructive whole. While the structural contrasts between the *Movements* and Variations are defined, naturally, by their very titles, it is nonetheless evident that in avoiding any kind of literal repetition, the Variations go considerably further in explorations of form than did, say, the repeated opening 22 measures of *Movements,* or the strophic symmetry of part IV of that work. Most probably, the only particular features discernible as having been inherited from the *Movements* are the structural-phraseological concerns first displayed in those compositional afterthoughts, the interludes between the five parts. And as for the future, one can be certain that whatever Stravinsky's next orchestral or instrumental composition may be, its inheritances, reminiscences and consolidations will be as little susceptible of specific prognostication as is the next day's weather to the toiling, nightly weatherman.

SOME NOTES ON STRAVINSKY'S
REQUIEM SETTINGS

CLAUDIO SPIES

STRAVINSKY's most recent religious works, *Introitus T. S. Eliot in memoriam* and *Requiem Canticles,*[1] are settings of various passages from the Latin texts comprised in the Roman Catholic Mass for the Dead and the Burial Service. In the *Introitus,* the entire opening section of the Requiem Mass is set—with apposite use of the third person singular, as required by the dedication. The texts for the *Requiem Canticles* were selected from the Introit and Sequence of the Mass, and conclude with the entire Responsory *Libera me* from the Burial Service. Both works, completed respectively on 17 February 1965 and 13 August 1966, are chronologically adjacent—except for the 17-measure orchestral *Canon on a Russian Popular Tune* (at T[1])—but not as intimately related to one another as might at first be assumed. For while they share a primordial concern with strophic designs, the use of refrains, and schemes of alternation between contrasting elements (defined by textural, timbral and registral traits), as well as characteristics obviously attributable to their texts, they can be proved not to stem from a common compositional (or even precompositional) impulse.

The *Introitus* unfolds in three strophes alternating sentences sung as a single choral line and sentences spoken together rhythmically by both choral sections, with the final strophe repeating the opening sentence of the first in two-part counterpoint and omitting choral speech. This structure is consistently accompanied by an amalgam of timpani coperti and their doubling-sustaining single viola and single contrabass; it is also embedded in and interwoven with self-sufficient instrumental music serving the purposes of introduction, cadence, interlude, conclusion, and punctuation by means of a refrain. To this end, the four participating instrumental duos achieve the combinations indicated in the diagram on page 99. The asymmetrical aspect of this overall design is proposed most clearly by the sung choral rhythms shown in Ex. 1. For the sake of reference, this design can be abbreviated *a + a + b,* provided that its funda-

---

[1] The *Requiem Canticles,* dedicated "to the Memory of Helen Buchanan Seeger," received their first performance on October 8, 1966, at Princeton University.

1.	piano-harp + tam-tams			mm.* 1-2 (introduction) * 9-10 (mid-point punctuatio * 32-33 between sung phrases * 46-47 of each choral strophe
2.			timpani + viola-contrabass	3-7, 11-15; (strophe 1) 26-30, 34-39; (strophe 2) 42-45, * 48-49. (strophe 3)
3.		tam-tams		7-8 (punctuation connectin 30-31 sung phrases and the 45 refrain listed in 1.)
4.	piano-harp + tam-tams		+ viola-contrabass	* 16-17 (accompaniment to 40-41 choral speaking)
5.	piano-harp		+ viola-contrabass	* 18 (cadence)
6.			viola-contrabass	19-25 (interlude)
7.	harp	+ timpani + viola-contrabass		* 50-53 (coda)

mentally strophic nature be kept in proper perspective, whereby *b* represents an element of only limited contrast. Asymmetry is further abetted both by unrecapitulated instrumental events, such as the interlude (mm. 19-25) and its immediately preceding cadence, and by the singular, eloquently ascending coda. At the same time, strophic recapitulations abound; they are, in fact, preponderant. The one rhythmic element that occurs in both chorus and instruments is the quarter-note triplet (first in the tenors, m. 8), whose reappearance in the second phrase of each strophe, and in an unchanging instrumental context, lends it formal weight (mm. 13, 38, 49).

In the program notes for the *Introitus* it is stated: "No novelty will be found in the manipulation of the series except, perhaps, in chord structure where, however, it is less a question of seriation than of choice...."[2] If this ambiguous explanation were to be somewhat expanded, it could be shown to mean, in the first place, that the chordal structures alluded to are at least partly derived by juxtaposing and combining related two-note or three-note fragments at independent transposition levels; that such fragments can represent selected adjacencies in the set; and that furthermore the choices in question are geared toward establishing per-

[2] Igor Stravinsky and Robert Craft, *Themes and Episodes*, New York, Alfred A. Knopf, 1966, pp. 62-63.

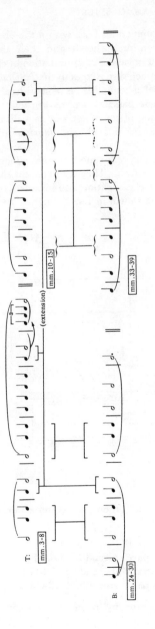

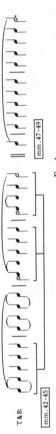

Ex. 1

ceptibly patterned melodic connections both within the chord successions themselves, and between such chords and their immediately
preceding or subsequent choral phrases. An examination of chord structures, as well as of other instrumental passages in the *Introitus* which are
not—or not *conventionally*—"twelve-countable" is of considerable interest,
if also rather tantalizing. (These passages are marked with an asterisk
on the above table of instrumental combinations, as well as on tables
further on, concerning set-usage in both the *Introitus* and *Requiem
Canticles*.)

The three opening piano-harp chords state a rhythm which will recur
with every appearance of this refrain. They also contain three of four
specific melodic features whose classification and instances of returning
throughout the composition are shown in Ex. 2.

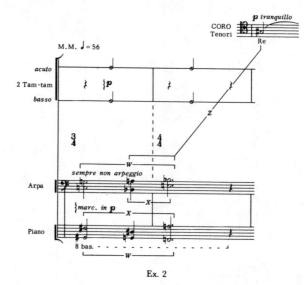

Ex. 2

Ascent or descent by stepwise motion encompassing a minor third, in
either top or lowest part:

$$(W)$$

mm. 1–2: top part: ascending: G-A-B♭
bass part: descending: G♯-G-F
46–47: bass part: ascending: A♯-C-C♯

Motion by consecutive minor thirds, by tritone, or by a combination of
minor third and tritone:

(X)

mm. 1–2: inner parts: Bb-E
                          F♯-D♯-A
     9–10: bass part: D♯-A-F♯ (piano)
    16–18: bass part: G-C♯-A♯ (piano-harp)
    32–33: bass part: A♯-E-A♯ (piano) [see (Y)]
       49: inner part: E-A♯-G-C♯ (viola)
    51–53: top part: E-(F♯)-G-A♯-E (viola)
            inner part: Gb-A-Eb (harp)

Ascent and return (as if to and from an upper neighboring-tone), in the top part:

(Y)

mm. 9–10: C♯-D-C♯
    32–33: F♯-Bb-F♯ (harp → piano)
    46–47: B-C♯-B

Ascent and descent (or vice versa) by whole-tone and half-tone (or vice versa), in the top part:

(Z)

mm. 1–3: A-Bb (harp) → G♯ (tenors)
    8–9: D♯ (tenors) → C♯-D (harp)
   16–18: C♯-B♯-D (piano-harp)
   46–47: C♯-B (harp) → C (tenors)

Stravinsky made a revision of the refrain-chords in mm. 32–33 between the printing of the *Introitus'* proofs and the publication of the score. A comparison between the discarded and revised versions reveals the significance of the rewritten top and lowest parts at this juncture. (See Ex. 3.)

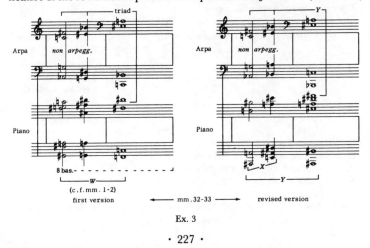

first version ←— mm.32-33 —→ revised version

Ex. 3

These chords contain more factors than any others in the piece, except the unrelated (i.e., non-refrain) chords in mm. 40–41. They may be conjectured, therefore, to occupy a slightly biased central position, and their placement at mid-point in the printed score is a felicitous metaphor. It is understandable that Stravinsky would prefer not to recapitulate the opening bass-line here, but to stress X (with the same pitch-classes as in the harp in mm. 1–2) by imbuing it with the characteristic of Y. At the same time, it is clear that the discarded triadic outline in the top part would have conveyed much less structural meaning than the simultaneous use of two forms of Y in the extreme parts, or the containment of all three chords within crucially placed high and low B♭'s.

Pitch-connections among contiguous phrases or segments of this music—other than those already accounted for—are made in the simplest way through registrally defined "common tones" (e.g., the tenors' C♯, m. 15 to the top C♯ in the next measure), or half-step motion (e.g., mm. 18–19), while octave-transfer (mm. 39–40) is reduced to a self-evident minimum by the composition's restricted range. Within this range, moreover, certain pitches and pitch-relations acquire hierarchical status and infuse the *Introitus* with harmonic priorities. B-flat is in the center, and with its upper and lower fifths immediately next, the related sphere F♯-*C♯*-G♯, as well as a few other symmetrically disposed areas, could perhaps too easily encourage the inference of a not altogether novel scheme! Nevertheless, these fifth-related axes are in evidence throughout, and they manifest their purpose in the following ways:

Cadences on B♭ at phrase-endings:	mm. 18
	30
Cadences on B♭ in the refrain-chords:	33
Phrases contained within B♭'s in outer parts:	50–53: the coda's lowest B♭ (m. 50) is reflected by the viola (m. 52) before proceeding to the closing chord;
	32–33 (cited above)
E♭ is the lowest pitch in the piece:	9
E♭ is the initial octave of the 3rd strophe:	42
E♭ is the initial highest pitch in the coda:	50
E♭ is the final lowest pitch in the coda:	53
F is the lowest pitch at the end of the introd.:	2 (while B♭ is the highest)

(cont. on p. 104)

Cadence "in" C♯:	38–39 (though the basses' melodic cadence is "in" B♭)
Strong G♯-D♯ fifth at the end of the first phrase:	7–8
Strong F♯-C♯ fifth:	10

But the prominence of fifths and fourths in the *Introitus* is more readily referable to the set itself, and to its particular, carefully circumscribed employment. As in most of Stravinsky's twelve-tone pieces of smaller dimension,[3] the complete set is stated only in its untransposed forms, and although the first hexachord of P yields its complement at I[7], no compositional use is made of this property. (See Ex. 4.) The melodic features previously discussed can, as it happens, be traced to the set. (See Ex. 5.)

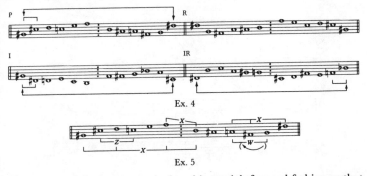

Ex. 4

Ex. 5

All choral set-statements are deployed in straightforward fashion so that both of the more symmetrically related strophes take up all four forms, and the final strophe, with its prevalence of repeated pitches, uses only one set-form per part. There is no transference whatever of set-factors between the two choral parts, just as there is none between any choral part and any complete sets stated in the instrumental ensemble throughout. There is elegance in Stravinsky's avoidance of having mid-points in the choral strophes coincide too obviously with set-endings (see mm. 7–10 and 30–34). In the instruments, complete sets unfold as successive dyads (viola-contrabass) with occasional "hold-overs" in the timpani. (Only one set-factor in the whole composition is assigned to the timpani without being sustained by a string instrument: the B in m. 5.) The exception to this dyadic deployment occurs in mm. 40–41, where the two chords divide P into its hexachords. A summary of set-usage follows:

[3] *Epitaphium, Anthem: The Dove Descending, Elegy for J.F.K., Fanfare for a New Theater, The Owl and the Pussycat.*

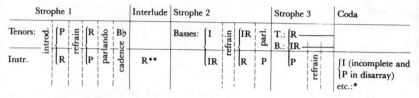

	Strophe 1	Interlude	Strophe 2		Strophe 3	Coda
Tenors:	introd. [P refrain [R parlando Bb cadence		Basses: [I refrain [IR parl.		T.: [R ——— B.: [IR ———	
Instr.	[R refrain [P	R**	[IR	[R P	[P refrain	{I (incomplete and {P in disarray) etc.:*

** R:5 = A♯; the viola's G♯ in m. 21 is a misprint.

By superimposing set-forms in this way, Stravinsky skirted the hazard of excessive duplication among parallel or adjacent set-factors. This explains his not having, for example, combined P and I anywhere within the three strophes. At the same time, in giving R and IR to the chorus, he makes direct reference to three duplications by writing them as octaves (see mm. 42, 43, and 45).

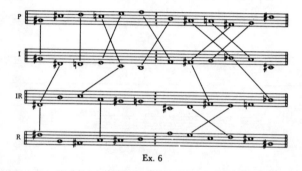

Ex. 6

If it were assumed for a moment that the *Introitus* was to have been merely the first part of a larger composition, then it should be reasonable to expect that an array of set-transpositions would have been required to expand upon available (and already exploited) possibilities of set-combinations and juxtapositions. (Even in the event that such precompositional explorations might have yielded desired results, it would still be feasible for the *Introitus* to have been planned on only the four basic set-forms, though, undoubtedly, as a movement of a larger work, it would thereby have become unique among Stravinsky's twelve-tone works.) Taking a cue from the charts used in Stravinsky's recent compositions, it would then be natural for such additional resources to be based on hexachordal transposition-rotation, as shown in Ex. 7. It will be recognized that each of the enclosed trichordal adjacencies outlining minor, major, or augmented triads would connote great serial inconvenience and harmonic monotony (or, at best, ambivalence) in a work of any length. If the hexachords guilty of such triadic content are

Ex. 7

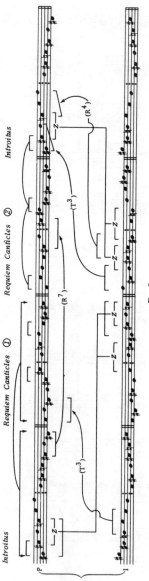

Ex. 8

therefore removed from among the material made available in the chart, the remainder—only one hexachord per original hexachord—represents too meager an increase over previously used material to justify any imputation of the chart's usefulness and, by extension, any assumption of a precompositionally projected larger work. The *Introitus* is therefore unquestionably an independent conception, even if at the time of its composition Stravinsky was already contemplating a larger Requiem setting.

A comparison of P and I forms between the sets of the *Introitus* and *Requiem Canticles* reveals a good many similarities. (See Ex. 8.) For what it may be worth, the comparison between the Primes of the *Introitus, Elegy for J. F. K.,* and *Requiem Canticles* (*1*) shows even more pronounced similarities: the first two share five hexachord factors, and sequential features in the *Elegy's* set become even more sharply profiled in *Requiem Canticles* (*1*), since they are symmetrically divided by the hexachordal bar. (See Ex. 9.)

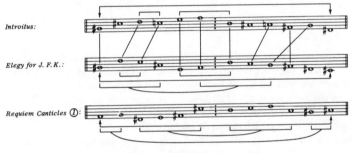

Ex. 9

The more germane comparisons, however, are to be made between sets of the *Requiem Canticles,* for the presence of two distinct sets is surely the most surprising technical feature of this work. In both, P and I forms manifest common traits, either among P sets or among P-I "crossovers," and are shown below (Ex. 10)—without inversional reflections —together with two such instances of extensive pitch-duplications resulting from transposition in one set.

Now, in order to reason out the genesis of the *Requiem Canticles'* set-usage, it is tempting to suppose that set (*2*) was formulated first. (The following tables were copied from Stravinsky's charts.[4] The set-denomi-

---

[4] The similar table for the *Introitus* (Ex. 7) was decidedly *not* copied and may in fact have had no prior existence even in a composers' scratch-pad. The evidence it provided is adduced in relation to the obviously similar limitations of *Requiem Canticles* (*2*).

Ex. 10

nations used here are slightly different from the composer's nomenclature, and his charts do not include numbering of rotations. But Stravinsky numbered the two *Requiem Canticles* sets as shown in Ex. 11.) The deficiencies of set (*2*), though not as serious as those displayed in the *Introitus'* table, nevertheless effectively curtail transposition-rotations in P^a, R^b, I^a, and IR^b to one in each, besides enabling discretely rotated hexachords of identical set-forms to constitute transposed twelve-tone sets in only two instances: $R_4{}^a–R_1{}^b$ and its inversion. On the other hand, set (*1*) is free of cumbrously triadic formations; permits three twelve-tone associations between discretely rotated hexachords in P, and two in R: $P_2{}^a–P_3{}^b$; $P_3{}^a–P_5{}^b$; $P_4{}^a–P_1{}^b$ and $R_3{}^a–R_5{}^b$; $R_4{}^a–R_3{}^b$;—plus their concomitant inversions;[5] provides Stravinsky with two useful sets of verticals; and implies in its interval-structure a distinctive harmony which will characterize large portions of the music. If, then, set (*1*) was devised as a *remedial* addition, that action must have antedated the composition of any of the choral movements in the *Requiem Canticles,* with the possible exception of the *Dies irae*. And since the central Interlude is the only movement among the nine in which complete set-forms of (*1*) and (*2*) are stated—albeit *concurrently* only in mm. 166–172—it would by necessity have been the first section of music to be written on

[5] I.e., hexachordally rotated contents of: P^1, P^2, P^{11} and R^8, R^{10}; I^{11}, I^{10}, I^1 and IR^4, IR^2.

Ex. 11

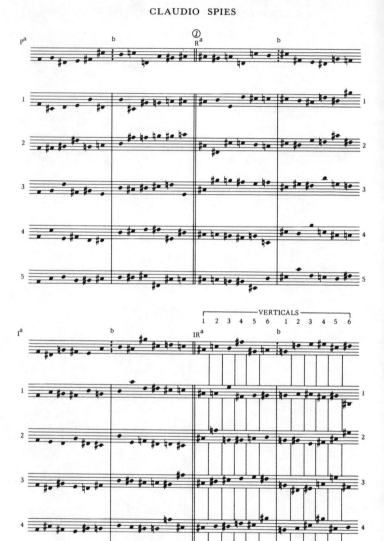

Ex. 11 (*cont.*)

the basis of any such precompositional conjunction, if only by virtue of irresistible curiosity. A *primary* initial assumption of two sets, however, is improbable in the extreme. More likely, Stravinsky composed a section, or more—perhaps the Prelude, which uses only (2)—before deciding to incorporate a separate "other" set among his roster of materials.

Requiem Canticles was planned and brought into being as an assemblage of nine movements whose brevity rested on the premise that the texts were to be segments of, or sentences from—rather than liturgically complete—prayers.[6] The formal design is symmetrically conceived: six vocal movements separated at mid-point by an instrumental Interlude and flanked by an instrumental Prelude and Postlude; an overall harmonic framework with F at either end and "F-derived" relations, as well as other immediate or longer-range pitch-connections, toward the middle; a tempo scheme whereby most movements are closely linked, either through identical or similar speed of beats; strophic construction or schemes of simple alternation among texturally–rhythmically defined elements throughout eight movements. (See table on p. 238.)

The table of instrumental and vocal distribution on page 239 will summarize textural elements in alternation, and set-usage, i.e., complete (*1*) or (*2*), either as discrete or complementary hexachords.

Symmetries in the larger sphere are also, naturally, reflected within movements. Each strophic design achieves a symmetrical effect, particularly when it also involves such exact melodic repetition—more than once—as to suggest an equivalence between "strophe" and "refrain" (see, for instance the Prelude). By the same token, schemes of alternation can connote the $a + a + b$ shape previously described. The *Exaudi* could be seen as an interlocking of two $a + a + b$'s: three choral phrases and, on the other hand, a "constant" repeated orchestral texture with a contrasting conclusion. And concluding phrases or codettas are, of course, the best suited occasions for the articulation of limited contrast. Sometimes Stravinsky devises a short passage within a strophe and makes of

[6] The one exceptionally complete—and more than complete—text is *Libera me*. Stravinsky must have consulted the Eulenburg Edition's pocket score of the Verdi *Requiem* for this, since it corresponds as little to the liturgical prescription as his own. He may also have been prompted by the first 10 and final 7 measures in Verdi's *Libera me* to convey the large amount of text by means of a rapidly murmuring, rhythmically unspecific choral mass, with simultaneously chanting solo voices. The concluding quarter-triplets + half-note fermata are, at any rate, as good as an acknowledged quotation. There is one other curious detail: both composers changed the order of the words "Dies illa, dies irae" to the more familiar version in the Sequence. However inadvertent Verdi's "mistake" might have been, it was justified by the large recapitulation occurring at that point. Stravinsky's overall design excludes any recapitulation of this sort; in fact, the words "Requiem aeternam" do not *return* here because they were not set at the very beginning of *Requiem Canticles*! As for the textual dislocation "Dies irae, dies illa," it was remedied before the first rehearsal.

PRELUDE	♪ = 250 (5 ♪'s = beat: 50)	F (Vlc., Cb.): first pitch stated; : lowest pitch in the final chord
		A♯–C (Vl. solo → Vla. sola): stressed through reiteration
EXAUDI	♪ = 104 (♩ = 52)	A♯ (Hp.): first pitch stated
		D♯ (Fl.): highest orchestral pitch; : highest choral pitch; (Bn. 2): lowest orchestral pitch at the beginning
		E♯ (A.) / A♯ (T.) : connection to
DIES IRAE	♪ = 136 (♩ = 68); (♩ ♫: ♩ = 34) i rae (mm. 83–84)	E♯ (S. T.) / A♯ (A.): first choral pitches (+ F♯ (B.)) (Cb., Vlc., Pno.) : first orchestral pitches; : last choral and orchestral pitches
		C / F (Fls., Xyl.): (m. 88)
		D♯ (Trb.): lowest pitch, middle section
(attacca)		(↑)
TUBA MIRUM	♪ = 136	C → F → A♯ → D♯ . . . C → C♯ → A♯ → (E♯) → G♯ (Baritone)
		G♯ / C♯ (Bar., Bn.): final fifth
INTERLUDE	♪ = 104 (♩. ♩: ♩. = 34⅔)	G / C (Fls., Hns., E♭ / F / B♭ Timp.): refrain A♭ / C♯ / D♯ (Bns.): final pitches
REX TREMENDAE	♩ = 104–106	A♯ (A.): first choral pitch
		E♯ (Fl.): highest pitch; also final highest pitch
		C (Vlc.): lowest pitch
		C (Tr.) : (m. 216; → E♯ / F (S. + A.) see Ex. 12) A♯
		D♯ (Cb.): final lowest pitch
LACRIMOSA	♪ = 132	F (Contralto): first pitch of solo part
		D♯ (Picc.): highest pitch
		A♯ (Cb.): lowest pitch
		G (Trb.): final lowest pitch
LIBERA ME	♩ = 170 circa (beat: ♩ = 85; ♩. = 42½)	G (S. A. T.) C / C (B.) C
		D♯ (S.): highest pitch
POSTLUDE	♩ = 40 (beat: ♪ = 80)	F–G♯–B♯–F (Hn.): sustaining pitches
		F (Hn.): lowest final pitch

PRELUDE	(2)	strings only	a) "ripieno": repeated ♪'s, *staccato;* b) sustaining soli; 2 vl., vla., vlc.-cb., entering cumulatively.
EXAUDI	(1)	Chorus; 3 fl., 2 bn.; 1 hn. (sord.); hp.; strings	a) hp. → strings, winds; b) chorus alone, then doubled; strings alone at the end.
DIES IRAE	(2)	chorus; 3 fl., alto fl.; 4 hn. (sord.),*** 2 tr., 2 trb.; pno., xyl., timp.; strings	a) orchestral refrain; b) choral refrain (sung); c) choral speech + fls., pno., xyl.; d) choral speech + 2 trb.
TUBA MIRUM	(2)	baritone solo; 2 bn.***; 2 tr., 1 trb.	a) 2 tr., trb.; b) baritone + 2 tr., trb.; baritone + bns. at the end.
INTERLUDE	(1 & 2)	3 fl., alto fl., 2 bn.; 4 hn.; timp.	a) refrain chords; b) alto fl., 2 bn.; c) all fls.
REX TREMENDAE	(1)	chorus; 3 fl.; tr., trb.; strings	a) chorus + (doubling) brass; b) chorus + orchestra; c) 3 fl., strings; chorus and brass (not doubling).
LACRIMOSA	(1)	contralto solo; picc., 2 fl., alto fl.; 2 cb.***; hp.; 3 trb. (sord.); strings (no cb.)	a) contralto + hp.; cb.; ⌐ picc., all fl.; b) vla.-vlc. pizz.-string harmonics; c) 3 trb.; contralto + hp., vla.-vlc. arco-*secco,* then ↓.
LIBERA ME	(2)	chorus, *parlando;* 4 soli, chanting; 4 doubling hn (sord.)***	
POSTLUDE	*	picc., 2 fl., alto fl.; 1 hn.***; pno., hp., celesta, vibraphone, chimes	a) picc., all fls.; hn.; pno., hp.; b) hn.; celesta, vibraphone, chimes; final tutti chord.

*** These parts were originally entrusted to a harmonium, purely for sustaining purposes. However, Stravinsky fortunately reassigned them even before hearing a rehearsal.

it a self-contained, beautifully balanced entity; such is the uncomplicated, perfect quantitative symmetry in this phrase. (See Ex. 12.) An independently strophic arrangement can also be located within a scheme of alternation. Among the more remarkable new instrumental combinations used in *Requiem Canticles* are the four flutes in the Interlude.

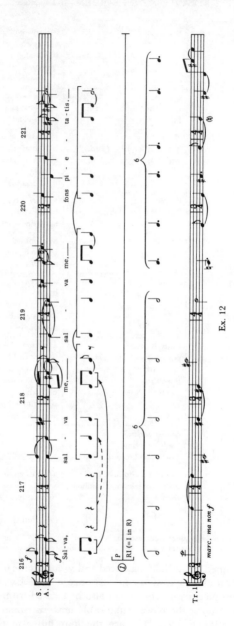

Ex. 12

The following (Ex. 13) is extracted from the relevant passage, showing that these two strophes are practically identical and that they exemplify Stravinsky's habitual hexachordal transposition-rotation.

Ex. 13

The melodic unwinding of a few successive phrases may be so contrived as to suggest, practically, structural independence. Such is the $a + a + b$ in the contralto's last three phrases in the *Lacrimosa*. The intervallic balances within these lines, between their beginnings, and in their structuring are of admirably lucid subtlety; it is not without reason that this is among the most eloquent moments in the whole work. (See Ex. 14.)

Ex. 14

It is self-evident, however, that the several strata of symmetrical intent are invariably buttressed by asymmetrical factors. Among internal "threes," it is *always* the last strophic utterance that affirms the entastic bias. In this respect, the prevalent construction in the *Requiem Canticles* can be quite directly related to Sections VII, VIII, and IX of the *Variations*,[7] despite any obvious dissimilarities.

Yet it is the explicit concern with structural symmetries that establishes an inescapable relation between the *Requiem Canticles* and its more extensive forerunners among Stravinsky's religious Latin settings. The clearest link is evidently with *Threni*, a much larger work, but one also structured in "threes," on many concentric levels, and one, moreover, that stands in as sharp rhythmic and phraseological contrast to its immediate orchestral successor, *Movements*, as *Requiem Canticles* does to its predecessor, *Variations*. But *Threni*'s amplitude was textually conditioned;

[7] See 210–22.

the spacious canonic writing in the *Querimonia,* and its structurally constant triple iteration of the Hebrew verse numbers throughout the two larger movements stood in direct reference to demands made upon timing and proportioning by such a lengthy text. It is only in *De Elegia Prima,* whose text is relatively short, that orchestral refrain elements (of equal melodic content) are to be found—although these are never restated without some change—and only in *De Elegia Quinta* that these are subtly echoed in the brief *parlando* return of mm. 385–387 and 391–393. In other words, choral-instrumental alternations, as well as strophic designs in *Threni* are gauged primarily to the necessities of the text and largely duplicate, and elaborate upon, its structure. The requirements suggested by the texts chosen for *Requiem Canticles* were, by definition, much more modest, and the plan of short movements entailed inevitable limitations in formal design. It may be said in this regard that the extraordinary compression of the *Variations* finds its reflection of sorts in the severe formal circumscription of the *Requiem Canticles.*

Granted that Stravinsky has in the last decade made a sharp distinction in his rhythmic usage between a purely orchestral medium and one involving choral activity,[8] the general rhythmic and timing procedures in *Requiem Canticles* should cause no particular surprise. Indeed, its three orchestral movements' structural, rhythmic, and recapitulative traits are a vital contributing agent toward the unity of the whole work, and they cannot sensibly be considered in any other light. It should be borne in mind, furthermore, that in composing this music, as also the *Introitus,* Stravinsky acted in keeping with his allegiance to a traditionally hieratic manner of dealing with liturgical texts. Still, this did not prevent him— any more than in his other compositions on liturgical texts—from making an occasional, circumspect allusion in the *Requiem Canticles:* the outburst of *Dies irae,* the requisite scoring of *Tuba mirum,* the apposite (and only) choral largeness in the *Rex tremendae,* the inflection of the word *Lacrimosa,* the congregational prayer-murmuring in the *Libera me,* and the doubly knelling Postlude. Lastly, it should be unnecessary, in this connection, to adduce in any detail the feeling of loss that the passing of many friends has caused Stravinsky in the years of his great age.

The serial practices in *Requiem Canticles* bespeak strophic and alternating designs so that particular hexachords or complete set-presentations occur either in layers or in successive stages of deployment. In the Prelude, for example, the "ripieno" sixteenths take up P and R while the soli each state their hexachordal conjunctions of discrete rotations,

---

[8] The only movement to show some greater degree of rhythmic complexity among all of Stravinsky's choral music is *A Sermon,* mm. 12–19, 21–23; 45–50, 53–59. It may well be for pratical reasons of performance that this movement has remained unique.

including one transposition that does not appear in the chart. (It is noteworthy that the few such transpositions throughout *Requiem Canticles* all occur in disarray or incompleteness.) Stravinsky does not miss the opportunity to present adjacently those hexachords of similar rotation which—only in set (2)—can be joined through a common factor: $I_5{}^a$–$I_5{}^b$ in the Prelude, and $P_5{}^a$–$P_5{}^b$, twice, in the *Dies irae*. In the *Rex tremendae,* the eighth-note repeated chords in strings and flutes consist of independently successive trichords (one group for flutes, one for strings) culled from I^a rotations. Only the final chord is a verticalized full hexachord. Recapitulation on the basis of a given instrumental combination, rather than melodic or rhythmic return, may be supported by a clear relation between set-forms employed. For example, the phrase for alto flute and bassoons beginning at m. 152 states (*1*): P and R, before continuing with discrete hexachords from (*2*) for bassoons alone. The Interlude ends with the same instrumental ensemble, this time stating (*1*): R and IR (mm. 197–202).

As in all of Stravinsky's larger recent works, there are some idiosyncratic practices which make twelve- (or six-) counting extremely difficult. Instances of such usage are more often to be found in chords whose pitch content does not correspond partially or entirely to any of the available hexachord types, and whose identity amid the serial apparatus could be open, at least *theoretically,* to question. If it is remembered, however, that Stravinsky's verticals, independent hexachordal rotation schemes, and frequent eschewal of the total chromatic (at least in its ordinarily inevitable association with twelve-tone practice) represent his personally worked-out components of serial technique—toward ends, after all, desirable to *him*—then the correct naming of serial idiosyncrasies becomes, merely, the ability to "look at the series" as he did, at a given moment. It is an ancillary consideration that by being "looked at" in different ways, the series may thus yield either patterned components or arbitrary, unrelatable fragments. But there are in the *Requiem Canticles* some linear puzzles as well. The tenors at the opening of the *Rex tremendae,* for instance, sing a succession of pitches that can only be called a sequence of three chromatically descending major thirds, followed by a minor third at a similar rate of descent (mm. 204–207). To be sure, some of these pitch-classes could be octave or unison doublings of factors in the orchestral chords, but they cannot all be accounted for in this way. The astonishment is the greater, however, at the tenors' subsequent entry (mm. 210–213) which is again sequential for two measures, this time describing chromatic descents that fill in the span of a major third before resuming hexachordal syntax in the last two measures. Nevertheless, there are easily recognizable hexachordal elements in this odd passage: the major third—occuring often enough with different uses of (*1*): P, and, in the second of these sequences, the familiar trichord constituting (*Z*).

But the most elusive music is contained in those movements whose harmonic emphasis is sustained by an absence of rhythmically differentiated counterpoint: the *Libera me* and Postlude. The four-part simultaneities in the *Libera me* are not as difficult (or impossible) to relate to the serial chart as the eight, seven, five, and four-factor whole-note chords in the Postlude. One may surmise that in these harmonic movements hexachordal elements were variously conjoined, and that the large chords in the Postlude represent juxtapositions of verticals and selected hexachord fragments. One clue resides, however, in the pervasive quarter-note whole-tone harmony; it points to set (*1*) as the source. At the same time, this music is the *Requiem Canticles'* strongest gesture in support of an overall tonal plan: the *Libera me* is in C, and its bass-line could be interpreted as moving from C to F and back to C. The triadic outline of the horn's held notes in the Postlude summarizes the overall scheme by recalling the bass A♭ in the Interlude's refrain-chord; the C in the *Tuba mirum, Rex tremendae* and *Libera me;* the last F as the *specific* pitch with which the composition begins, as well as the other, more centrally located, F's of importance. But perhaps the most beautiful recall is in the final chord itself: its factors: A♯, B♯ and C♯ represent the first six and the tenth notes of the solo violin's opening phrase in mm. 4–7!

The combinatorial aspect of set (*1*) is never given full expression, but there are two crucial occasions on which at least trichordal fragments of P and I^5 could be cited as evidence of the set's being put to this specific use: the sung choral refrain utterances in the *Dies irae* entail a total of six pitch-classes in parallel rising succession; the superposed fifths in the Interlude's distinctive refrain-chord denote adjacent set-factors. (See Ex. 15.)

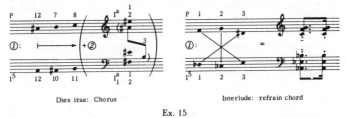

Dies irae: Chorus   Interlude: refrain chord

Ex. 15

The *Lacrimosa,* among all nine movements, is the most meticulously and ingeniously organized. Each of its vocal and instrumental participants is —either singly or not—given an unvarying role within four independently operating serial structures, and each structure is circumscribed to a particular group of rotating hexachords or verticals. Further, two such groups of hexachords are stated in a succession whereby orders are alternately read in the usual manner, and from right to left. In the case of the contralto's part, for instance, this guarantees pitch-connections between one rotation and the next, when these happen to conjoin at the left edge; and in order to provide this advantage, Stravinsky gives her a spiral ascent of all hexachords in $[(I):]$ IR^b, starting at the *end* of $IR_5{}^b$. Once this group of orders has been exhausted after the conclusion of her fourth phrase (m. 247), she sings a spiral consecution of all descending hexachords in IR^a, beginning, again, with the last pitch of IR^a. It is only between the last two phrases that her pitch-connected A♯ moves up an octave (see Ex. 14)—and for good reason. Verticals, first in IR^b and later (m. 245) in IR^a, are assigned to the flute ensemble's sustaining notes during the alto's phrases,[9] and also to these instruments' chords in combination with string harmonics, at the end of her phrases. (They occur in all seven phrases but the last.) Muted trombones punctuate the form between all phrases save the concluding two; they state the hexachords of I^a, though not in an orderly (i.e., strictly patterned) sequence —$I_1{}^a$, I^a, $I_3{}^a$, $I_2{}^a$, $I_5{}^a$ and $I_4{}^a$. Finally, the contrabass + harp and lower strings (pizz.) are given an independently unfolding spiral of R^a hexachords, starting at the top right edge. The fact that the first two orders are read in the same way (r. to l.) will be significantly reflected later. But the main purpose behind the consecutive retrogradation at this point must have been, in the first place, to move from the initial low B to C (m. 238), rather than to an A♯, already stated in the second phrase (m. 235), and secondly, to permit the bass-register fifth D-A (m. 235) to move up a semi-tone through the A♯ link in the harp (mm. 246–248). By the beginning of the contralto's second, descending, spiral, the contrabass + harp have begun "regular" spiral motion, with $R_2{}^a$. The final stages of this extraordinary mechanism, which is to say, the last two phrases, are shown on pp. 247–48, and the excellent reason for the unretrograded last hexachord in this spiral is indicated with arrows. The relationship between the contralto's line and the *secco* dyads (mm. 257 on) is splendidly highlighted by means of the last three rotations of R^a, through their abundance of minor and major seconds.

Enough said—the *Lacrimosa* is a paragon in this serene and deeply moving composition.

---

[9] A few are incomplete verticals, and the "unison" A♯ vertical of IR^a is omitted. The corresponding "unison" G's in verticals IR^b occur while the contralto is still threading her way up IR^b hexachords, but there is no collision.

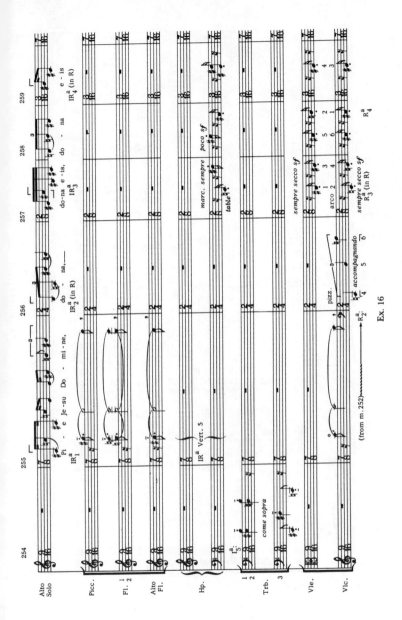

Ex. 16

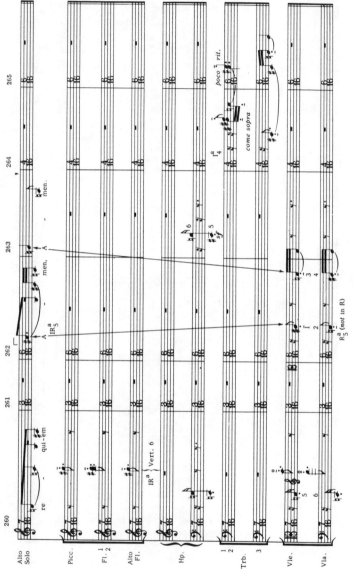

Ex. 16 (cont.)

While singleness of textural and rhythmic make-up in the chanted portion of the *Libera me* might initially discourage an assumption of any structural patterning in Stravinsky's serial choices, the succession of hexachordal units nevertheless reveals an "independent" design whose balances and artificial symmetries could be referred both to the composer's long-standing predilection for imposing arbitrary limits upon his selection of those materials available toward particular ends—in this case, the harmonic stresses on C and F—and to his obvious delight in the concealment of such patterning.

Stravinsky's greatest assets in hiding hexachordal identity are the prevalent octave or unison doublings—except for the F♯'s in m. 272, all such doublings represent mere duplication of a factor within single hexachords—, and truncation of hexachords by either one or two initial, or final, factors. At the same time, his means of emphasizing the one reiterated text-line is a correspondingly exact musical recurrence (mm. 270–271; 278–279).

The design contained in hexachord-successions is subsumed as follows:

m.	266	: ⌈IR_4^b	(lacking 5–6: D♯, C♯)	initial dyad: C-G
mm.	267–269:	⌊IR_3^b		initial factor: C
mm.	270–271:	⟨I_4^a⟩ ⎫		initial factor: E♯ (=F)
mm.	272–273:	I_4^b ⎭		
mm.	274–275:	I_3^a ⎫		initial factor: E♯
mm.	276–277:	I_3^b ⎭	(lacking 6: G)	
mm.	278–279:	⟨I_4^a⟩		(initial factor: E♯)
mm.	280–284:	I^a		initial factor: E♯
mm.	285–286:	⌈R_2^b	(lacking 1: D)	
mm.	287–288:	⌊R_3^b		final factor: B♯ (=C)

The score of *Requiem Canticles* was published several months after the writing of this article. It shows a few notational changes which were incorporated for the sake of clarity. Among these, for example, the last four measures of the *Lacrimosa* (see Ex. 16) are now given time signatures that concur with the way in which they are to be beaten; i.e., $\frac{3}{8}$, $[\frac{3}{8}]$, $\frac{2}{8}$, and $\frac{3}{8}$.

EDITIONS OF STRAVINSKY'S MUSIC

CLAUDIO SPIES

THROUGHOUT his long career, Stravinsky's music was published by a relatively small number of firms, and by far the greater portion of his published œuvre has remained in the control either of the original publishers or their direct affiliates and successors. Such problems and controversies as might arise from comparisons between many competing editions of the works of composers long since in the public domain cannot therefore often occur in Stravinsky's case; there are, in fact, only one or two works to whose editions that kind of comparison could be applied, and even then only to a limited extent. For those of his compositions that have come into the public domain—less through negligence on Stravinsky's own part, I would guess, than through the vagaries of international copyright practices—the norm has been the photographically reproduced reprint, rather than the newly engraved, newly edited, ostensibly *new* edition—the reason for this being purely economic.

In this survey, editions of Stravinsky's music currently available in the U.S. will be grouped according to publishers (i.e., *who* published *what*), rather than compositional chronology or genre and medium. Works that have been published hitherto only in formats other than those conventionally understood by the term "music publications"— in other words, pieces published in books or as adjuncts to books, in newspapers, and in journals—will not be dealt with here. An Appendix lists all publications currently in print. Dates of composition, whenever indicated, invariably appear in square brackets; dates of recomposition, revision, or reworked instrumental setting of Stravinsky's own works, in simple parentheses; dates of publication, without parentheses, except in those instances which may require a distinction to be made between an original date of publication and one of subsequent republication.

None of Stravinsky's hitherto published works is at present *totally* unavailable; in one form or another, each one of his compositions hitherto published is obtainable. (In using such terms as "published" and "publication," I refer unequivocally and exclusively to that which is commercially available for purchase.) Whatever may be currently unobtainable, or rare, is so only because it is either an unreprinted (or originally unpublished) first version of a composition subsequently revised (or recomposed) and available in this later state, or an unpublished (or unreprinted), "rental only," later version of a work available in its original (or earlier) form. I cite the following as examples:

Symphonies of Wind Instruments [1920]; Chester: score never published; Edition Russe de Musique: piano reduction (Lourié) 1926.

Symphonies of Wind Instruments (1947); Boosey & Hawkes: score 1952; no piano red. published.

Canon on a Russian Popular Tune (1965) (for orchestra); B. & H.: unpublished, rental only. (Based on *Final Hymn* from *Firebird*.)

Three Little Songs ("*Souvenir de mon Enfance*"), orchestral version (1929-30); B. & H.: unreprinted, rental only.

Three Little Songs ("*Souvenir de mon Enfance*"), voice & piano [1913]; B. & H.: reprinted.

There are, then, to begin with, two large, general categories: those works, on the one hand, whose editions have remained *essentially* unchanged since their first publication—no matter whether they may subsequently have been reprinted by other publishers—and those works, on the other hand, whose editions have undergone greater or lesser transformation as a result of Stravinsky's having rescored, revised, and recopyrighted them. In the interests of concision, I will subsume the former under Category A, and the latter under B. (In stressing the word *essentially*, above, I allude to those predictable and necessary corrections which are often, yet not often enough, undertaken in a second printing. When mistakes in a first printing are trivial and easy to correct, the corrected second printing can hardly be equated with a "new" edition. If, however, mistakes in a first printing are both numerous and non-trivial, publishers are apt to become more hesitant about their correction, for the simple reason that such correction might call for nothing less than a new layout, involving, to whatever extent, newly engraved plates and even, possibly, new pagination. It may readily be inferred, then, that whenever such a "corrected" new edition of a piece of music is contemplated, it could additionally provide its composer with the opportunity for including a few emendations or some changes in notation, thereby justifying the use of the rubric *revised version*, and also, perhaps, of a new copyright. It will be advisable, therefore, to keep in mind the difference between editions brought into existence primarily through a

CLAUDIO SPIES

criterion of *rectification,* and those that have resulted from actual *recomposition.*)

CATEGORY A

These editions may be more easily surveyed if we remember that at various times during his career Stravinsky was published mainly by one particular firm, and that contractual arrangements of this kind could cover a fairly long period. From 1946 on (i.e., through 1968), for example, Stravinsky published all his new compositions through Boosey & Hawkes—the only exceptions being those instrumental reworkings of compositions originally published (prior to 1946) by firms other than Boosey & Hawkes (or Edition Russe de Musique) and including, in one instance, a work by another composer.

1. Of all the new works published by Boosey & Hawkes after 1946, only two went through significantly corrected editions following their first printing: the *Concerto in D* for string orchestra, 1947 (elongations in the last movement) and *Threni,* 1958 (inclusion of dotted bar-lines and time-signatures in previously unbarred sections); yet in several other instances, errata lists were provided for printings following the first. If there is one among Stravinsky's works belonging to this period which is in serious need of a corrected edition, it is the study score of *The Rake's Progress,* 1962, whose publication was intended as a surprise for the composer's 80th birthday. This edition, though engraved from Stravinsky's manuscript, did not take into account a vast number of local emendations and corrections which had already been carefully incorporated into the performing material (including the rental full score) some ten years earlier. Needless to say, the occasional aspect of this edition prevented its being properly proof-read by the composer. The result was, and remains, unfortunate.

1a. When those of Stravinsky's compositions that had originally been published by Edition Russe de Musique between the years 1912 and 1934 were assimilated into the catalogue of Boosey & Hawkes in 1947, this transfer called for eventual republication (either as unchanged reprints, or as completely new and revised editions) of a very large segment of his output during that particular (and purely coincidental) 22-year period, although it must be added that Stravinsky published a considerable number of other works of this time through other firms—principally J. & W. Chester, and Schott.

1b. Boosey & Hawkes also took on the reprinting of two early pieces originally published by Jurgenson, Moscow. Of all the works transferred from other firms, Boosey & Hawkes reprinted only the following in unchanged fashion:

Two Songs, Op. 6 (Gorodetzky)
Three Movements from Petrushka (piano)
Russian Dance from *Petrushka* (violin & piano)
Two Poems of Balmont
Three Japanese Lyrics (voice and piano reduction)
Three Little Songs ("*Souvenir de mon Enfance*")
Song of the Nightingale (score; piano reduction)
Three Pieces for String Quartet (score)
Suite Italienne (violin & piano)
Suite Italienne (cello & piano)
Russian Maiden's Song (violin & piano)
Piano Sonata
Serenade in A [1]
Pater Noster (Slavonic)
Ave Maria (Slavonic)
Divertimento (violin & piano)
Duo Concertant

2. Turning now to the compositions published by Chester (and/or by arrangement among Chester, Ad. Henn, and Philharmonia), in the years roughly between 1917 and 1922, we find not only that a bare minimum of these editions have gone through reprinting with adequate correction of their plentiful mistakes, and that uncorrected editions have never been supplied with errata lists, but also that in several cases the copyrights have been permitted to lapse in this country (while continuing in Europe), with the consequence that some of our local reprinting firms have been prompted to issue exact replicas of precisely those first printings most abundantly endowed with every imaginable sort of error, and a good many beyond that. (See in the Appendix: *Les Noces, Renard*.)

The preeminent instance of a composition that has been burdened with miserable editions is *Les Noces*. A partly corrected "new" printing has not removed nearly enough of the countless inconsistencies, misprints, errors, and omissions from this altogether shoddy production; only a *completely* remade, responsibly undertaken, new edition could do justice to this score. There is, however, no sign of any prospective fulfillment of such hopes; indeed, the distinguishing trait in Chester's recent reprinting of a few of their editions of Stravinsky is confined to the modish design of their wrappers. It is difficult to believe that a simple error in alignment, for example,

[1] Still including—as recently as 1964—a well-known misprint in m. 1.

in both score and piano reduction of *Berceuses du Chat* (III: m. 1), first perpetrated by Ad. Henn in 1917, has been negligently handed down through subsequent reprintings by Chester. (On second thought, it is easy to believe; glancing through a newly published volume of Beethoven's works for cello and piano [G. Henle, 1971], one discovers on pp. 82, 85, and 89 a piece of musical nonsense that had already been committed in the first publication of Op. 69 in 1809—and, of course, since then—and for whose correction Beethoven himself wrote twice to the publisher! See *The Music Forum*, II, 99-109.) Until circumstances allow for a thorough cleaning-up of Chester's editions of Stravinsky, such works as *Pribaoutki* and *Renard* will be known only with their abiding misprints—for, despite Stravinsky's emendations and occasional rebarring, Chester have not seen fit to publish the revised and corrected versions—and the utterly disreputable state of performing materials for *Les Noces* will continue to hamper responsible performances of this composition, while the impractical notation for percussion in *Histoire du Soldat* will persistently bedevil percussionists and conductors alike. Some anomalous and cumbersome splitting-up of a given work's editions between two firms—as in the case of *Pulcinella* (Boosey & Hawkes: full score, revised edition 1965; Chester: piano-vocal reduction 1920)—may then also be sensibly and equitably avoided.

3. The publications of Schott, to whom Stravinsky entrusted a number of works from 1910 on, feature a most encouraging contrast to the above-mentioned editions by Chester; Schott's editions of Stravinsky are virtually flawless and bespeak an unusual degree of attentiveness, competence and care. Only one work has undergone a new, amended edition (and not because of previously printed errors): the *Dumbarton Oaks Concerto*, recopyrighted in 1966, now includes those repeats in the last movement that correspond to the composer's own performances, and allows for the extra measure in the more accurately notated articulations between 64 and 65. If there is any place for cavil here, it would be to point out that the score of *Jeu de Cartes* is in need of dynamics for the strings between 46 and 49, in view of Stravinsky's unmistakable practice in concerts and recordings, and to raise a question over the repeat (not printed, but at least at one time taken by Stravinsky) of the music between 99 and 106. It would be nice, too, if the score of Stravinsky's arrangement for small orchestra of the *"Bluebird" Pas-de-Deux* from *The Sleeping Beauty* could include the missing flute passage, 1 m. after 4 (parenthetically, perhaps, since Stravinsky omitted it inadvertently), and

point out, likewise, other similar details in which this arrangement differs amusingly from the original.

3a. Among the compositions reprinted by Schott from original Jurgenson editions, the *Scherzo Fantastique* underwent small emendations in 1931, and this score has, in turn, been recently reprinted in study-score size, albeit without the remark concerning Stravinsky's transformation (in the performing parts only) of three harp parts into two. In several cases, such works have been locally and variously reprinted. (See Appendix.)

3b. During World War II Stravinsky published most of his new works through AMP, then the American representatives of Schott. After 1945, a few works composed between 1938 and 1944 were first published by Schott (e.g., *Symphony in C,* 1948; *Babel,* 1953), while other compositions of that period later reverted to Schott, usually reprinted from the original AMP editions. Of these, the following require special mention: the *Symphony in Three Movements* was reissued by Schott ca. 1959 in a newly engraved and very slightly amended edition, which has since been reprinted by Eulenburg; *Danses Concertantes,* recently reprinted from AMP in study-score size, fails (for no discernible reason) to include Stravinsky's hand-written note in facsimile on the fly-leaf and omits, as had the original edition, the repeat between 153 and the first measure of 157—a repeat which Stravinsky consistently observed; the *Ode* has also been re-issued in study-score size, and in a newly "autographed" (i.e., not engraved) format in which, oddly enough, the composer's subtitle, "Elegiacal chant in three parts" is translated as *"Tryptichon für Orchester,"* while the movement-headings, "Eulogy," "Eclogue," and "Epitaph" remain untranslated (and unchanged). The study-score reprints or reissues of *Scherzo Fantastique, Danses Concertantes, Ode,* and *Symphony in C* are in Schott's series "Music of the Twentieth Century."

4. Of the works published by AMP, two others have now reverted to Schott—the *Sonata for Two Pianos* and *Four Norwegian Moods*—but are still being sold in AMP editions, pending exhaustion of the present printings; the first of these works, as far as I can tell, was the only one of AMP's publications of Stravinsky to undergo a second (and corrected) printing. Four other works are the property of AMP, and will remain under that imprint: *Scènes de Ballet, Scherzo à la Russe,* the *Elegy* for viola, and the *Danse Sacrale*—of which latter, more below under Category B. I might add that these particular

scores were printed on extremely poor paper, and are therefore, understandably, after 25-odd years, simply falling apart.

There now remain those firms with only a very small quantity of Stravinsky publications.

5. From among works originally published by Jurgenson, Rob. Forberg have reprinted the *Symphony in E-flat* (with the revisions of 1914), and *Zvezdoliki* (*Le Roi des Étoiles*).

6. Belaieff, the original publishers of *Le Faune et la Bergère*, reprinted this work in the early 1960s. The *Ebony Concerto*, first published by Charling, has been reprinted very recently, in a larger format, by Morris. And finally, Breitkopf & Härtel, the publishers of Sibelius' *Canzonetta*, Op. 62a, also published Stravinsky's arrangement (1963) of this piece for clarinet, bass clarinet, four horns, harp and contrabass.

CATEGORY B

If distinctions between criteria of *rectification* and *recomposition* are taken into account, the list in the Appendix under Category B will show a minority of editions to have been called into existence by the former, while the result of the latter—the recomposed scores— can be divided into two groups: first, works originally written for a medium not generically different from that of their later versions (i.e., reorchestrations, or rescorings involving a reduction in instrumentation); and secondly, works arranged for chamber ensembles, or for orchestra, from original versions either for piano or a differently constituted chamber ensemble. Publications of excerpted and rescored pieces from larger compositions, as well as arrangements— for example, for piano and violin—of such excerpts also belong to this second group. It is among the recomposed scores of the first group, however, that Stravinsky's published music has at times been up against a considerable problem. In some cases, that problem has been happily solved; in others, it might eventually be tackled with success, while in the particular instance of one composition it is beyond hope of solution. I am referring to the availability, at present, for purposes of comparison, of scores both in their original states and their subsequently reworked versions. Some publishers have shown little or no concern over matters of this sort, since they apparently equate a reworked composition in their catalogue with that composition's only commercially valid state, as if that composition had had no prior existence whatsoever. Other publishers have seized upon the chance to reprint a first state of a composition which has been superseded by a substantially revised version, although such reprinting has only very rarely been undertaken with any attendant requisite thoughtfulness. Naturally, for Stravinsky himself, the aim of a reworked score was—regarding whichever of its particulars—an improvement on the original state and on however many intervening stages there may have been.

The financial misfortune that befell *Firebird, Petrushka,* and *The Rite of Spring*—precisely those works that could have yielded the most impressive, dependably long-lasting revenue in royalties—was caused by complexities in international copyright, yet was itself not the only cause for Stravinsky's having reworked and rescored those compositions. Proceeding as before, in Category A, the problem mentioned above may be appreciated with peculiar vividness as it applies to these three ballets.

1b. *Petrushka,* in its original version, has long been available in a Kalmus reprint which incorporates a number of misprints from the Edition Russe score. The only existing corrected reprint was published in 1967 by Norton, in the series *Norton Critical Scores.* The additional fact of Boosey & Hawkes' recently corrected printing of the revised version (1946) places both orchestral states of this work in a felicitous position. Consequently, this problem does not apply here, and need not be expected to do so in future.

As if reflecting, with consummate irony, some sixty years' worth of pervasively silly journalistic splutterings about Stravinsky's principal *scandale*-provoking composition, *The Rite of Spring*'s editions are currently beset by so massive a tangle of confusions, contradictions, and conflicting evidence, that there is no likelihood of foreseeable repair. Ever since the score was first published in 1921, a succession of partly corrected, minimally amended editions has been printed on the basis of the original Edition Russe edition. The first published edition, heavily loaded with misprints and mistakes, has been reprinted (without corrections) by Kalmus. The first of Boosey & Hawkes' various printings of this work included a few emendations that had already been incorporated into a second edition by Edition Russe, shortly after the score's first publication. However, Boosey & Hawkes' first printing added quite a few other emendations, some of which are immediately identifiable because they are printed in English rather than in Italian. All previous mistakes were left uncorrected, and this edition became known (later) as the "1947 revised version." A subsequent edition went about correcting some of the many mistakes that had been handed down thus far, and was named "revised 1947 version, reprinted with corrections 1965." Substantially, this was still no more than a corrected, amended reprint, and it left several details in some doubt. (See, for instance, the inherited slurs for the trumpets between 132 and 133, which only partly correspond to Stravinsky's recording of 1960, and are in direct conflict with his recording of 1940, as well as with his often-stated preference for no slurs in this passage.) When Stravinsky reorchestrated the *Danse Sacrale* (1943), he intended this new scoring to substitute for the original one, and from then on conducted *The Rite of Spring* only with the reorchestrated *Danse Sacrale*. Had an agreement between AMP and Boosey & Hawkes permitted a new edition of *The Rite of Spring* to include the reorchestrated *Danse Sacrale*, such an edition might indeed reasonably have been expected. As it is, however, the newly engraved Boosey & Hawkes edition dated 1967 again reprints the old version of the *Danse Sacrale*, besides featuring a number of emendations of very dubious authenticity. This edition corrects a few slips that had been left over (such as the trumpet slurs mentioned above), but it leaves unanswered the basic question of a thorough representation of Stravinsky's wishes, as well as suggesting the question as to why the trouble should have been taken to engrave what is no more than yet another stop-gap score of this work. In the meantime, International has reprinted a beautifully engraved score of presumable East European origin, which corresponds in detail, although not in layout, to the Boosey & Hawkes "revised 1947 version, reprinted with corrections 1965."

Although *The Rite of Spring* is in fact the only one of Stravinsky's works an edition of whose sketches has been published thus far (Boosey & Hawkes, facsimile edition, 1969), and while the future may yet provide for as nearly authentic an edition of this work as possible, that authenticity will nevertheless have to be circumscribed within Stravinsky's abiding dissatisfaction with the state of *The Rite of Spring* as a whole. Had he proceeded from the rescoring of the *Danse Sacrale* to a revision of the complete work, we might indeed have had a "final" score. Stravinsky contemplated such a revision, and even considered enlarging the orchestra for it. Clearly, then, the problem in this case will remain, by definition, insoluble, and whatever revisions were prevented from being written down by Stravinsky's fear of too little time for the task must now remain conjectural.

3a. *Firebird* has fared almost as well as *Petrushka*, so far as reliable editions of its various reworkings and transformations are concerned.

Those currently missing stages (i.e., the inadvertently omitted music between 157 and 182 in the Kalmus reprint of the *First Suite* (1911); and the *Berceuse* for reduced orchestra, of the same year) are likely to be reprintable in the event that a completely documented *Firebird* may some day be published, and that documentation may then also include the *Canon on a Russian Popular Tune*.

The unending saga of printing errors and oversights unfortunately applies to many of the publications in Category B. Three examples will suffice for the moment:

1b. In the revised editions of *Pulcinella* and of the *Pulcinella Suite*, changes in dynamics in mm. 17-18 of the *Serenata* are as conspicuously lacking as they were evident in all of Stravinsky's performances of this music. What is puzzling here is that these changes were already lacking in the Edition Russe score of 1924, but had been explicitly incorporated into the *Suite for violin & piano after themes, fragments and pieces by Pergolesi* (1925) and into both cello and violin versions of the *Suite Italienne*.

The *Four Etudes for Orchestra*, reprinted with corrections and recopyrighted in 1971, retain some mistakes, one of the more serious of which is the indication on p. 17 of a first and second ending. Stravinsky's recording confirms that the four measures after 6 are simply to be repeated, without further ado.

6. In the *Tango* for piano, a misprinted D above middle C, in the top line, on the third eighth of mm. 10 and 11, has crept into both currently available recordings of this piece. That this D was always meant to be an F is not only dictated by common musical horse-sense, but is made unmistakably clear by Stravinsky's own instrumentation (1953), and by the large (ugly) orchestration (not by Stravinsky) published by Mercury, 1941.

The mere recital of mistakes would, of course, be pointless, were it not possible to infer some reasons for their persistent occurrence in so many of Stravinsky's published works, and were the inference not to suggest some specific remedial action, even at this late date. Certainly, a good deal of evidence supports the notion of a rather widely differing degree of professional thoughtfulness, care, and competence among publishers, yet very little is actually known about Stravinsky's personal assumption of direct responsibility for proofreading, or for delegating such labors to individuals qualified to do the job acceptably. It is difficult not to suspect, indeed, that for a long period during his residence in Europe he either refused to be bothered with proofreading, or assigned it to careless assistants without checking results prior to actual printing. Nevertheless, misprints and mistakes in his published music were extremely annoying to him; there was not a rehearsal that I can remember in which publishers were not roundly cursed for such errors. Looking back over the various and frequent circumstances which permitted oversights, inaccuracies, omissions, and inconsistencies to remain uncorrected (rather than being immediately and permanently remedied) throughout an exceptionally long career, it is reassuring, at least, that for most of the works written after 1962, Stravinsky relied upon a composer and student of his music for proof-reading and elimination of errors from scores in process of publication. It is only to be regretted that he had not previously availed himself of this kind of attentive assistance for such chores.

In considering any possible future editions of Stravinsky's works—and I am thinking only of such publications as might propose to present his works in scrupulous correctness, with all desirable scholarly and editorial efficiency brought into play—sources of the usual kind will have to be supplemented by all available specific (and reliable) indications of his performance practice, as may be gleaned both from his recordings and from markings he made on his own personal copies of printed scores. Since Stravinsky's inclination was always toward reticence in providing his written music with dynamic shadings or subtle tempo inflections, his demonstrated—and indeed, variable—preferences in performing it are crucial for filling any gaps in this respect. Moreover, relevant markings and annotations made by Stravinsky on score copies belonging to his musical associates, as well as notes taken down by these individuals concerning specific points at rehearsals attended by (and commented on by) Stravinsky must be taken into account as important ancillary sources. All such additional source materials will then confirm and explain divergences, for example, between editions of Stravinsky's music, as they now exist, and his own recordings. (In *Le Faune et la Bergère,* for instance, the measures omitted in the second and third songs, in the recording of 1964, indicate a solution prompted by Stravinsky's impatience over some musical redundancies afflicting this early composition.) What may be predicted, at any rate, for the immediate future is the first publication of a number of small, occasional pieces, of sundry (and newly discovered) juvenilia, as well as of arrangements and orchestrations hitherto left unprinted. Once that aspect of Stravinsky's catalogue has been suitably exploited, and once the inevitable parade of

EDITIONS OF STRAVINSKY'S MUSIC

biographies will have provided an appropriate impetus, some more serious publishing venture may yet be called into existence. When this occurs, the time will have come for a thorough, general cleaning-up, so that such fictitious and/or nominal editors as "Albert Spalding, N. Y.," "F. H. Schneider," and "Julia A. Burt, N. Y." may be excused from further service on the opening pages of scores whose copyrights had once had to be protected in this manner.

It is no exaggeration to suggest that there is hardly a single work by Stravinsky whose current published state is representative of notational sufficiency, to the extent that *it alone* might be trusted to imply all the particulars which Stravinsky might have found desirable for its performance, at the same time as to prohibit all those other aspects in execution which he might have abhorred. If the other side of that coin is the continuing unsatisfactory condition of notation *per se*—in the sense that a notion of dependable notational comprehensiveness is now as remote, or even as absurd as, or more remote and absurd than, ever—there may be expected to endure that necessary, habitual process of filling-in through sheer guesswork; which expectation can only elicit my slim yet persistent hope in the survival of the educated guess.

Publishers and abbreviations:

Associated Music Publishers, Inc., New York	AMP
Autograph Editions, New York	Autograph
M.P. Belaieff, Leipzig; currently Bonn	Belaieff
Boosey & Hawkes, Ltd., London	B. & H.
Breitkopf & Härtel, Wiesbaden	Br. & H.
Broude Brothers, New York	Broude
Chappell & Co., Ltd., London	Chappell
Charling Music Corporation, New York	Charling
J. & W. Chester, Ltd., London	Chester
Edition Russe de Musique, Berlin/Paris	Ed. Russe
Ernst Eulenburg & Co., Mainz	Eulenburg
Rob. Forberg, Bad Godesberg	Forberg
Wilhelm Hansen, Copenhagen	Hansen
Ad. Henn, Geneva	Henn
International Music Company, New York	International
P. Jurgenson, Moscow	Jurgenson
Edwin F. Kalmus, Commack, N.Y.	Kalmus
Leeds Music Corporation, New York	Leeds
E. B. Marks Music Corporation, New York	Marks

Mercury Music Corporation, New York	Mercury
Edwin H. Morris & Co., Inc., New York	Morris
W. W. Norton & Co., New York	Norton
Omega Music Co., New York	Omega
G. Schirmer, Inc., New York	Schirmer
B. Schott's Söhne, Mainz	Schott
Editions de la Sirène, Paris	Sirène
Wiener Philharmonischer Verlag	Philharmonia

Original publishers and publication dates are given within square brackets, *before* subsequent publishers, whenever necessary. The term "score" denotes miniature or study score, for the sake of convenience. Most works published in miniature score by B. & H. are also obtainable in full score. "Full score" indicates that *only* a full score is published. "Red." = reduction; when a red., or piano-vocal score, is by Stravinsky it is mentioned without parentheses; when anonymous, it is enclosed within parentheses; otherwise, its author's name appears in parentheses. Arrangements, other than reductions for 1 or 2 pianos, are indented and placed next to their source compositions.

<h4 style="text-align:center">CATEGORY A</h4>

1. *Praeludium* for Jazz Ensemble [1937] (1953); B. & H.: full score 1968
   Concerto in D (string orch.) [1946]; B. & H.: score 1947; revised edition ca. 1950
   Orpheus [1947]; B. & H.: score 1948; piano red. (Spinner) 1948
   Mass [1944-48]; B. & H.: score 1948; piano-vocal red. (Spinner) 1948
   The Rake's Progress [1948-51]; B. & H.: score 1962; piano-vocal red. (Spinner) 1951
       Lullaby (two recorders) (1960); B. & H. 1960
   Cantata [1951-52]; B. & H.: score 1952; piano-vocal red. 1952
   Septet [1952-53]; B. & H.: score 1953; 2-piano red. 1953
   Three Songs from William Shakespeare [1953]; B. & H.: score 1954; piano red. 1954
   In Memoriam Dylan Thomas [1954]; B. & H.: score 1954; piano red. 1954
   Greeting Prelude [1955]; B. & H.: full score 1956
   Canticum Sacrum [1955]; B. & H.: score 1956; piano-vocal red. 1956
   J. S. Bach: Choral Variationen ("Vom Himmel hoch") [1955-56]; B. & H.: score 1956; Bach's original included
   Agon [1953-57]; B. & H.: score 1957; 2-piano red. 1957
   Illumina nos (Gesualdo) [1957]; B. & H. 1957 (see *Tres Sacrae Cantiones* below)
   Threni [1957-58]; B. & H.: score 1958; revised printing ca. 1962; piano-vocal red. (Stein) 1958
   Movements [1958-59]; B. & H.: score 1960; red. 2 pianos 1960
   Epitaphium [1959]; B. & H. 1959
   Double Canon [1959]; B. & H. 1960
   Tres Sacrae Cantiones (Gesualdo) [1959]; B. & H. 1960
   Monumentum (Gesualdo) [1960]; B. & H.: score 1960

A Sermon, a Narrative, and a Prayer [1960-61]; B. & H.: score 1960; (piano-vocal red.) 1961

Anthem "The Dove Descending" [1962]; [Faber & Faber] B. & H. 1962

The Flood [1961-62]; B. & H.: score 1963; (piano-vocal red.) 1963

Abraham and Isaac [1962-63]; B. & H.: score 1965; (piano-vocal red.) 1965

Elegy for J.F.K. [1964]; B. & H. 1964; two versions: for baritone, and for mezzo-soprano

Fanfare for a New Theatre [1964]; B. & H. 1968

Variations [1963-64]; B. & H.: score 1965

Introitus T.S. Eliot in Memoriam [1965]; B. & H.: score 1965

Requiem Canticles [1965-66]; B. & H.: score 1967; (piano-vocal red.) 1967

The Owl and the Pussy-cat [1966]; B. & H. 1967

Two Sacred Songs (Hugo Wolf) [1968]; B. & H.: full score 1969

1a. *Two Songs* (Gorodetzky), Op. 6 [1907-08]; [Jurgenson 1912] B. & H. 1953

1b. *Three Japanese Lyrics* [1912-13]; [Ed. Russe, 1913] B. & H.: full score 1955 (together with *Two Poems of Balmont*); likewise piano red.

Sonata for Piano [1924]; [Ed. Russe, 1925] B. & H. reprint

Serenade in A [1925]; [Ed. Russe, 1926] B. & H. reprint

Duo Concertant [1931-32]; [Ed. Russe, 1933] B. & H. reprint

2. *Pribaoutki* [1914]; [Henn, 1917] Chester (and Philharmonia): score, no date; piano red. 1924

Berceuses du Chat [1915]; [Henn, 1917] Chester (and Philharmonia): score, no date; piano red. 1923

Renard [1915-16]; [Henn, 1917] Chester (and Philharmonia): score, no date; piano-vocal red. reprinted 1956, with an English translation, but omitting the Russian text. Score reprinted by Kalmus

Song of the Volga Boatmen [1917]; Chester: score 1920

Les Noces [1914-23]; Chester (and Philharmonia): score, no date; partly corrected reprint; piano-vocal red. 1922. Reprinted by Kalmus: all (original!) performing materials, full score, choral score, piano-vocal red., and score

Histoire du Soldat [1918]; Chester (and Philharmonia): score 1924. Reprinted by Kalmus: all performing materials, full score, score; International, score

   Grande Suite (8 pieces); Chester 1922; rental only; piano red. 1922
   Suite for Clarinet, Violin & Piano (5 pieces) (1919); Chester 1920. Reprinted by International

Ragtime [1918]; [Sirène, 1919] Chester (and Philharmonia): score 1920; piano red. 1920

Piano-Rag-Music [1919]; Chester 1920

Three Pieces for Clarinet [1919]; Chester 1920. Reprinted by Omega, 1949, and by International

3. *Fireworks,* Op. 4 [1908]; Schott 1910: score, no date; 4-hand piano red. (Singer). Reprints: Kalmus (full score); International

Concerto in D (violin & orch.) [1931]; Schott: score 1931; piano red. 1931

Concerto for Two Pianos [1931-35]; Schott 1936

Jeu de Cartes [1936]; Schott: score 1937; piano red. 1937

Concerto in E flat—Dumbarton Oaks [1937-38]; Schott: score 1938; corrected edition 1966; 2-piano red. 1938

Symphony in C [1938-40]; Schott: score 1948; reissued, no date

Pas-de-Deux ("Bluebird") (Tchaikovsky) [1941]; Schott: score 1953

Babel [1944]; Schott: score 1953; short score 1952

3a. *Scherzo Fantastique*, Op. 3 [1907-08]; [Jurgenson] Schott: score 1931; reissued, no date

3b. *Danses Concertantes* [1941-42]; [AMP: full score 1942; 2-piano red. (Dahl) 1944] Schott: score reprint, no date

Circus Polka [1942]; [AMP: full score 1944; version for piano 1942; (versions for violin and piano, and 2 pianos)] Schott: score reprint, no date

Ode [1943]; [AMP: score 1947] Schott: score, new edition 1968

Symphony in Three Movements [1942-45]; [AMP: score 1946] Schott: engraved score, no date. Reprinted by Eulenburg

4. *Four Norwegian Moods* [1942]; AMP: score 1944, not reprinted [2]

Scherzo à la Russe [1944]; [Chappell 1945] AMP: score (orch. version only) 1946, not reprinted; 2-piano red. 1946

Scènes de Ballet [1944]; [Chappell 1945] AMP: score 1946, not reprinted

Sonata for Two Pianos [1943-44]; [Chappell 1945] AMP 1945; later printing corrected [2]

Elegy [1944]; [Chappell 1945] AMP 1945

5. *Symphony in E-flat*, Op. 1 [1905-07]; [Jurgenson 1914] Forberg: score (with revisions of 1914) 1964; Kalmus: reprint, full score

Zvezdoliki ("Le Roi des Étoiles") [1911-12]; [Jurgenson 1913] Forberg: score 1971; piano red. reprint, no date

Four Études for Piano, Op. 7 [1908]; [Jurgenson 1910] Reprints: Kalmus; International

6. *Le Faune et la Bergère*, Op. 2 [1906]; Belaieff 1913; score reprint, no date (without Russian text); piano red. 1908, reprinted

The Star-Spangled Banner [1941]; Mercury: full score 1941; piano red. 1941

Ebony Concerto [1945]; [Charling: Score 1946] Morris: score reprint, no date

Canzonetta (Sibelius) [1963]; Br. & H.: full score 1964

1a. *Two Songs* (Verlaine), Op. 9 [1910]; [Jurgenson 1911] B. & H. 1954, with revisions

Orchestral version (1951); B. & H.: full score 1953

1b. *Petrushka* [1910-11]; [Ed. Russe 1912; 4-hand piano red.] Reprints: Norton Critical Scores, corrected 1967; Kalmus (full score, score)

Revised version (1946); B. & H.: score 1948; reprinted with corrections 1965; 4-hand piano red. 1948

---

[2] These works are now owned by Schott, but have not been reprinted; the AMP editions are still being sold.

Three Movements from Petrushka (1921); [Ed. Russe 1922] B. & H. reprint; International, reprint

Russian Dance (violin and piano) (1932); [Ed. Russe 1933] B. & H. reprint

Two Poems of Balmont [1911]; [Ed. Russe 1912] B. & H. reprint

    Version for chamber ensemble (1954); B. & H.: full score 1955 (together with *Three Japanese Lyrics*)

The Rite of Spring: Sketches [1911-1913]; B. & H. 1969

The Rite of Spring [1911-13]; [Ed. Russe: score 1921; 4-hand piano red. 1913] Reprint of first edition: Kalmus (full score, score); B. & H. reprint of 4-hand piano red., no date; B. & H.: score, reprint of amended edition (1921), no date ("revised 1947 version"); B. & H.: full score, revised (1947) version, with corrections 1965; B. & H.: score, revised (1947); newly engraved edition 1967, 1969; International: reprint of Eastern European score corresponding to revised version (1947), but differently engraved

    Danse Sacrale (1943); AMP: score 1945, not reprinted

Three Little Songs ("*Souvenir de mon Enfance*") [1913]; [Ed. Russe 1914] B. & H. reprint

    Orchestral version (1929-30); [Ed. Russe: rental score 1934] B. & H. reprint, rental only

The Nightingale [1908-09; 1913-14]; [Ed. Russe: Piano-vocal red., no date] B. & H.: score, revised edition (1962); piano-vocal red., revised 1962, without Russian text (i.e., with English, French and German translations.)

    Song of the Nightingale (1917); [Ed. Russe: score 1921; piano red. 1927] B. & H.: score, reprint; piano red., reprint

    Song of the Nightingale and *Chinese March* (violin & piano) (1932); [Ed. Russe]

Three Pieces for String Quartet [1914]; [Ed. Russe: score 1922] B. & H. reprint

    Four Études (1914-1928); [Ed. Russe: rental score] B. & H.: score, reprint 1947; revised version (1952) with corrections, 1971

Étude for Pianola [1917]; B. & H.: version for two pianos (Soulima Stravinsky) 1951. (See *Four Études*, above.)

Pulcinella [1919-20]; [Ed. Russe: rental score 1924] B. & H.: full score, revised edition 1965; Chester: piano-vocal red. 1920

    Suite (ca. 1922); [Ed. Russe: score 1924] B. & H.: score, revised edition 1949

    Suite for violin & piano, after themes, fragments and pieces by Pergolesi (1925); [Ed. Russe 1926]

    Suite Italienne (cello & piano) (1932); [Ed. Russe 1934] B. & H. reprint

    Suite Italienne (violin & piano) (1933); [Ed. Russe 1934] B. & H. reprint

Symphonies of Wind Instruments [1920]; [Ed. Russe: piano red. (Lourié) 1926] Chester: no score published

    Revised version (1947); B. & H.: score 1952

Mavra [1921-22]; [Ed. Russe: rental score 1925; piano-vocal red. 1925] B. & H.: score, revised version (1947) 1969; piano-vocal red. reprinted

CLAUDIO SPIES

(i.e., without corresponding revisions) 1956 with English, French and German translations, but omitting the Russian text

   Russian Maiden's Song (violin & piano) (1937); [Ed. Russe 1938] B. & H. reprint

   Russian Maiden's Song (cello & piano) [Ed. Russe] B. & H.

Octet [1922-23]; [Ed. Russe: score 1924; piano red. Lourié] B. & H.: score, revised version (1952) 1952; piano red. (Lourié) reprint

Piano Concerto [1923-24]; [Ed. Russe: full score 1936; red. 2 pianos 1924] B. & H.: score, revised (1959) 1960; 2-piano red. reprint

Pater Noster [1926]; [Ed. Russe 1932] B. & H.: reissued 1967; Latin version (1949) 1949

Credo [1932]; [Ed. Russe 1933] B. & H.: Latin version (1949) 1949

   Russian Credo, new version (1964); B. & H. 1966

Ave Maria [1934]; [Ed. Russe 1934] B. & H.: reissued 1967; Latin version (1949) 1949

Oedipus Rex [1926-27]; [Ed. Russe: rental score 1927; piano-vocal red. 1927] B. & H.: score, revised version (1948) 1949; piano-vocal red.

Apollo [1927-28]; [Ed. Russe: rental score 1928; piano red. 1928] B. & H.: score, revised version (1947) 1949; piano red.

Le Baiser de la Fée [1928]; [Ed. Russe: rental score 1928; piano red. 1928] B. & H.: score, revised version (1950) 1952; piano red.

   Ballad (violin & piano) (1947); B. & H. 1951

   Divertimento (1934); [Ed. Russe 1938] B. & H.: score, revised version (1949) 1950

   Divertimento (violin & piano) (1932); [Ed. Russe] B. & H. reprint

Capriccio [1928-29]; [Ed. Russe: rental score 1930; red. 2 pianos] B. & H.: score, revised version (1949) 1952; red. 2 pianos. Reprinted by International

Symphony of Psalms [1930]; [Ed. Russe: score 1932; piano-vocal red. (Soulima Stravinsky)] B. & H.: score, revised version (1948) 1948; piano-vocal red. (S. Stravinsky) revised, 1948

Perséphone [1933-34]; [Ed. Russe: rental score 1934; piano-vocal red. (S. Stravinsky) 1934] B. & H.: score, revised version (1949) 1950; piano-vocal red. (S. Stravinsky)

2. *Three Easy Pieces* [1914-15]; [Henn 1917] Chester, no date. Reprinted by Omega, 1949; International

Five Easy Pieces [1915-16]; [Henn 1917] Chester 1917. Reprinted by Omega 1949; International

   Suite No. 1 (1917-25); Chester (and Philharmonia): score 1926; re-issued. Reprinted by Kalmus (full score, score)

   Suite No. 2 (1921); Chester (and Philharmonia): score 1925; re-issued. Reprinted by Kalmus (full score, score)

Three Tales for Children [1915-17]; Chester 1920

   Tilimbom (voice and orchestra) (1923); Schott, rental

Four Russian Songs [1918-19]; Chester 1920

   Four Songs (voice, flute, harp, guitar) (1953-54); Chester: score 1955. (See *Three Tales for Children,* above.)

Four Russian Peasant Songs [1914-17]; Chester 1932; Schott ("*Unterschale*"), no date; Marks 1950, English and French, Russian text omitted

       Version with 4 horns (1954); Chester 1958, with English words only

The Five Fingers [1921]; Chester 1922. Reprinted by Kalmus; Omega.

       Eight Instrumental Miniatures (1962); Chester: score 1963

3a. *Pastorale* [1907]; [Jurgenson 1910] Schott (also Chester). Reprinted by
    G. Schirmer

       Version for soprano and four woodwinds (1923); Schott, no date

       Version for violin and piano (1933); Schott 1934

       Version for violin and 4 woodwinds (1933); Schott 1934

   Firebird [1909-10] [Jurgenson: full score; piano red. 1910] Schott: piano
    red. reprint, no date. Score reprinted by Broude, no date; Kalmus

       First Suite (1911); [Jurgenson 1912] Reprinted by Kalmus: full score

       Berceuse (reduced winds) (1911); [Jurgenson 1912]

       Suite (reduced orchestra) (1919); Schott 1920. Reprinted by Kalmus
       (full score, score)

       Ballet Suite (1945); Leeds: score 1947; Schott: newly engraved score,
       no date

       Prélude et Ronde des Princesses (violin & piano) (1926); Schott,
       no date

       Berceuse (violin & piano) (1926); Schott, no date

       Berceuse (further transcription, violin & piano) (1932); Schott
       1932, reprint 1960

       Scherzo (violin & piano) (1933); Schott 1933, reprint 1961

       Canon on a Russian Popular Tune (1965); B. & H.: rental only

6.   *Concertino for String Quartet* [1920]; Hansen: score 1923; piano red.
    (Lourié)

       Concertino for 12 Instruments (1952); Hansen: score 1953

   Tango for piano [1940]; Mercury 1941

       Version for chamber orchestra (1953); Mercury: score 1954

IGOR STRAVINSKY: A DISCOGRAPHY
OF THE COMPOSER'S .PERFORMANCES

DAVID HAMILTON

Since the beginning of the twentieth century, many composers who were also performers have been persuaded to make recordings of their own music. Certainly no major figure has produced such an exhaustive documentation of this kind as did Igor Stravinsky — not surprisingly, for on numerous occasions he made clear his concern with the limitations of musical notation as a means for fixing a performance tradition for his music.[1] Before the perfection of the techniques of electrical sound recording, he was led to the player-piano roll,[2] but after 1926 the phonograph record provided a considerably more satisfactory medium for the purpose. Over a period of more than forty years, he committed to discs virtually all of his major theater, orchestral, and chamber works (and, in his days as a concert pianist, not a few of the piano works).

In later years, as is well known, Robert Craft was very active in assisting Stravinsky at rehearsals, concerts, and recording sessions. That some portions of rehearsal takes conducted by Craft were used in the final edited versions of Stravinsky's later recordings seems not improbable, and doubtless specific details about these matters will be made public by those with firsthand knowledge. I have mentioned here, in footnotes, certain recordings made by Craft in Stravinsky's presence, and attempted to clarify some apparent misattributions. That Stravinsky was frequently dissatisfied with his later recordings and with the conditions of tension and pressure under which they were made is also not a secret — and should be fairly evident from the recordings themselves; again, that is a story for others to tell in detail.

The purpose of the present listing is to define, for students of the subject and for libraries and other institutions desiring a comprehensive collection in this area, the extent and limits of the commercially recorded material relevant to the study of Stravinsky's performance

---

[1] See *An Autobiography*, New York, 1936, p. 101; Stravinsky and Robert Craft, *Conversations with Igor Stravinsky*, Garden City, N.Y., 1959, p. 139; *Dialogues and a Diary*, Garden City, N.Y., p.33.

[2] The present discography does not deal with Stravinsky's piano rolls, as they are not accessible for study at the present time. A list of them may be found in Appendix D of Eric Walter White, *Stravinsky: The Composer and His Works*, London and Berkeley, 1966, p. 573; I am informed that this listing is not entirely correct.

practice. It is a revision of one first published in *Perspectives on Schoenberg and Stravinsky* (Princeton, 1968), and later, in a slightly revised and corrected form, in the booklet accompanying Columbia album set D5S-775. As before, I have the pleasant duty of expressing my gratitude to many persons who have assisted me. Mr. Stravinsky and Mr. Craft examined an early draft; Mr. John McClure and his staff at Columbia Records provided comprehensive information about their recordings; Professor Claudio Spies and Mr. Steven Smolian checked drafts and filled in gaps; Miss Ida Rosen and Messrs. Samuel Dushkin, Paul Jacobs, Jean Morel, Eric Walter White, and Donald Mitchell assisted in diverse ways with information and advice. After two revisions, a compiler begins to aspire to genuine completeness and correctness; if that ideal state has still not been attained, it is not for the lack of generous assistance, nor is it the fault of those who so willingly gave such assistance.

A note on procedure. In general, only the most recent American catalogue numbers are listed. Details of earlier issues may be found in *The World's Encyclopaedia of Recorded Music* (compiled by F. F. Clough and G. J. Cuming, London, 1952; supplements, 1953 and 1957) and in back issues of the Schwann LP record catalogue; readers in Europe are referred to their local equivalents of that catalogue for information.

Unless otherwise indicated, all listings refer to 12-inch, 33⅓ RPM microgroove recordings; numbers in roman type indicate monophonic recordings, while italics refer to stereo. The symbol 10" is self-explanatory; the mark *78* denotes a 78 RPM recording. In the case of multiple-record sets, the number of records is indicated by a digit preceding the abbreviation for the manufacturer's name. The following abbreviations are used:

Col.	Columbia Records (U.S.A.)
Fr. Col.	French Columbia
Merc.	Mercury Records (U.S.A.)
Ser.	Seraphim (division of Angel Records, U.S.A.)
USSR.	Amalgamated Unions Gramophone Studio (Soviet state label)[3]
Vds M.	Voix de son Maitre (France)
Vic.	RCA Victor (U.S.A.)
Vox.	Vox Productions (U.S.A.)

[3] I have been unable to ascertain whether these records are still available; they were presumably issued in 1963, but the continuing availability of Soviet recordings seems to be a problematic matter. Note that Soviet records have two numbers, one for each side.

An asterisk following a catalogue number indicates that the record was discontinued by the manufacturer as of June 1, 1972.

The order of listing is based on the catalogue of works in Eric Walter White's book.[4] To avoid cluttering the listings with distinctions between different versions of various works, these are only mentioned where there seems a possibility of confusion; in general, all recordings made after Stravinsky had completed a revised edition may be assumed to use that revision.

The dates for the prewar recordings have been arrived at by comparison of the matrix numbers, by reference to the published writings of Stravinsky, and through the recollections of persons concerned in the recordings; some of these remain tentative. Information about the American Columbia sessions was provided by Columbia Records.

A. ORIGINAL WORKS

The Faun and the Shepherdess, Op. 2 (1906)

> Mary Simmons (m-s, in Russian), CBC Symphony Orchestra— Igor Stravinsky (May 7, 8, 1964—Toronto)   Col. *MS-7439*

Symphony in E♭ major, Op. 1 (1905-07)

> Columbia Symphony Orchestra—Igor Stravinsky (May 2, 1966 —Hollywood)   Col. *MS-6989*

Pastorale (1907)

—Arr. for violin & wind quartet (1932)

> Samuel Dushkin, wind quartet—Igor Stravinsky (1933— Paris)   *78:* 10″ Col. 17075-D*
> Joseph Szigeti, Mitchell Miller (ob), R. McGinnis (cl), D. Gassman (Eng hn), Sol Schoenbach (bsn)—Igor Stravinsky (Feb. 9, 1946—New York)   10″ Col. ML-2122*
> Israel Baker, Columbia Chamber Ensemble—Igor Stravinsky (Oct. 26, 1965—Hollywood)   Col. *M-30579*

Scherzo Fantastique, Op. 3 (1908)

> CBC Symphony Orchestra—Igor Stravinsky (Dec. 1, 1962— Toronto)   Col. *MS-7094*

Fireworks, Op. 4 (1908)

> Philharmonic-Symphony Orchestra of New York—Igor Stravinsky (Jan. 28, 1946—New York)   Col. ML-4398*
> Moscow State Philharmonic Symphony Orchestra—Igor Stravinsky (October 1962—concert, Moscow)   USSR. 33D-010936
> Columbia Symphony Orchestra—Igor Stravinsky (Dec. 17, 1963—New York)   Col. *MS-7094*

The Firebird (1909-10)

—Complete ballet

[4] See note 2 above.

Columbia Symphony Orchestra—Igor Stravinsky (Jan. 23-25, 1961—Hollywood   Col. *MS-6328*

—First suite for orchestra (1911), and Berceuse and Finale from Second suite (1919)

Orchestra—Igor Stravinsky (1927—Paris)   *78*: 4-Col. M-115*

—Third suite for orchestra (1945) (connecting interludes omitted)

Philharmonic-Symphony Orchestra of New York—Igor Stravinsky (Jan. 28, 1946—New York)   Col. ML-4882*

—Third suite for orchestra (1945) (with connecting interludes)

Columbia Symphony Orchestra—Igor Stravinsky (Jan. 23, 24, 1967—Hollywood)   Col. *MS-7011*

. . . *Scherzo* and *Berceuse* only

—Arr. for violin & piano by Stravinsky & Dushkin (1933)

Samuel Dushkin, Igor Stravinsky (1933—Paris)

VdsM. 2C 061-11300

Two Poems of Verlaine, Op. 9 (1910)

—Arr. for baritone & orchestra (1951)

Donald Gramm, Columbia Symphony Orchestra—Igor Stravinsky (Dec. 1964 & 1966—New York)[1]   Col. *MS-7439*

Petrushka (1910-11)

—Abridged recording of original version[2]

Orchestra—Igor Stravinsky (June 27, 28, 1928—London)

78: 3-Col. M-109*

—Suite from original version[3]

Philharmonic-Symphony Orchestra of New York—Igor Stravinsky (Apr. 29, 1940—New York)   Col. ML-4047*

—Revised version of complete ballet (1946)

Columbia Symphony Orchestra—Igor Stravinsky (Feb. 12, 15, 17, 1960—Hollywood)[4]   Col. *MS-6332*

—Suite from revised version[5]

Moscow State Philharmonic Symphony Orchestra—Igor Stravinsky (October 1962—concert, Moscow) USSR. 33D-010933

[1] The orchestral part was recorded in December 1964, and the vocal part overdubbed in 1966.

[2] In addition to several minor cuts, this recording omits the Waltz in Scene 3 and the "Peasant with Bear" and "Gypsies and a Rake Vendor" episodes from Scene 4; the final episode is replaced by the concert ending.

[3] Includes Scene 1, from the Charlatan's entrance; Scene 2 complete; and Scene 4, beginning from the "Wet-Nurses' Dance" but omitting the final episode, which is replaced by the concert ending.

[4] A "suite" from this recording is issued on Col. *MS-7011;* Scene 3 is omitted, and the final episode is replaced by the concert ending.

[5] Includes Scene 1, from the Charlatan's entrance; Scene 2 complete; and Scene 4, with the concert ending replacing the final episode.

. . . Russian Dance only
— Arr. for violin & piano by Stravinsky & Dushkin (1932)
    Samuel Dushkin, Igor Stravinsky (1933 — Paris)
                        VdsM. 2C 061-11300

Two Poems of Balmont (1911)
— Arr. for high voice & 9 instruments (1954)
    Marni Nixon (s, in English), chamber ensemble — Igor Stravinsky (July 28, 1955 — Hollywood)   Col. CML-5107

Zvezdoliki (1911-12)
    Festival Singers of Toronto (in Russian), CBC Symphony Orchestra — Igor Stravinsky (Nov. 29, 1962 — Toronto)
                        Col. *CMS-6647*; *M-31124*

The Rite of Spring (1911-13)[6]
    Symphony orchestra — Igor Stravinsky (1928 — Paris)
                      78: 5-Col. M-129*

    Philharmonic-Symphony Orchestra of New York — Igor Stravinsky (Apr. 29, 1940 — New York)   Col. ML-4882*
— with revised version of *Danse sacrale* (1943)
    Columbia Symphony Orchestra — Igor Stravinsky (Jan. 5, 6, 1960 — New York)   Col. *MS-6319*

Three Japanese Lyrics (1912-13)
    Marni Nixon (s, in English), chamber ensemble — Igor Stravinsky (July 28, 1955 — Hollywood)   Col. CML-5107

Three Little Songs ("Souvenirs") (1913)
— Arr. for soprano & small orchestra (1933)
    Marilyn Horne (m-s, in English), chamber orchestra — Igor Stravinsky (July 28, 1955 — Hollywood)   Col. CML-5107
    Cathy Berberian (m-s, in Russian), chamber orchestra — Igor Stravinsky (Dec. 11, 1964 — New York)   Col. *MS-7439*

The Nightingale (1908-14)
    (In Russian) Soloists, Chorus & Orchestra of The Opera Society of Washington — Igor Stravinsky (Dec. 29, 31, 1960 — Washington, D. C.)   Col. *MS-6327**
    Cast:
        The Fisherman   Loren Driscoll (t)

---

[6] A talk by Stravinsky, *Apropos of Le Sacre,* recorded December 8, 1959, in New York, was issued in Col. *D3S-614**, a three-record deluxe album set also containing the later recordings of *Petrushka* and *The Rite of Spring.*

    A recording of *The Rite of Spring* by the USSR State Symphony Orchestra, conducted by Robert Craft, was made at a Moscow concert in Autumn 1962, and issued on USSR. 33D-010935/6. See Stravinsky and Craft, *Retrospectives and Conclusions,* New York, 1969, pp. 123ff.

The Nightingale	Reri Grist (s)
The Cook	Marina Picassi (s)
The Chamberlain	Kenneth Smith (bs)
The Bonze	Herbert Beattie (bs)
The Emperor	Donald Gramm (bs)
1st Japanese Ambassador	Stanley Kolk (t)
2nd Japanese Ambassador	William Murphy (bs)
3rd Japanese Ambassador	Carl Kaiser (t)
Death	Elaine Bonazzi (a)

Chorus Master: John Moriarty

. . . *Air of the Nightingale* and *Chinese March* only
—Arr. for violin & piano by Stravinsky & Dushkin (1932)
Samuel Dushkin, Igor Stravinsky (1933—Paris)
78: Col. 68334-D*

Three Pieces for String Quartet (1914)
—Arr. for orchestra: see below, Four Studies for Orchestra (1928)
Pribaoutki (1914)
Cathy Berberian (m-s, in Russian), chamber ensemble—Igor Stravinsky (Dec. 11, 1964—New York)   Col. *MS-7439*

Three Easy Pieces for Piano Duet (1914-15)
—Arr. for orchestra: see below, Suite No. 2 for Small Orchestra (1921)

Cat's Lullabies (1915-16)
Cathy Berberian (m-s, in Russian), three clarinets—Igor Stravinsky (Dec. 14, 1964—New York)   Col. *MS-7439*

Renard (1915-16)
(In English) George Shirley (t), Loren Driscoll (t), William Murphy (b), Donald Gramm (bs), Toni Koves (cimbalom), Columbia Chamber Ensemble—Igor Stravinsky (Jan. 26, 1962—New York)   **Col.** *M-31124*

Five Easy Pieces for Piano Duet (1916-17)
—Arr. for orchestra: see below, Suite No. 2 for Small Orchestra (1921) & Suite No. 1 for Small Orchestra (1925)

Three Tales for Children (1915-17)
—Nos. 1 & 2 arr. for soprano & 3 instruments: see below, Four Songs (1953-54)

Four Russian Peasant Songs (1914-17)
—with accompaniment of four horns (1954)
Chorus (in English), four horns—Igor Stravinsky (July 28, 1955—Hollywood)   Col. CML-5017
Gregg Smith Singers (in Russian), Columbia Symphony Or-

chestra members—Igor Stravinsky (Aug. 20, 1965—Holly-
wood)   Col. *M-31124*

The Wedding (1914-17)[7]

(In English) Kate Winter (s), Linda Seymour (m-s), Parry
Jones (t), Roy Henderson (bs), chorus & ensemble—Igor
Stravinsky (July 10, 1934—London)   *78:* 3-Col. M-204*
(In English) Mildred Allen (s), Regina Sarfaty (m-s), Loren
Driscoll (t), Robert Oliver (bs), American Concert Choir,
Samuel Barber, Aaron Copland, Lukas Foss, Roger Sessions
(pfs), Columbia Percussion Ensemble—Igor Stravinsky (Dec.
21, 1959—New York)   Col. *MS-6372**

Study for Pianola (1917)

—Arr. for orchestra: see below, Four Studies for Orchestra (1928)

The Soldier's Tale (1918)

—Concert Suite

Darrieux (vn), Boussagol (cbs), Godeau (cl,), Dherin (bsn),
Foveau (tpt), Delbos (tbn), Jean Paul Morel (percussion)—
Igor Stravinsky (1932—Paris)   *78:* 3-Col. M-184*
Alexander Schneider (vn), Julius Levine (cbs), David Oppen-
heim (cl), Loren Glickman (bsn), Robert Nagel (tpt), Erwin
Price (tbn), Alfred Howard (perc)—Igor Stravinsky (Jan. 27,
1954—New York)   Col. ML-4964*
Israel Baker (vn), Richard Kelley (cbs), Roy D'Antonio (cl),
Don Christlieb (bsn), Charles Brady (tpt), Robert Marsteller
(tbn), William Kraft (percussion)—Igor Stravinsky (Feb. 10,
13, 1961—Hollywood)[8]   Col. *MS-6272; MS-7093*

Rag-Time (1918)

Chamber ensemble—Igor Stravinsky (c. 1934—Paris)
                                                          78: Col. 68300-D*
Toni Koves (cimbalom), Columbia Chamber Orchestra—Igor
Stravinsky (Jan. 26, 1962—New York)   Col. *M-30579*

Four Russian Songs (1918-19)

—Nos. 1 & 4 arr. for soprano & 3 instruments: see below, Four Songs
(1953-54)

Piano-Rag Music (1919)

Igor Stravinsky (pf) (c. 1934—Paris)   Ser. 60183

---

[7] A recording in Russian of *The Wedding,* conducted by Robert Craft and supervised
by Stravinsky, was made in New York on December 21, 1965, and released on Col.
MS-6991.

[8] The sections of the score omitted from the concert suite were recorded at the same
time, so that a release of the complete work, with the spoken parts overdubbed, is
possible.

Pulcinella (1919-20)
— Complete ballet score
>Mary Simmons (s), Glenn Schnittke (t), Phillip MacGregor (bs), Cleveland Orchestra — Igor Stravinsky (Dec. 14, 1953 — Cleveland)   Col. ML-4830*
>Irene Jordan (s), George Shirley (t), Donald Gramm (bs), Columbia Symphony Orchestra — Igor Stravinsky (Aug. 23, 1965 — Hollywood)   Col. *MS-6881*

— Nos. 5-8 of concert suite (c. 1922)
>Orchestra — Igor Stravinsky (1927 & 1932 — Paris)
>>*78*: 2-Col. X-36*

— Complete recording of concert suite (1947 revision)
>Columbia Symphony Orchestra — Igor Stravinsky (Aug. 25, 1965 — Hollywood)[9]   Col. *MS-7093*

— *Suite Italienne* for violin & piano (c. 1933)
. . . Nos. 2 & 5 only
>Samuel Dushkin, Igor Stravinsky (1933 — Paris)
>>*78*: Col. 68238-D (in set M-199)*

Concertino for String Quartet (1920)
— Arr. for 12 instruments (1952)
>Columbia Chamber Ensemble — Igor Stravinsky (Oct. 26, 1965 — Hollywood)   Col. *M-30579*

Symphonies of Wind Instruments (1920)[10]
>Wind ensemble of NWDR Orchestra — Igor Stravinsky (October 1951 — Cologne)   Col. ML-4964*

The Five Fingers (1920-21)
— Arr. for orchestra: see below, Eight Instrumental Miniatures (1962)

Suite No. 2 for Small Orchestra (1921)
>CBC Symphony Orchestra — Igor Stravinsky (Mar. 30, 1963 Toronto)   Col. *CMS-6648*

Mavra (1921-22)
>(In Russian) Susan Belink (s), Mary Simmons (m-s), Patricia Rideout (a), Stanley Kolk (t), CBC Symphony Orchestra — Igor Stravinsky (May 7, 8, 1964 — Toronto)   Col. *MS-6991*

. . . *Parasha's Song* ("Russian Maiden's Song") only

---

[9] At this session, only the passages necessary to "patch" material from the complete recording (see above) were recorded. Apparently the two measures preceding No. 65 in the score of the Suite were overlooked at this time and have been spliced in from another performance.

[10] A recording of the Symphonies of Wind Instruments, conducted by Robert Craft in the composer's presence, was made on October 11, 1966, in New York, but has not yet been released.

—Arr. for violin & piano by Stravinsky & Dushkin (1937)
   Joseph Szigeti, Igor Stravinsky (May 9, 1946—New York)
                                                    Col. ML-4398*
Octet for Wind Instruments (1922-23)
   Marcel Moyse (fl), Godeau (cl), Dherin (bsn), Piard (bsn),
   Foveau (tpt), Vignal (tpt), Lafosse (tbn), Delbos (tbn)— Igor
   Stravinsky (1932—Paris)   78: 2-Col. X-25*
   Julius Baker (fl), David Oppenheim (cl), Loren Glickman (bsn),
   Sylvia Deutscher (bsn), Robert Nagel (tpt), Ted Weis (tpt),
   Erwin Price (tbn), Richard Hixon (tbn)—Igor Stravinsky (Jan.
   26, 1954—New York)   Col. ML-4964*
   James Pellerite (fl), David Oppenheim (cl), Loren Glickman
   (bsn), Arthur Weisberg (bsn), Robert Nagel (tpt), Ted Weis
   (tpt), Keith Brown (tbn), Richard Hixon (tbn)— Igor Stravinsky
   (Jan. 5, 1961—New York)   Col. MS-6272; M-30579
Concerto for Piano and Wind Orchestra (1923-24)
   Soulima Stravinsky, RCA Victor Symphony Orchestra—Igor
   Stravinsky (Feb.1949—New York)   10" Vic. LM-7010*
   Philippe Entremont, Columbia Symphony Orchestra—Igor
   Stravinsky (May 13, 1964—New York)   Col. MS-6947*
Serenade in A (1925)
   Igor Stravinsky (pf) (c. 1934—Paris)   Ser. 60183
Suite No. 1 for Small Orchestra (1917-25)
   CBC Symphony Orchestra—Igor Stravinsky (Mar. 29, 1963—
   Toronto)   Col. CMS-6648
Pater Noster (1926)
   Festival Singers of Toronto (in Slavonic)—Igor Stravinsky
   (May 7, 8, 1964—Toronto)   **Col. M-31124**
—New version with Latin text (1948)[11]
   Choir of the Church of the Blessed Sacrament, New York—
   Igor Stravinsky (Feb.24,25, 1949—New York)
                                         10" Vic. LM-7010*
Oedipus Rex (1926-27)
   Jean Cocteau (narrator, in French),[12] Martha Mödl (m-s),
   Peter Pears (t), Helmut Krebs (t), Heinz Rehfuss (b), Otto von
   Rohr (bs), Cologne Radio Symphony Orchestra and Chorus—
   Igor Stravinsky (Oct. 8, 1951—Cologne)   Col. ML-4644*
   John Westbrook (narrator, in English), Shirley Verrett (m-s),
   George Shirley (t), Loren Driscoll (t), Donald Gramm (bs),
   Chester Watson (bs), John Reardon (b), Orchestra & Chorus

[11] The recording does not correspond to the published score of this revision, and apparently represents a preliminary stage in the underlay of a Latin text.
[12] Cocteau's speaking voice was recorded separately, in Paris during June 1952.

of The Opera Society of Washington — Igor Stravinsky (Jan. 20, 1962 — Washington, D. C.)   **Col.** *M-31129*

Apollo Musagetes (1927-28)

    RCA Victor Orchestra — Igor Stravinsky (Apr. 17, 1950 — New York)   Vic. LM-1096*

    Columbia Symphony Orchestra — Igor Stravinsky (Jan. 29 & Dec. 11, 1964 — New York)   Col. *MS-6646*

The Fairy's Kiss (1928)

— Complete ballet

    Cleveland Orchestra — Igor Stravinsky (Dec. 11, 1955 — Cleveland)   Col. ML-5102*

    Columbia Symphony Orchestra — Igor Stravinsky (Aug. 19, 20, 1965 — Hollywood)   Col. *MS-6803*; 3-Col. *D3S-761*

— *Divertimento* (1934)

    Victor Symphony Orchestra — Igor Stravinsky (1940 — Mexico City)   78: 3-Vic. (Mexico) M-931*

    RCA Victor Symphony Orchestra — Igor Stravinsky (1947 — Hollywood)   Vic. LVT-1029*

Four Studies for Orchestra (1928)

    CBC Symphony Orchestra — Igor Stravinsky (Nov. 29, Dec. 1, 1962 — Toronto)   Col. *CMS-6648*

Capriccio for Piano & Orchestra (1928-29)[12]

    Igor Stravinsky (pf), Straram Orchestra — Ernest Ansermet (1930 — Paris)   Ser. 60183

Symphony of Psalms (1930)

    Alexei Vlassoff Choir, symphony orchestra — Igor Stravinsky (Feb. 1931 — Paris)   78: 3-Col. M-162*

    Chorus, Columbia Broadcasting Symphony Orchestra — Igor Stravinsky (Dec. 19, 1946 — New York)   Col. ML-4129*

    Festival Singers of Toronto, CBC Symphony Orchestra — Igor Stravinsky (Mar. 30, 1963 — Toronto)   Col. *MS-6548*

Concerto in D for Violin & Orchestra (1931)

    Samuel Dushkin, Lamoureux Orchestra — Igor Stravinsky (1932 — Paris)   Vox VLP-6340*

    Isaac Stern, Columbia Symphony Orchestra — Igor Stravinsky (June 29, 30, 1961 — Hollywood)   Col. *MS-6331*

Duo Concertant (1931-32)

    Samuel Dushkin, Igor Stravinsky (1933 — Paris)   Ser. 60183

---

[13] The recording on Columbia *MS-6947*, by Philippe Entremont, with the Columbia Symphony Orchestra — Robert Craft, was not recorded "under the supervision of the composer," as the liner notes have it; Stravinsky was not present at this recording session.

Joseph Szigeti, Igor Stravinsky (Oct. 11, 13, 1945 – New York)
Col. ML-2122*

Credo (1932)

– New version with Slavonic text (1964)

Gregg Smith Singers – Igor Stravinsky (Aug. 20, 1965 – Hollywood) **Col. *M-31124***

Persephone (1933-34)

Vera Zorina (narrator), Richard Robinson (t), Westminster Choir, New York Philharmonic – Igor Stravinsky (Jan. 14, 1957 – New York) Col. ML-5196
Vera Zorina (narrator), Michele Molese (t), Gregg Smith Singers, Texas Boys' Choir, Columbia Symphony Orchestra Igor Stravinsky (May 4, 7, 1966 – Hollywood) Col. *MS-6919**

Ave Maria (1934)

Festival Singers of Toronto (in Slavonic) – Igor Stravinsky (May 7, 8, 1964 – Toronto) **Col. *M-31124***

– New version with Latin text (1948)[14]

Choir of the Church of the Blessed Sacrament, New York – Igor Stravinsky (Feb. 24,25, 1949 – New York)

10″ Vic. LM-7010*

Concerto for Two Solo Pianos (1931-35)

Igor & Soulima Stravinsky (1933 – Paris)[15]

78: 3-Fr. Col. LFX-951/3*

The Card Party (1936)

Berlin Philharmonic Orchestra – Igor Stravinsky (1938 – Berlin) Merc. MG-10014* & 10″ Cap. L-8028*
Cleveland Orchestra – Igor Stravinsky (Mar. 13, 1964 – Cleveland) Col. *CMS-6649*

Preludium (1937, rev. 1953)

Columbia Jazz Group – Igor Stravinsky (Apr. 27, 1965 – New York) Col. *M-30579*

Concerto in E♭ ("Dumbarton Oaks") (1937-38)

Dumbarton Oaks Festival Orchestra – Igor Stravinsky (May 28, 1947) Merc. MG-10014*
Columbia Symphony Orchestra members – Igor Stravinsky (Mar. 29, 1962 – Hollywood) Col. *CMS-6648*

[14] The recording does not correspond to the published score of this revision, and apparently represents a preliminary stage in the underlay of a Latin text.

[15] The sixth side of this set contained Mozart's Fugue in C minor, K. 426, played by the same performers. Despite Stravinsky's statement (*Dialogues and a Diary*, p. 75) that this set "was never released because of the war," it seems that it had some circulation in France immediately before the war. Along with the Mexican Victor set of the Divertimento from *The Fairy's Kiss*, it is probably the rarest of Stravinsky's recordings.

Symphony in C (1938-40)

    Cleveland Orchestra—Igor Stravinsky (Dec. 14, 1952—Cleveland)   Col. ML-4899*

    CBC Symphony Orchestra—Igor Stravinsky (Dec. 2, 3, 1962—Toronto)   Col. *MS-6548*

Tango (1940)

—Arr. for chamber ensemble (1953)

    Columbia Jazz Group—Igor Stravinsky (Apr. 27, 1965—New York)   Col. *M-30579*

Danses Concertantes (1941-42)[16]

    RCA Victor Chamber Orchestra—Igor Stravinsky (1947—Hollywood)   Vic. LVT-1029*

Circus Polka (1942)

    Philharmonic-Symphony Orchestra of New York—Igor Stravinsky (Feb. 5, 1945—New York)   Col. ML-4398*

    CBC Symphony Orchestra—Igor Stravinsky (Mar. 29, 1963—Toronto)   Col. *CMS-6648*

Four Norwegian Moods (1942)

    Philharmonic-Symphony Orchestra of New York—Igor Stravinsky (Feb. 5, 1945—New York)   Col. ML-4398*

    CBC Symphony Orchestra—Igor Stravinsky (Mar. 29, 1963—Toronto)   Col. *M-30516*

Ode (1943)

    Philharmonic-Symphony Orchestra of New York—Igor Stravinsky (Feb. 5, 1945—New York)   Col. ML-4398*

    USSR State Symphony Orchestra—Igor Stravinsky (October 1962—concert, Moscow)   USSR. 33D-010935

    Cleveland Orchestra—Igor Stravinsky (Mar. 13, 1964—Cleveland)   Col. *M-30516*

Babel (1944)

    John Colicos (narrator), Festival Singers of Toronto, CBC Symphony Orchestra—Igor Stravinsky (Nov. 29, 1962—Toronto)   **Col.** *CMS-6647; M-31124*

Scherzo à la Russe (1944)

    RCA Victor Symphony Orchestra—Igor Stravinsky (1947—Hollywood)   10″ Vic. LM-7010*

    Columbia Symphony Orchestra—Igor Stravinsky (Dec. 17, 1963—New York)   Col. *MS-7094*

---

[16] The recording on Columbia *M-30516*, incorrectly labeled as conducted by Stravinsky was made by the Columbia Symphony Orchestra—Robert Craft, in Legion Hall, Hollywood, during January 1967.

Scènes de Ballet (1944)

    Philharmonic-Symphony Orchestra of New York — Igor Stravinsky (Feb. 5, 1945 — New York)   Col. ML-4047*

    CBC Symphony Orchestra — Igor Stravinsky (Mar. 28, 1963 — Toronto)   Col. *CMS-6649*

Symphony in Three Movements (1942-45)

    Philharmonic-Symphony Orchestra of New York — Igor Stravinsky (Jan. 28, 1946 — New York)   Col. ML-4129*

    Columbia Symphony Orchestra — Igor Stravinsky (Feb. 1, 1961 — Hollywood)   Col. *MS-6331*

Ebony Concerto (1945)

    Woody Herman (cl) and His Orchestra — Igor Stravinsky (Aug. 19, 1946 — Hollywood)   Col. ML-4398*

    Benny Goodman (cl), Columbia Jazz Group — Igor Stravinsky (Apr. 27, 1965 — New York)   Col. *MS-6805; M-30579*

Concerto in D ("Basel") (1946)

    John Corigliano (vn), Michael Rosenker (vn), RCA Victor Orchestra — Igor Stravinsky (Feb.1949 — New York) Vic. LM-1096*

    Columbia Symphony Orchestra — Igor Stravinsky (Dec. 17, 1963 — New York)   Col. *M-30516*

Orpheus (1947)

    RCA Victor Symphony Orchestra — Igor Stravinsky (Feb. 23, 1949 — New York)   Vic. LM-1033*

    USSR State Symphony Orchestra — Igor Stravinsky (October 1962 — concert, Moscow)[17]   USSR. 33D-010933/4

    Chicago Symphony Orchestra — Igor Stravinsky (July 20, 1964 — Chicago)   Col. *MS-6646*

Mass (1944-47)

    Choir of the Church of the Blessed Sacrament, New York, wind ensemble — Igor Stravinsky (Feb. 24, 25, 1949 – New York)   10″ Vic. LM-17*

    Columbia Symphony woodwinds and chorus — Igor Stravinsky (June 9, 1960 — Hollywood)   Col. *MS-6992*[18]

[17] The passage from No. 13 in the score to 1½ measures before No. 16 is omitted in this recording.

[18] Early copies of Col. *MS-6992* (and some, possibly all, copies of its mono equivalent, Col. ML-6392*) erroneously contained a different version of the Mass, recorded on October 11, 1966, in New York, under the direction of Robert Craft; the composer was present for part of this session. Although these copies were officially called back, a number evidently remain in circulation; they may be distinguished by the stamper suffix "1A" following the matrix number (XXSM 117085) embossed on the record just outside the label (copies with suffixes "2A" and higher contain the 1960 Stravinsky version). The alto soloist in both recordings is the same; the labels (although not the jackets) distinguish two different soprano soloists in the Gloria: Annette Baxter in 1960, Linda Anderson in 1966.

The Rake's Progress (1948-51)

Soloists, Chorus & Orchestra of The Metropolitan Opera Association—Igor Stravinsky (Mar. 1, 8, 10, 1953—New York)

3-Col. SL-125*

Cast:

Anne Truelove	Hilde Gueden (s)
Mother Goose	Martha Lipton (m-s)
Baba the Turk	Blanche Thebom (m-s)
Tom Rakewell	Eugene Conley (t)
Sellem	Paul Franke (t)
Nick Shadow	Mack Harrell (b)
Truelove	Norman Scott (bs)
The Keeper	Lawrence Davidson (bs)

Soloists, Sadlers Wells Opera Chorus, Royal Philharmonic Orchestra—Igor Stravinsky (June 16-20, 22, 23, 1964—London)

3-Col. *M3S-710*

Cast:

Anne Truelove	Judith Raskin (s)
Mother Goose	Jean Manning (m-s)
Baba the Turk	Regina Sarfaty (m-s)
Tom Rakewell	Alexander Young (t)
Sellem	Kevin Miller (t)
Nick Shadow	John Reardon (b)
Truelove	Don Garrard (bs)
The Keeper	Peter Tracey (bs)

Cantata (1951-52)

Jennie Tourel (m-s), Hugues Cuenod (t), New York Concert Choir, Philharmonic Chamber Ensemble—Igor Stravinsky (Dec. 22, 1952—New York) Col. ML-4899*

Adrienne Albert (m-s), Alexander Young (t), Gregg Smith Singers, Columbia Chamber Ensemble—Igor Stravinsky (Nov. 27, 1965—Hollywood) Col. *MS-6992*

Septet (1952-53)

David Oppenheim (cl), Loren Glickman (bsn), John Barrows (hn), Alexander Schneider (vn), Karen Tuttle (va), Bernard Greenhouse (vc), Ralph Kirkpatrick (pf)—Igor Stravinsky (Jan. 27, 1954—New York) Col. CML-5107

Columbia Chamber Ensemble—Igor Stravinsky (Oct. 27, 1965—Hollywood) Col. *MS-7054*

Three Songs from William Shakespeare (1953)

Grace-Lynne Martin (s), Arthur Gleghorn (fl), Hugo Raimondi (cl), Cecil Figelski (va)—Igor Stravinsky (Sept. 13, 1954—Hollywood) Col. CML-5107

Cathy Berberian (m-s), chamber ensemble — Igor Stravinsky
(Dec. 14, 1964 — New York)   Col. *MS-7439*

Four Songs for Voice, Flute, Harp, and Guitar (1953-54)
Marni Nixon (s, in English), Arthur Gleghorn, Dorothy
Remsen, Jack Marshall — Igor Stravinsky (July 28, 1955 —
Hollywood)   Col. CML-5107
Adrienne Albert (m-s, in Russian), Louise di Tullio, Dorothy
Remsen, Laurindo Almeida — Igor Stravinsky (Nov. 30, 1965
— Hollywood)   Col. *MS-7439*

In Memoriam Dylan Thomas (1954)
Richard Robinson (t), chamber ensemble — Igor Stravinsky
(Sept. 13, 1954 — Hollywood)   Col. CML-5107
Alexander Young (t), Columbia Chamber Ensemble — Igor
Stravinsky (Nov. 27, 1965 — Hollywood)   Col. *MS-6992*

Greeting Prelude (1955)
Columbia Symphony Orchestra — Igor Stravinsky (Dec. 17,
1963 — New York)   Col. *CMS-6648*

Canticum Sacrum (1955)[19]
Richard Robinson (t), Howard Chitjian (b), Los Angeles
Festival Symphony Orchestra & Chorus — Igor Stravinsky
(June 19, 1957 — Los Angeles)   Col. *CMS-6022*

Agon (1953-57)
Los Angeles Festival Symphony Orchestra — Igor Stravinsky
(June 18, 1957 — Los Angeles)   Col. *CMS-6022*

Threni (1957-58)
Bethany Beardslee (s), Beatrice Krebs (a), William Lewis
(t), James Wainner (t), Mac Morgan (b), Robert Oliver (bs),
Schola Cantorum, Columbia Symphony Orchestra — Igor
Stravinsky (Jan. 5, 6, 1959 — New York)   Col. *CMS-6065*

Movements (1958-59)
Charles Rosen (pf), Columbia Symphony Orchestra — Igor
Stravinsky (Feb. 12, 1961 — Hollywood)

Col. *MS-6272; MS-7054*

Epitaphium (1959)
Arthur Gleghorn (fl), Kalman Bloch (cl), Dorothy Remsen
(harp) — Igor Stravinsky (Jan. 25, 1961 — Hollywood)

Col. *MS-6272; MS-7054*

[19] A recording of the *Canticum Sacrum* and the arrangement of Bach's Chorale
Variations. with Jean Giraudeau (t), Xavier Depraz (bs), Elisabeth Brasseur Chorale,
and an orchestra conducted by Robert Craft, was issued on Westminster XWN
18903*. The liner of the original French Véga release stated that these recordings
were made under the composer's supervision; the date of the recordings is Dec.
3, 1956.

Double Canon (1959)

> Israel Baker (vn), Otis Igleman (vn), Sanford Schonbach (va), George Neikrug (vc) — Igor Stravinsky (Jan. 25, 1961 — Hollywood)   Col. *MS-6272; MS-7054*

A Sermon, a Narrative, and a Prayer (1960-61)

> John Horton (narrator), Shirley Verrett (m-s), Loren Driscoll (t), Festival Singers of Toronto, CBC Symphony Orchestra — Igor Stravinsky (Apr. 29, 1962 — Toronto)
>
> Col. *CMS-6647; MS-7054*

Anthem: "The Dove descending . . ." (1962)

> Festival Singers of Toronto — Igor Stravinsky (Apr. 29, 1962 — Toronto)   Col. *CMS-6647; MS-7054*

Eight Instrumental Miniatures (1961-62)

> CBC Symphony Orchestra members — Igor Stravinsky (Apr. 29, 1962 — Toronto)   Col. *CMS-6648*

The Flood (1961-62)

> Lawrence Harvey (narrator), Sebastian Cabot (Noah), Elsa Lanchester (Noah's Wife), Paul Tripp (Caller), Richard Robinson (t, Satan), John Reardon & Robert Oliver (b & bs, The Voice of God), Columbia Symphony Orchestra & Chorus — Igor Stravinsky & Robert Craft (Mar. 28, 31, 1962 — Hollywood)   Col. *MS-6357**

Elegy for J. F. K. (1964)
— version for mezzo-soprano

> Cathy Berberian (m-s), Paul Howland, Jack Kreiselman, Charles Russo (cls) — Igor Stravinsky (Dec. 14, 1964 — New York)   Col. *MS-7054*

Fanfare for a New Theatre (1964)

> Robert Heinrich, Robert E. Nagel (tpts) — Igor Stravinsky (Dec. 11, 1964 — New York)   Col. *MS-7054*

Variations (1965)

> Columbia Symphony Orchestra — Igor Stravinsky (Aug. 26, 1965 — Hollywood)   Col. UNRELEASED[20]

Introitus (1965)

> Gregg Smith Singers, Columbia Symphony Orchestra members — Igor Stravinsky (Aug. 26, 1965 — Hollywood)
>
> Col. *MS-7386*

---

[20] This recording was presumably unsatisfactory and will not be released; a recording of the *Variations* conducted by Robert Craft was made at the New York session of October 11, 1966, and issued on Columbia *MS-7386*.

Gregg Smith Singers, Columbia Symphony Orchestra members — Igor Stravinsky (Feb. 9, 1966 — Hollywood)

Col. UNRELEASED[21]

B. ARRANGEMENTS OF WORKS BY OTHER COMPOSERS

Song of the Volga Boatmen, arranged for winds and percussion (1917)
Moscow State Philharmonic Symphony Orchestra — Igor Stravinsky (October 1962 — concert, Moscow) USSR. 33D-010936

Pas de Deux ("Bluebird") from Tchaikovsky's *The Sleeping Beauty,* arranged for small orchestra (1941)
Columbia Symphony Orchestra — Igor Stravinsky (Dec. 17, 1963 — New York) Col. *CMS-6649*

The Star-Spangled Banner, harmonized and orchestrated (1941)
Festival Singers of Toronto, CBC Symphony Orchestra — Igor Stravinsky (May 7, 8, 1964 — Toronto) Col. *M-31124*

Chorale Variations on *Vom Himmel hoch* by J. S. Bach, arranged for chorus & orchestra (1955-56)[22]
Festival Singers of Toronto, CBC Symphony Orchestra — Igor Stravinsky (Mar. 30, 1963 — Toronto) Col. *CMS-6647; M-31124*

Monumentum pro Gesualdo di Venosa ad C D annum (1960) (three madrigals recomposed for instruments)
Columbia Symphony Orchestra — Igor Stravinsky (June 9, 1960 — Hollywood) Col. *CKS-6318*

NOTE: The following album couplings of Stravinsky's later Columbia recordings have been issued:

3-Col. *D3S-614**: *Petrushka; The Rite of Spring; Apropos of Le Sacre* (talk by Stravinsky)

3-Col. *D3S-705: The Firebird; Petrushka; The Rite of Spring*

3-Col. *D3S-761: Pulcinella* (complete); *Apollo Musagetes; The Fairy's Kiss; Orpheus*

6-Col. *D5S-775: The Firebird* (1945 Suite); *Petrushka* (suite from 1946 version); *The Rite of Spring; The Soldier's Tale* (concert suite); *Pulcinella* (concert suite); *Apollo Musagetes;* Symphony of Psalms; Symphony in C; Symphony in Three Movements; record of rehearsal excerpts and "conversations," etc., from television programs.

2-Col. *MG-31202: The Firebird* (1945 Suite); *Petrushka* (suite from 1946 version); *The Rite of Spring*

[21] This recording was presumably less satisfactory than the first one and will not be released.
[22] See note 19 above.

NORTON PAPERBACKS ON MUSIC